The Origins of War

Selected Titles from the *Moral Traditions* Series

James F. Keenan, SJ, series editor

The Origins of War
A Catholic Perspective

Matthew A. Shadle

Georgetown University Press
Washington, D.C.

Library of Congress Cataloging-in-Publication Data

Shadle, Matthew Allen, 1979-
   The origins of war : a Catholic perspective / Matthew Allen Shadle.
     p. cm. — (Moral traditions series)
   Includes bibliographical references and index.
   ISBN 978-1-58901-735-1 (pbk. : alk. paper)
     1. War—Religious aspects—Catholic Church—History.   2. Catholic Church—Doctrines—History.   I. Title.
   BX1793.S485 2011
   261.8′73—dc22   2010037036

15 14 13 12 11   9 8 7 6 5 4 3 2
First printing

Printed in the United States of America

TABLE OF CONTENTS

PREFACE

THIS WORK, WHICH in an earlier form was my doctoral dissertation at the University of Dayton, was originally conceived in the early years of the first decade of the twenty-first century. The September 11 attacks had already been perpetrated, and NATO had already invaded Afghanistan and put in place a new government. Americans debated whether or not to go to war with Iraq, and after the war began, continued to debate the morality of that war. Catholic intellectuals were no different, and I passionately followed their arguments. I soon concluded, however, that advocates for and against the war were really talking past one another, not only because of their different approaches to moral reasoning about war, but also because of their different assumptions about the way states behave and the causes of conflict between states. For the most part, I found, these assumptions were adopted uncritically from outside sources and seemed to reflect ideas that did not fit well within the Catholic worldview. I decided to try to develop an understanding of state behavior that would adequately reflect the Catholic worldview, focusing especially on the origins of war.

Although this project arose out of debates over current events, I have tried to set aside my particular views on these events. I have also tried to avoid too much discussion of the issues of debate concerning moral reasoning about war. I believe that the arguments I make in this book do have implications for moral reasoning about war and for analyses of current events, but I did not want my own conclusions on these matters to get in the way of the insights that others with different views might gain from the following chapters.

I would like to thank the members of my dissertation committee: Dr. Dennis Doyle, Dr. Kelly Johnson, Dr. Margaret Karns, Dr. Therese Lysaught, and especially my director, Dr. William Portier, for their advice, suggestions, and criticisms as I wrote my dissertation and for their guidance through the dissertation-writing process.

I would also like to thank my colleagues in the Division of Philosophy, Theology, and Religion at Loras College for allowing me to teach there as I finished my dissertation and for offering me support and advice as I completed the process of turning my dissertation into a book. Thanks are also due to Carol

Oberfoell, the Division's academic secretary, who helped me with many of the practical details of preparing the manuscript.

I would like to thank my family and my wife's family for their words of encouragement, and finally I thank my wife, Gisella Aitken-Shadle, for her love and support.

INTRODUCTION

"Building peace . . . depends upon the progress of research about it. Scientific studies on war, its nature, causes, means, objectives and risks have much to teach us on the conditions for peace."
—Pope John Paul II, "1982 World Day of Peace Message"

"Theology cannot choose to be either influenced or not influenced by other disciplines. The choice lies rather between being unconsciously affected by such influences or critically aware of them."
—Gerald O'Collins, SJ, *Fundamental Theology*

CONTEMPORARY CATHOLIC INTELLECTUALS have failed to give an adequate account of the origins of war. Despite important contributions to debates over the morality of war and to the establishment of peace, Catholics have not developed a convincing account of why nations come into conflict with each other in the first place. Of course, Catholics who write on war have assumptions about the reasons for conflict; these assumptions guide their judgments on the morality of war and on what should be done to prevent it, yet they are almost always drawn uncritically from the field of international relations theory or from mainstream foreign policy debates. Because these assumptions about the origins of conflict are accepted uncritically, Catholic authors often do not perceive that such assumptions rest on theories about human nature or the nature of politics that do not fit easily, if at all, into the Catholic worldview. Contemporary Catholics lack an account of war's origins that is consistent with their fundamental beliefs, which is a problematic situation if Catholics maintain that those fundamental beliefs have any relevance for human social life.

Fortunately, this state of affairs need not be the case, for three reasons. First, great Christian minds of the past have reflected on the origins of war, and these seeds from the Catholic tradition can provide a valuable starting point for a contemporary account of war's origins. Because of an overwhelming emphasis on the moral dimensions of war in contemporary discussions, no doubt inspired by the emergence of total war and nuclear weapons in the twentieth century,

Catholics of the past century have neglected what these past writers have had to say about why humanity resorts to war. Second, two significant developments in twentieth-century Catholic theology—a growing awareness of historical consciousness, or historicity, and a renewed sense of the integral relationship between human nature and grace—provide essential perspectives on human nature, considered both individually and socially, that are necessary for an adequate account of war's origins. Third, new voices in the field of international relations theory emerging in the last thirty years, particularly the movement known as constructivism, present a way of understanding international politics much more amenable to the Catholic worldview than the theories uncritically accepted in most recent Catholic analyses of war.

OUT OF DIVISION, UNITY

There is currently a great diversity of Catholic opinion on the morality of war, and the debate leading up to the Iraq War of 2003 made this diversity, at least among American Catholics, abundantly clear. Conservative Catholics, who pride themselves on their faithfulness to the official teachings of the Church, found themselves at odds with Pope John Paul II, who strongly condemned the war, although a minority of conservative writers also opposed the war. The majority of liberal Catholics, who normally have no qualms about dissenting from papal teachings, ended up agreeing with John Paul about the war, claiming that the United Nations inspections for Iraq's weapons of mass destruction needed to be given more time and that a war would lead to disproportionately destructive consequences. Pacifist Catholics rejected the very notion that a war against Iraq could be just. The disagreements among these different groups of Catholics were often rancorous and uncharitable.

These divisions were nothing new, however, having been present within the American Catholic Church since at least the 1960s. Pacifism had existed within the Catholic Church long before the 1960s, for example, in the Catholic Worker movement founded by Dorothy Day and Peter Maurin in the 1930s. This perspective became much more widespread among Catholics after the Second Vatican Council (1962–65) and was even supported by a handful of the bishops at the council. The looming threat of nuclear war, made very apparent by the Cuban missile crisis of 1962, contributed to a new openness to pacifism. Most of the bishops, however, and Popes John XXIII and Paul VI, remained committed to the just war theory, which claims that in certain limited situations, the use of military force may be justified. In the United States, the Vietnam War further widened the gulf between these perspectives. Many Catholics became involved with the antiwar movement and were drawn toward pacifism. The Catholic Worker movement became more prominent, and other Catholic pacifists such as Daniel and Philip Berrigan became well known. Others, some of whom had originally defended the legitimacy of the Vietnam War, concluded that even if that particular war was unjust, the Catholic Church should not abandon the principle that in other cases war might be justified. This debate between pacifists and supporters of the just war tradition continued in the following decades, but more and more, those who supported the just war theory also disagreed among themselves over such questions as the use of nuclear weapons as a deterrent, the role of international institutions, and more recently, the legitimacy of pre-emptive war. J. Bryan Hehir on the liberal side and George Weigel on the conservative side are probably the leading representatives of these competing points of view.

These divisions among American Catholics reflect fundamental disagreements about the morality of war. Of course, the primary disagreement between pacifists and believers in the just war theory is over whether war can ever be morally legitimate. Liberal and conservative defenders of the just war ethic differ over such issues as how to determine the justice of a cause for war, the balance of legitimate authority between national leaders and international organizations, and the relative importance of the destructive effects of war. The differing presuppositions that lie behind the opposing arguments in the American Catholic debate about the morality of war probably serve to make the debate as it currently stands irresolvable.

I would argue, though, that behind the incommensurate positions of Catholic pacifists and the various supporters of the just war theory on the *morality* of war lay some common presuppositions about the *origins* of war that have largely remained unexamined and fit uneasily within a broader Catholic perspective. Catholic thinking about war and its origins has been influenced by certain precepts of modern political thought, which emerged in earlier centuries as part of an explicit rejection of the Christian political tradition of the past and which, generally speaking, Catholics have rejected as incompatible with their faith. In their writings, both the hierarchical leaders of the Catholic Church and Catholic intellectuals have vigorously contested these ideas. Nevertheless, views on the origins of war based on these presuppositions have been uncritically accepted in both the official teaching of the Catholic Church and in the writings of Catholic intellectuals.

How We Got Here

The purpose of this book is to show how this situation came about, and also to explore the resources in the Catholic tradition that can be employed to develop a more adequate perspective on the origins of war. Therefore a significant portion of the book looks back on that tradition. The early Christians had a distinctive, if not fully developed, account of the origins of war. Drawing on biblical themes, church fathers such as Justin Martyr, Tertullian, Origen, and Lactantius claimed that war had demonic origins. They did not mean this in the simplistic sense that those engaged in war acted at the suggestion of the devil, but rather that the religious and cultural practices of pagan societies cultivated vices in their participants, making them more susceptible to committing evil actions. One of the results of this process, which according to the fathers was demonically inspired, was war. This demonic theory of war's origins allowed the church fathers to speak of forces transcending the individual as an essential source of war without ignoring individual responsibility. The theory left unanswered the question, particularly relevant after the conversion of Europe to Christianity, of why war continued among Christians despite the disappearance of pagan religion. The great Augustine attempted to resolve these questions with his brilliant claim that all sin is a form of idolatry.

In the Middle Ages, Christian writers continued to reflect on war's origins, although distinct areas of emphasis began to emerge. In his *Policraticus*, the twelfth-century English writer John of Salisbury described the vices that rulers are tempted to develop within the royal court that will lead them to become tyrants and engage in unjust wars. Although the thirteenth-century theologian Thomas Aquinas did not specifically write on the origins of war, his moral theology centering on virtue, vice, and the natural law established a theoretical framework that could be useful for an examination of war's origins. Finally, in the writings of the poet Dante Alighieri and the lawyer Pierre Dubois, this period also saw the first serious Christian reflection on how political institutions could help to establish peace.

Beginning in the early sixteenth century, modern political thought was a conscious reaction against the Christian vision of politics developed in earlier centuries, including the way it understood the origins of war, although it had roots in the medieval Christian tradition and Christian thinkers adopted some of its themes as their own. The medieval thinkers William of Ockham and Marsilius of Padua developed ideas that would go on to influence Niccolò Machiavelli, the true originator of modern political thought. Machiavelli concluded that Christian understandings of politics were impossibly moralistic and ignored the true motivations of political actors: power and survival. Christian writers such as the Renaissance humanists Desiderius Erasmus and Juan Luis Vives and the natural law jurists Francisco Suarez and Hugo Grotius incorporated some aspects of the earlier Christian tradition but also adopted characteristically modern notions into their thought on war. Modern political thought developed in several directions, including those represented by giants such as Thomas Hobbes, John Locke, Immanuel Kant, John Stuart Mill, and Karl Marx, but thinkers in all these strands, following Machiavelli, shared certain presuppositions that shaped how they understood the origins of war. These presuppositions—including the denial that human nature is oriented toward an end, in particular God; the belief that human political life can be understood without reference to humanity's relation to God; and the belief that politics can be studied as a science free from any philosophical presuppositions, based only on observation—marked an explicit rejection of the earlier Christian tradition.

In the twentieth century the field of international relations theory emerged as a distinct academic discipline, and the various strands of modern political thought coalesced into three major schools: liberalism, realism, and Marxism. Liberalism is characterized by the beliefs that states behave in a generally rational way, that war is primarily caused by the lack of international institutions to help states resolve their conflicts, and that establishing adequate international institutions will make war unlikely. Realists, on the other hand, emphasize states' desire for power and security and are skeptical that international institutions will be able to tame those desires. For their part, Marxists claim that conflicts among states are primarily caused by economic exploitation, either within a particular state or among states. In the past few decades, variations of these schools have emerged, such as neoliberalism, neorealism, and world-systems theory, but the basic orientations have remained the same, and these major schools of thought continue to be based on the presuppositions that modern thinkers developed in earlier centuries.

In the 1980s and 1990s, certain international relations theorists became dissatisfied with the dominant theories in the field and developed an approach describing how the identities, interests, and norms that shape the behavior of states are formed by the interactions of states and by domestic forces. Calling themselves constructivists, these theorists challenged the way the mainstream theories of international relations understood the interests of states. These interests, they argued, are socially constructed, leading to a much more complex picture of international politics than earlier theories had proposed. The constructivist approach suggests that war has its origins in the conflicting identities, interests, and norms of states and some nonstate actors, and that war itself is governed by a set of culturally formed norms.

Although by no means religiously motivated, constructivism can prove useful for Catholics interested in understanding international politics, including war, because it challenges contemporary views on the origins of war precisely at the points where modern political thought differs from the Catholic worldview. Constructivism provides a tool for Catholics who wish to develop an understanding of the origins of war that is consistent with Catholic positions challenging modern presuppositions about politics. Two changes in Catholic theology in the past few decades are particularly important for such a task. First, Catholic theologians have begun to take historicity—that is, the ways in which our beliefs and actions are shaped by our time, place, and culture—more seriously. This development is particularly important for understanding the cultural influences that lead two or more groups to go to war. Second, over the course of the twentieth century, Catholic theologians shifted their treatment of the relationship between human nature and grace toward what they perceived to be a position consistent with the tradition: that humanity's calling toward a supernatural destiny, communion with God, is an integral part of their being, not something added on to an already-complete human nature. The struggle between sin and grace that marks each person's response to this calling penetrates all aspects of the person's existence, including human political life. Therefore, a Catholic way of understanding war's origins must take into account the way that the relations among states are part of this broader theological drama.

Looking at what Catholic leaders have in fact said about the origins of war, however, one finds that their views have been deeply shaped by theories, particularly liberalism, that are based in large part on those very modern presuppositions about politics to which they object. Intellectuals such as Jacques Maritain and John Courtney Murray adopted into their ethical and political thought elements of liberalism that influenced their views on war and peace. Over the course of the twentieth century and through the influence of thinkers like Maritain and Murray, the popes' thinking on matters of war and peace gradually converged with liberalism. On the one hand, they increasingly recognized the importance of human rights and democracy as necessary for the establishment of peace. On the other hand, especially beginning with Pope John XXIII, they adopted typically liberal views about the rational behavior of states and the possibilities for peace provided by international institutions. This convergence with liberal theory continued into the papacy of Pope John Paul II, despite significant changes in papal theology that would suggest the opposite course, and is also evident in the writings of contemporary authors such as Hehir and Weigel.

Now is the time for Catholics to rethink how they understand the origins of war. Contemporary theology can provide powerful insights into the origins of war. The constructivist approach to international relations adds a theoretical framework that harmonizes with and reinforces these theological principles. And Catholics who wish to develop a perspective on war's origins consistent with their faith do not have to create something out of nothing: There is a long tradition of Christian reflection on the origins of war on which they can draw and that should guide them, a tradition that begins with the Bible.

. . . .

CHAPTER ONE

FROM THE BIBLE
TO THE MIDDLE AGES

IN RECENT DECADES scholars looking back on the Christian tradition have focused on the ethical aspects of war, tracing three strands of thought: pacifism, the just war tradition, and the crusade.[1] In a century that suffered the horrors of the two world wars, when nuclear weaponry has threatened humankind's very existence, and when international organizations have at least held out the prospect of a world without war, it is understandable that Christians would mine their tradition for insights into the morality of war. Yet in the history of Christian thought, there is also a tradition of reflection on the origins of war that has been largely ignored by recent scholars but that is essential for understanding the Christian attitude toward war in its entirety, and is therefore key if Catholics today wish to develop a truly Christian perspective on war and its origins.

The roots of the Christian tradition of thinking about the origins of war are found in the Bible, and the first sprouts of the tradition emerged in the thought of the church fathers. Passages in both the Old and New Testaments suggest that the origins of violence and injustice can be found in idolatry. The church fathers developed the idea of idolatry as the source of war as part of their apologetic against pagan Roman culture. As Christianity became dominant throughout Europe, however, this line of thought was transformed and taken in new directions, particularly by medieval theologians and writers.

WAR IN THE BIBLE

The Bible has always been the starting point for Christian thinking about war. Some have used the holy wars of the Old Testament to justify war, although for many they remain troubling. The words of Jesus in the Gospels have inspired pacifists throughout the centuries, whereas those committed to the just war theory have tried to situate those sayings in the context of other New Testament passages and natural law thinking. Besides being a source of reflection on the morality of war, however, the Bible also provides insight into the origins of war. It is clear that the Old Testament finds the source of evils, including war, in idolatry, whether that of Israel or its neighbors. This theme is taken up again in the New Testament and forms the foundation for future thinking on the origins of war.

Old Testament History

The holy wars of the Old Testament have been of particular interest to scholars. The characteristics that distinguish the holy war from other wars are the cultic activities prior to the battle and the *herem*, or ban, the total annihilation of the populace of the city being attacked. In a holy war, God fights on behalf of the Israelites, and at times even in place of them. For example, after the Israelites are saved from the Egyptians, they sing: "The LORD is a man of war; the LORD is his name" (Exod. 15:3; all biblical citations are from the RSV); in 2 Kings 18–19, God kills the invading Assyrians with a plague. Although the concept of holy war was shared by other Near Eastern cultures such as Ugarit, Mari, Egypt, Assyria, and Moab, the Israelite conception had several distinguishing characteristics: In Israelite culture, warriors were not considered the primary heroes, holy war imagery is at times used by the prophets against Israel itself, and sometimes God alone acts as warrior.[2]

Gerhard von Rad has traced the history of the holy war among the Israelites. Biblically, the earliest holy wars are found in the book of Joshua, in which the Israelites militarily conquer Canaan; yet Joshua was written much later than the events it describes, and biblical scholars have given various accounts of the actual history of this period. The book of Judges, however, according to von Rad, presents a fairly accurate description of Israelite warfare during the twelfth century BC, and therefore provides our earliest historical account of Israelite holy war. Von Rad states that the Israelite holy wars of this period were primarily defensive, as the Israelites responded to the provocations of their neighbors. Significantly, the author of Judges usually describes these provocations as arising from the idolatry of these tribes, therefore making idolatry the origin or cause *of* war, rather than a cause *for* war, as the holy war is typically characterized.[3]

The emergence of the Israelite monarchy in the late eleventh century BC led to changes in the way the Israelites waged war. According to von Rad, the holy war died out during the rule of Kings Saul and David because of institutional changes brought about by the monarchy, especially the replacement of the older militia with a standing army.[4] As T. R. Hobbs notes, it was also during the period of the monarchy that offensive wars became more prominent. For example, the wars of David are neither defensive nor holy wars, but wars to establish an empire.[5]

The holy war experienced a revival, however, under King Josiah in the seventh century BC as part of his deuteronomistic reforms. Josiah instituted sweeping reforms against paganism in the kingdom of Judah, and this antipagan fervor carried over into his foreign policy. This religious revival helped Josiah muster a militia after the Judean army had been wiped out by the Assyrians, and Josiah began to expand Judah's borders, taking advantage of the decline of the Assyrian Empire. For the first time the idolatry of Israel/Judah's neighbors served as a cause *for* war, and the holy war became a cultic punishment for their sins. This version of the holy war was then read back into Israelite history, as Joshua was written at this time.[6]

The holy war is also related to a broader Old Testament theme, Israel's struggle with idolatry. Whether waged defensively or offensively, the holy war served to protect Israelite society from the idolatry of its neighbors. In the period of the Judges, the Israelites' defensive holy wars not only ensured their physical survival, but were also a safeguard against the alien ways, both political and religious, of their neighbors. Later under King Josiah, this wariness of foreign gods and kings was simply used to justify offensive actions on the part of Israel. On the other hand, in the deuteronomistic history, spanning from Joshua to 2 Kings, the Israelites' own idolatry is the cause of their weakness before their enemies. In Judges, the idolatry of the Israelites leads to the breakdown of their society and their vulnerability to attacks. The book 2 Kings attributes the fall of both Israel and Judah to the idolatry promoted or tolerated by a series of evil kings, culminating in King Manasseh of Judah, who in the seventh century BC "did much evil in the sight of the LORD, provoking him to anger," including desecrating the temple in Jerusalem and sacrificing his own son, leading to the destruction of Judah by the Babylonians (2 Kings 21:6). Therefore the ultimate origin of Israel's wars could be found not only in the idolatry of Israel's neighbors, but also in Israel's own idolatry.[7]

The logic of this connection between idolatry and war lies in the Old Testament conviction that God created the world in an orderly fashion, and idolatry, or turning away from God, puts this order in jeopardy. The creation account of Genesis 1:1–2:4a presents creation as ordered and peaceful, in contrast to the violence of other creation stories, such as the Babylonian *Enuma Elish*, in which the god Marduk defeats the goddess Tiamat in battle and creates the world from her corpse. In the Old Testament, peace and justice are essential aspects of God's creation, and violence and injustice are, in a sense, ruptures of that order.[8] Turning away from God, either through idolatry or refusing to acknowledge God, violates this order and invariably leads to injustice. For example, in Exodus, the Pharaoh oppresses the Israelites because he does not know God: "Who is the LORD, that I should heed his voice and let Israel go? I do not know the LORD, and moreover I will not let Israel go" (Exod. 5:2).[9] It is not surprising, then, that the Israelites would conclude that their neighbors' aggression was rooted in their idolatry, or that the Israelites' own idolatry could lead to civil strife or invasions from their neighbors.

The Old Testament Prophets

The Hebrew prophets' admonitions about war reflect the changing Israelite views on war outlined earlier. According to Hobbs, the pre-exilic prophets' protests against war represent a condemnation of the offensive, imperial warfare of the early monarchy.[10] On the other hand, von Rad points out that Isaiah uses holy war language in chapter 31 to encourage Israel in its struggle with Assyria. Isaiah, however, is urging the Israelites to reject an alliance with Egypt against Assyria, and to instead trust in God, who will fight on behalf of Israel. Because of their pride, the Israelites trust in their own deeds rather than in God.[11] This theme is echoed by the post-exilic prophet Zechariah: "Not by might, nor by power, but by my Spirit, says the LORD of hosts" (Zech. 4:6).[12] Jeremiah also uses holy war language, but in judgment on the people of Israel themselves, reflecting the theme that Israel's own idolatry will bring destruction upon itself.[13]

The prophets called Israel to trust in God not only to defeat their foes but also to bring about peace. According to the prophets, rather than relying on themselves, the Israelites must trust in God, who will usher in a messianic age of peace and justice. This hope is expressed by Isaiah: "He shall judge between the nations, and shall decide for many peoples; and they shall beat their swords into plowshares, and their spears into pruning hooks; nation shall not lift up sword against nation, neither shall they learn war any more" (Isa. 2:4). But the prophets did not uniformly share Isaiah's belief that God would act in the place of Israel in establishing peace. The post-exilic prophetic vision of peace often involves Israel's violent subjugation of its neighbors.[14] The prophet Joel reverses Isaiah's prediction: "Beat your plowshares into swords, and your pruning hooks into spears; let the weak say, 'I am a warrior'" (Joel 3:10).

The prophets also develop the notion of idolatry as the source of Israel's woes. The theme of idolatry as the source of Israel's vulnerability to its neighbors pervades the prophetic writings.[15] The eighth-century prophet Hosea emphasizes the Israelites' lack of knowledge of God—"There is no faithfulness or kindness, and no knowledge of God in the land" (Hosea 4:1)—warning that Israel's unfaithfulness will lead to its fall before Assyria. In the seventh century Jeremiah also prophesies against the idolatry of Judah, arguing that it will lead to the destruction of Jerusalem by the Babylonians (Jer. 10–11). The author known as Second Isaiah provides several scathing attacks on idolatry. He writes, "All who make idols are nothing, and the things they delight in do not profit; their witnesses neither see nor know, that they may be put to shame," and later continues, "They know not, nor do they discern; for he has shut their eyes, so that they cannot see, and their minds, so that they cannot understand" (Isa. 44:9, 18). Writing during the Babylonian Exile, Second Isaiah suggests that the Israelites suffered the destruction of their homeland because of their idolatry, but now the Babylonians will fall because of their own idolatry and the Israelites will be liberated.

The prophets connect idolatry with violence and injustice in a more complete way than do the historical books of the Old Testament. The prophet Amos accuses the Israelites of injustice, writing that they "trample the head of the poor into the dust of the earth, and turn aside the way of the afflicted," and links this with an accusation of idolatry: "They lay themselves down beside every altar, upon garments taken in pledge" (Amos 2:7–8). In Isaiah 2, the wealthy are led to idolatry because of their love for their material goods, contributing to the corruption of society and eventually to the fall of Israel to the Assyrians.[16] The Old Testament connection between war and idolatry, or turning away from God, is carried over into and transformed in the New Testament.

The Gospels

From the time it was written, the New Testament has been scoured for clues as to the proper Christian attitude toward the morality of war. When those thinking about war have looked to the Gospels, most often they have turned to the sayings of Jesus, particularly in the Sermon on the Mount, yet the meaning of Jesus's sayings is highly contested.[17] Debates over what the Gospels say about the morality of war will continue, but the Gospels also provide insights into war's origins. The Gospels take up from the Old Testament the belief that lack of knowledge of God leads to evil.[18]

The emphasis on knowledge of God is particularly evident in the Gospel of John, which presents a stark contrast between knowledge and lack of knowledge, light and darkness. In the opening of the Gospel we are told that Jesus is "the light of men. The light shines in the darkness, and the darkness has not overcome it" (John 1:4–5). John adds: "The true light that enlightens every man was coming into the world. He was in the world, and the world was made through him, yet the world knew him not. He came to his own home, and his own people received him not. But to all who received him, who believed in his name, he gave power to become children of God; who were born, not of blood nor of the will of the flesh nor of the will of man, but of God" (John 1:9–12). In one of his discourses, Jesus links light and darkness with good and evil deeds (John 3:19–21). When Jesus is on trial before Pontius Pilate, the conflict between truth and untruth reaches its culmination.[19] Jesus says to Pilate, "For this I was born, and for this I have come into the world, to bear witness to the truth. Every one who is of the truth hears my voice," and Pilate responds, "What is truth?" (John 18:37–38). Although the Gospel of John does not speak about war, its claim that evil is caused by lack of knowledge of God is clearly related to the Old Testament view that evils such as war have their origins in turning away from God, particularly in the form of idolatry.

This contrast between knowledge and ignorance is developed in the First Epistle of John. Knowledge of God is demonstrated by following the commandments (1 John 2:3–6). The author continues, "He who does not love does not know God; for God is love" (1 John 4:8). Knowledge of God has been given by Jesus Christ, the Son of God (1 John 5:20). To follow Jesus Christ is to walk in the light, while to sin is to walk in darkness (1 John 1:5–7). Elsewhere John writes, "He who loves his brother abides in the light, and in it there is no cause for stumbling. But he who hates his brother is in the darkness and walks in the darkness, and does not know where he is going, because the darkness has blinded his eyes" (1 John 2:10–11). One also finds the metaphor of blindness in the Gospel of Mark. In Mark 8:22–26 and 10:46–52, Jesus heals two physically blind men, but between these episodes Jesus's disciples show real blindness: They are unable to see who Jesus is and what he must accomplish. Although neither 1 John nor the Gospels of Mark and John relate lack of knowledge of God to idolatry, this connection is made in the Pauline epistles.

The Pauline Epistles

Christian thinkers have turned to the epistles of Paul not so much for statements on violence and war, but rather for Paul's treatment of political authority and its relation to the cosmic order established by God. In the Epistle to the Romans, Paul writes: "Bless those who persecute you; bless and do not curse them. . . . Repay no one evil for evil, but take thought for what is noble in the sight of all. If possible, so far as it depends on you, live peaceably with all. Beloved, never avenge yourselves, but leave it to the wrath of God; for it is written, 'Vengeance is mine, I will repay, says the Lord'" (Rom. 12:14, 17–19). Yet immediately afterward, Paul writes, "Let every person be subject to the governing authorities. For there is no authority except from God, and those that exist have been instituted by God," and he adds, "[the ruler] does not bear the sword in vain; he is the servant of God to execute his wrath on the wrongdoer" (Rom. 13:1, 4). Paul here establishes a dichotomy—between the nonresistance of everyday Christian citizens and the sword of the government—that would be formative in Christian thinking about war. Despite the authorities' power to bear the sword, Paul insists that only Christ can establish true peace; Rome's claim to have established real peace is idolatrous.[20]

Entities known as the "powers" play an important role in Paul's account of the Gospel. The powers are invisible realities that are manifested in political authority and other institutions; Anthony J. Tambasco writes, "The powers are not persons in a world apart from the material, but neither are they only symbols of a purely material reality. They are real, immaterial, invisible dimensions of the concrete manifestations of power in human history."[21] The powers are not evil in their essence, because they are created by God: "For in him all things were created, in heaven and on earth, visible and invisible, whether thrones or dominions or principalities or authorities—all things were created through him and for him" (Col. 1:16). Yet the powers have rebelled against God.[22] In the final analysis Christians do not struggle against political leaders and institutions, against "flesh and blood," "but against the principalities, against the powers, against the world rulers of this present darkness, against the spiritual hosts of wickedness in the heavenly places" (Eph. 6:12). Christ, however, has ultimately overcome the powers. In 1 Corinthians it seems that Christ will destroy the powers (1 Cor. 15:24–7), whereas in Ephesians it seems the powers will be converted (Eph. 3:10). The rebellion of the powers against God's order has led to chaos and violence; peace exists only when Christ restores the original order established by God.[23]

Surely passing themselves off as gods is part of the rebellion of the powers, and Paul often touches on the topic of idolatry. Idolatry is among the "works of the flesh" that Paul lists in Galatians (Gal. 5:20). Before warning the Corinthians against eating meat sacrificed to idols, Paul writes, "Therefore, my beloved, shun the worship of idols" (1 Cor. 10:14). In his letter to the Romans, Paul closely links idolatry with other sins: "Therefore God gave them up in the lusts of their hearts to impurity, to the dishonoring of their bodies among themselves, because they exchanged the truth about God for a lie and worshipped and served the creature rather than the Creator, who is blessed forever!" (Rom. 1:24–5).

Although Paul did not write specifically of war, his conception of idolatry as a cause for evil links him back to the Old Testament theme connecting idolatry and war. The Bible does not present a unified view on the morality of war, but it does provide a suggestive perspective on war's origins. The Hebrew prophets and the Gospel of John clearly place the origins of evil in turning away from or failing to know God, and for the prophets and the apostle Paul, turning away from God is embodied in the practice of idolatry. In the historical books of the Old Testament, the idolatry of Israel's neighbors led them to wage unjust wars on Israel, and conversely Israel became subject to attack by its neighbors when it fell into idolatry. The explicit connection between idolatry and war is not found in the New Testament, but the fathers of the church took up this theme.

THE CHURCH FATHERS ON WAR AND ITS ORIGINS

Perhaps no topic in the history of Christian thought on war has received as much attention as the church fathers' attitude toward war. Prior to the rise of Constantine in the early 300s, the church fathers were unanimously opposed to war, although Christian practice was not so consistent.[24] Scholars have paid relatively little attention to what the church fathers thought about the origins of war, however. In fact, the fathers developed a sophisticated and surprisingly unified view on the origins of war. Drawing on the biblical themes already outlined, the fathers traced the origins of violence and war to the idolatrous practices of pagans.

The Pre-Constantinian Fathers

The early fathers of the church claim that war is the result of pagan religion, particularly focusing on the Romans, and they further claim that pagan religion is inspired by demons. According to Justin Martyr (c. 100–c. 165), the demons came to the world and through magic convinced humans to worship them as gods.[25] The North African Tertullian (c. 160–c. 230), on the other hand, states that overzealous admirers deified heroes of the distant past, and demons took advantage of the situation by pretending to be those gods.[26] In his *Apology*, Tertullian surveys the literature of Roman religion and with painstaking argument shows the absurdity of the myths invented about these heroes and the ways in which demons have deceived the pagans.

Many of the early fathers see the demons as a cause of evil behavior, especially through the influence of pagan religion. Tertullian writes, "The breath of demons and [fallen] angels induces the corruption of the mind by foul passions, by dread derangements of the mind, or by savage lusts accompanied by manifold perversities," including sacrifices to idols.[27] Irenaeus (c. 125–c. 202), the bishop of Lyons, echoes this theme.[28] Justin writes that because Christians expose their lies, the demons inspire the authorities to put Christians to death, and even to put to death those, like Socrates, who discovered aspects of the truth before the time of Christ.[29] Origen (c. 185–c. 254) also links persecution with the demons, even claiming that demonic influence can be seen in the faces of the judges who condemn Christians to death.[30]

Both Justin and Origen also explicitly link the demons with war. Justin writes that "partly by magic writings, partly by the fear they instilled into them and the punishments they inflicted on them, and partly by instructing them in the use of sacrifices, incense, and libations," "among men [the demons] engendered murders, wars, adulteries, all sorts of dissipation, and every species of sin."[31] Likewise, Origen argues that Christians do more good for the empire than soldiers do, because when they pray, they "vanquish all demons who stir up war, and lead to the violation of oaths, and disturb the peace."[32] Here Origen echoes Paul's belief that Christians do not fight against flesh and blood, but against the powers. Justin and Origen's claim that ultimately idolatry is the source of war also parallels the Old Testament connection between idolatry and war, although without the central focus on the particular political community of Israel.

Justin contrasts the Christian way of life with that of the pagans. According to Justin, Christians live by a set of practices, including the worship of God, sharing with the poor, and love for enemies, that are the opposite of those inspired by demons.[33] Elsewhere he writes, "We who delighted in war, in the slaughter of one another, and in every other kind of iniquity have in every part of the world converted our weapons of war into implements of peace—our swords into ploughshares, our spears into farmers' tools—and we cultivate piety, justice, brotherly charity, faith, and hope," which come from God through Jesus Christ.[34]

Despite proposing a demonic influence on the exercise of Roman political authority, particularly in the Roman practices of war and persecution, the early church fathers do not associate political authority itself directly with the demonic. One of the few direct connections between the demonic and political authorities is made by Irenaeus of Lyons, and that is to show that Satan lied when he offered Jesus all the kingdoms of the earth because really they belong to God.[35]

Other fathers reinforce this belief that God ordains political authorities. Tertullian claims that Christians pray for the emperor (including for "security at home" and "brave armies") because God has ordained the political authorities.[36] Christians can even say, "Caesar belongs more to us, since he has been appointed by our God."[37] Tertullian links the legitimacy of political authorities to the Pauline concept of the powers: "[God] existed before time and . . . has made the world a unified system of times [and] has ordained changes in the ruling powers during certain periods in the course of time."[38] Likewise Origen, a few years later, argues that God ordains rulers.[39] Tertullian and Origen recognize that even if rulers govern legitimately, this does not legitimize all of their actions, such as the persecution of Christians. Despite recognizing the legitimacy of political rulers, Tertullian seems to suggest and Origen explicitly states that Christians should not hold public office, a tension that would be resolved later in the Christian tradition.[40]

In the thought of the early church fathers, particularly Justin, Tertullian, and Origen, then, a Christian account of the origins of war began to emerge. Political authority itself is not evil and is not the source of war, but political authorities have been wrapped in a web of beliefs and practices that lead them to war. Demons were responsible for leading the Romans, among others, to worship them as gods. Religious practices and literature developed around this idolatrous worship. The demons' influence began to be felt throughout Roman culture as these pagan rituals and texts fostered the vices in the people, vices that are expressed in all areas of society. The pervasiveness of pagan religion and the concomitant vices made it much more likely that individuals would commit sinful actions, and also more likely that society as a whole would engage in wickedness, including war. The fathers also concluded that in contrast to pagan religious practices, Christian religious practices form virtuous people and therefore lead to peace.

The Post-Constantinian Fathers

The church underwent great changes in the fourth century as it went from being persecuted to being the official religion of the empire, yet in their writings touching on the origins of war, the fathers of this century wrote on similar themes. The line of thought on the origins of war developed by the earlier church fathers reached its culmination in the writings of Augustine and Paulus Orosius, but also began to lose its original relevance. In his *City of God*, Augustine created the most sophisticated critique of Roman paganism yet, and linked paganism and idolatry with the vices of the Romans. Yet as Christianity became more and more prevalent throughout Europe, it became less and less credible to blame wickedness, including war, on paganism and idolatry. This difficulty came to light in the *City of God* and in Orosius's *The Seven Books of History against the Pagans.*

In the *City of God*, written in the early fifth century, Augustine (354–430) takes up the themes of the previous fathers concerning paganism and wickedness. Augustine accepts the theory that "the gods were once human beings who received adulation from men who wished to have them as gods."[41] The demons "rejoice in the errors of mankind, and to further such errors put themselves forward to be worshipped by a thousand tricks designed to ruin and deceive."[42] The demons promote the vices among their worshippers through their example and through pagan religious practices, particularly the theatrical performances dedicated to the gods.[43] Perhaps more than earlier fathers, Augustine emphasizes the harmful role not only of pagan literature and philosophy in influencing people's behavior for the worse, but also of pagan religious practices themselves.

The pagans, according to Augustine, come into inevitable conflict with Christians. In fact, the pagan Romans are part of a larger community spread throughout history in opposition to the community of those faithful to God. Augustine writes, "We see that the two cities were created by two kinds of love: the earthly city was created by self-love reaching the point of contempt for God, the Heavenly City by the love of God carried as far as contempt of self."[44] Love of self and love of God are inner dispositions, but they are formed by practices, whether pagan rituals or the practices of the church. This does not mean that all members of the church are citizens of the Heavenly City; the good and the evil are mixed within the church on earth, separated only at the end of time.[45] Yet Christianity has the power to set people free from the domination of the demons.[46] This leads the pagans, influenced by the demons, to persecute the Christians.[47]

Augustine, like the earlier fathers, clearly links idolatry and war. Wars are the result of the self-love of the earthly city, which is fostered by idolatry.[48] Augustine writes that the civil wars that racked the Roman Republic in its last decades had their origins in the vices that had developed among the Romans because of their idolatry.[49] He makes this argument to show that calamities had befallen Rome even before the advent of Christianity, since some pagans blamed the Christians for the evils plaguing the empire in Augustine's own day.[50] Yet the very fact that calamities and wickedness, including war, continued even after Christians controlled the empire weakened the effectiveness of the fathers' explanation of war's origins.

This weakness is particularly evident in *The Seven Books of History against the Pagans* by Paulus Orosius, a disciple of Augustine. Orosius (c. 385–420) meant *Against the Pagans*, written around the same time as the *City of God*, to be an extension of Augustine's argument that there had been calamities and wars throughout pre-Christian history. This makes for grim reading. Orosius claims that it is perverse to blame the empire's misfortunes on God's faithful, because humanity has suffered since the sin of Adam and Eve.[51] Augustine and Orosius both admit that calamities, including war, continued even when society was predominantly Christian, and by the early fifth century it had become clear that even Christian rulers engaged in unjust wars; therefore the fathers' argument on the origins of war lost much of its force.

The connection between idolatry and wickedness survived, however, in Augustine's moral theology. For Augustine, drawing on the thought of the Platonist philosophers, evil is not a substance opposed to the good, but is rather the privation of good; evil is when something is less than it should be. Concerning human affairs, Augustine writes in *Free Choice of the Will*, "We usually speak of evil in two ways: first, when we say that someone has done evil; second, when someone has suffered something evil."[52] One is not necessarily doing evil when one causes someone or something to suffer evil; this is merely a result of creaturely finitude.[53] Sin is a defect, an evil, of the will.[54]

Since sin is a defect of the will, it must involve defective preferences and desires. Augustine concludes that sin is the pursuit of temporal goods to the neglect of the pursuit of God. He adds, "Every kind of wrongdoing, namely sin, is included, it seems to me, under this one class."[55] Temporal goods really are goods, but only the good person uses them rightly. The evil person "becomes subject to things which should be subject to him, making these goods his goal when, really, his true good should consist in assigning them their proper place and use."[56] In his *Confessions*, Augustine makes it clear that when a person becomes subject to temporal goods, this is really idolatry, because he has put these goods in the place of God.[57] He draws on Paul's claim that the wicked "worshipped and served the creature rather than the Creator," now suggesting that disordered love for a thing is a form of worship, even if no explicit idolatry is involved.

By describing how any sinful action could be considered a form of idolatry, Augustine shows how the earlier fathers' theory of the origins of war could still be true when Christians are responsible for unjust wars. In the Old Testament, it was the Israelites themselves who were often guilty of idolatry, and the Old Testament authors saw this infidelity as the source of Israel's woes, including military defeat at the hands of its their neighbors. The early church fathers continued to link war with the idolatry of the Romans, but unlike the Old Testament writers, they had little need to reflect on how members of their own community—in this case, Christians—could be responsible for unjust wars. By developing the Pauline idea that all sins are a form of idolatry and that therefore even Christians can engage in idolatry, Augustine is able to connect biblical and patristic thought. Augustine's moral theology also forms the background of his development of just war reasoning.[58] Unjust wars are caused by the idolatry of those who love violence and seek to unfairly dominate others. Even just wars can be considered to have their origins in idolatry because they are a response to the wickedness of others.

Augustine's reinterpretation of the biblical and patristic accounts of the origins of war ensured that two ideas that are crucial to developing a Christian view of war's origins were passed on. The first is that vices and sinful behavior, including unjust wars, are fostered by cultural and religious practices that turn people away from the true God. Conversely, Christian practices foster virtuous behavior and lead to peace. By expanding the meaning of "idolatry" to include all sinful actions, Augustine extended the usefulness of this idea. The second is that the origins of war can be found in forces or "powers" that transcend individuals and governments, but that nevertheless exist through the free choices of individuals. The origins of war cannot be attributed to any intrinsic evil located in the individual or the government.[59]

MEDIEVAL THOUGHT ON THE ORIGINS OF WAR

The centuries immediately after the fall of Rome were an unruly time and produced little in the way of Christian thought on war. The Roman Empire in the West fell before wave upon wave of invaders; as soon as one group of invaders settled down, they were terrorized by new groups. Goths, Franks, Huns, Angles, Saxons, Magyars, Vikings, and so on sought to carve out homes for themselves and permanently shaped the ethnic makeup of Europe. Eventually the invaders converted to Christianity. During the early Middle Ages, however, Christians were too busy fighting for their survival to think systematically about politics or war.

Once a semblance of order had been reestablished, Christians began to reflect on war once again, and three separate strands of thought emerged from the earlier tradition: one focusing on the origins of war in personal and cultural practices, one on moral reasoning about war, and one on the establishment of peace. Now that Christians could no longer claim paganism as the exclusive source of war, the medieval philosopher John of Salisbury sought its origins in the temptations of life in the royal court. Thomas Aquinas refined Augustine's just war doctrine while also providing valuable insights into the natural law and virtue. Other thinkers of the Middle Ages, such as Dante Aligheri and Pierre Dubois, began to think about institutional ways of establishing peace in Europe.

John of Salisbury and Thomas Aquinas

As the political situation in Europe became more stable, Christian political thought experienced a revival in the twelfth and thirteenth centuries, thanks largely to John of Salisbury and Thomas Aquinas. These two represent the sundering of two elements of Christian reflection on war that had been united in the thought of the fathers, particularly Augustine: first, the analysis and evaluation of the practices and beliefs that lead to war, and second, the development of moral principles applicable in situations of war. Whereas John of Salisbury wrote critically about the vices of the royal court developing at the height of the

Middle Ages, Aquinas refined moral concepts such as the natural law and the virtues, which were useful for analyzing both the morality and origins of war.

In his *Policraticus*, John of Salisbury (c. 1110–80) presents a conventional account of the purpose of political life. The prince's authority comes from God; he rules for the benefit of the people.[60] The magistracy and the army are the ruler's two hands, and with both hands, the ruler has the authority to kill.[61] The just ruler must sometimes resort to war for the maintenance of good order: "Whoever is desirous of peace is to prepare for war; whoever covets victory is to train his troops diligently; whoever wishes for good fortune is to fight by skill, not by chance."[62]

John distinguishes the good prince from the tyrant and argues for the right to overthrow a tyrant. Whereas the good prince rules for the sake of his people and executes the will of God, the tyrant rules for his own benefit. When the tyrant rules, "the grace of God is plainly being assailed and God is in a certain fashion being challenged to a battle," and whereas the prince is the image of the divine majesty, "the tyrant is an image of the strength of the Adversary and the depravity of Lucifer."[63] There are faint echoes of the biblical concepts of the holy war and the powers in John's statements. According to John, even the tyrant is a minister of God by whom "the evil are punished and the good are corrected and trained."[64] Here we find echoed the early church fathers' distinction between the perversions committed by the government and the government itself. Still, "it is not only permitted, but it is also equitable and just to slay tyrants. For he who receives the sword deserves to perish by the sword."[65] Therefore John contributes a strong defense of the overthrow of tyrants to Christian reflection on the morality of war, but his most important contribution to understanding the origins of war is his meditation on life in the royal court.

According to John, the flattery and viciousness of court life pose the danger of turning princes into tyrants, and the prince must fortify himself with virtues to resist such temptations. Although he had been trained in theology, John was a church official responsible for diplomacy between England and the papacy, and was acquainted with both King Henry II and Archbishop Thomas à Becket of Canterbury. John writes, "For in fact it is a frequent occurrence that a court either receives or creates vicious men, among whom transgressions increase in audacity since their vices are indulged by reason of their intimacy with the powerful."[66] The pride that comes from power is the root of all other vices.[67] Those with access to power are also led astray by wealth, "which turns one aside from the vision of truth."[68] The ruler must be careful to practice the virtues, which come only through God's grace.[69] The virtues and vices of a prince are not merely of personal concern, since the prince influences his people by his behavior.[70]

John's thoughts on the virtues and vices of rulers contributed to a Christian theory of war's origins. Although he did not explicitly claim that the vices of leaders lead to wars, as the Renaissance humanists would later do, John did say that a ruler becomes a tyrant when he is overcome by vices, and a tyrant makes war on his neighbors and his own people (not to mention God). John's description of the concrete practices that could lead Christian rulers to war is also significant, paralleling the concrete cultural and religious practices named in the church fathers' earlier treatment of the origins of war in pagan idolatry.

Whereas John of Salisbury's *Policraticus* is written as a practical guide for the Christian prince, Thomas Aquinas (1225–74) provided a much more theoretical account of the different types of law that would be influential in later Catholic thinking about war. Aquinas's theory of law, which he categorized as eternal, natural, human, and divine law, unites a description of the objective reality of human political life with normative judgments about political actions such as war. In Aquinas's view, moral right and wrong arise from human nature, as created by God. This includes the moral principles that govern political decision making, because politics is a natural part of human life. Therefore Aquinas created a synthesis of concrete observations of the realities of politics, philosophical reflection on human nature and political life, and moral judgments. He integrated this synthesis into his theology, showing how political life, among humanity's other pursuits, is finally fulfilled by humanity's ultimate end, communion with God. I will outline this synthesis in some detail because it was the breakdown of this synthesis in later centuries that led to the modern views of the origins of war to which Christians must now respond.

Natural law, according to Aquinas, consists in the moral precepts that arise out of human nature; it is part of God's order for the whole of creation. The eternal law is the order of all things that God has established, and "it is evident that all things partake somewhat of the eternal law, in so far as, namely, from its being imprinted on them, they derive their respective inclinations to their proper acts and ends." Rational creatures participate in the eternal law in a special way because they have the use of reason, and this is why they are governed by the natural law.[71] The first principle of the natural law is that "good is to be done and pursued, and evil is to be avoided," and for humans the good is determined by their "natural inclinations," including those we share with all created things, those we share with animals, and those unique to rational creatures.[72] Because humanity is created with a supernatural end, however, divine aid is also necessary to direct us to this end, the fulfillment of our nature.[73] Human laws make the natural law more specific and apply it to concrete circumstances, such as specifying the punishment for a crime.[74] Although human laws vary among societies, there is also a law of nations that includes "those things which are derived from the law of nature, as conclusions from premises . . . without which men cannot live together."[75] The law of nations is "in some way, natural to man" because it is derived from the natural law, but distinct from it.[76]

Aquinas outlines the purpose of government in his treatise *On Kingship, to the King of Cyprus.* Humanity is social by nature, according to Aquinas, because we need each other for protection and because one person is not able to do all of the things necessary for his or her well-being. It is also natural for society to have some form of government. The purpose of government is to serve the good of the society, and therefore a ruler is just or a tyrant based on whether he serves the common good or his own good.[77]

The government has an important role in helping persons achieve their final, supernatural end. As Aquinas writes: "Yet through virtuous living man is further ordained to a higher end, which consists in the enjoyment of God, as we have said above. Consequently, since society must have the same end as the individual man, it is not the ultimate end of an assembled multitude to live virtuously, but through virtuous living to attain to the possession of God." Because humans cannot attain this end by their own powers, however, it is not the role of the king to direct them toward it; that ministry is given to priests, who were commissioned by God and to whom the king ought to be subject. The king is responsible for the intermediate ends of social unity and peace, the virtue of the people, and the goods necessary for proper living, and therefore his responsibilities include providing for the well-being of the people, punishing vices and rewarding virtues, and defending society from aggression.[78] It is this responsibility of the ruler to defend society that is the basis of Aquinas's treatment of the just war.[79]

Aquinas says very little about the origins of war; however, he does address the origins of wickedness, including unjust wars, in the human heart. He primarily focuses on the source of individuals' evil actions, whether it is in ignorance or in free choice. More important for understanding the origins of war, however, is Aquinas's theory of the vices and virtues, or dispositions to do evil or good, respectively, which we develop through our actions.

The virtues and vices are habits, or dispositions, that lead to good or evil actions and are formed in us by good or evil actions.[80] The virtues and vices are found in the intellect, the will, and in the "sensitive appetites."[81] The cardinal virtues—prudence, justice, temperance, and fortitude—correspond to the perfection of human nature, but because humans are ordained to a supernatural end, the cardinal virtues alone are not sufficient, and therefore God gives us the theological virtues of faith, hope, and charity. This infusion of God's grace even transforms the cardinal virtues so that they are proportionate to our supernatural end.[82] The sacraments are the most important practices that form the theological virtues, and therefore it is the particular practices of the church that dispose men and women to be and do good.[83] Aquinas gives no corresponding account of the practices that form the vices, no doubt because they are so varied; thus his treatment of the vices lacks the concreteness found in John of Salisbury's description of how life in the royal court can create vices in rulers.

Nevertheless, Aquinas's theory of the vices and virtues, particularly as it relates to his theory of the natural law, is relevant for developing a Catholic perspective on war's origins. The virtues and vices are dispositions governing the very natural inclinations that form the basis of the natural law. Therefore the actions that form virtues and in turn result from the virtues are actions in accord with the natural law, and the converse is true concerning the vices. If the just war theory is derived from the natural law, as Aquinas claims, then it makes sense to conclude that making just decisions about war is in some way connected with the virtues, whereas making unjust decisions is connected with the vices. It might be that a ruler dominated by the vices, or in our democratic times a society dominated by the vices, is more likely to cause unjust wars. These vices are formed by concrete cultural practices, but Aquinas's theory of the vices is relatively abstract compared to the fathers' theory of the origins of war in pagan religious practices or John of Salisbury's reflections on the royal court. Aquinas is very clear, however, that it is the religious practices of Christianity that potentially form the virtues in us, and therefore contribute to truly peaceful behavior.

Dante Alighieri and Pierre Dubois

The poet Dante Alighieri and the lawyer Pierre Dubois, writing in the following century, both made a very different claim about peace, arguing that some kind of overarching political institution is necessary to establish peace among nations, and thus beginning a third strand of medieval Christian reflection on war. Dante and Dubois both looked back to the Roman Empire as an ideal of European and Christian unity and sought the means for reestablishing that unity in their own day. Dante, more well known for his *Divine Comedy*, argued for the political supremacy of the Holy Roman Emperor in his *Monarchia*. Dubois, on the other hand, sought to establish a council of Christian rulers and ecclesiastical officials. In their plans for unifying Europe and ending conflicts among Christians, Dante and Dubois also revealed their thoughts on the origins of war.

Dante Alighieri (1265–1321) was drawn into the Italian political conflicts of the late thirteenth and early fourteenth centuries, eventually taking a pro-imperial position in the conflict between emperor and pope. By the late thirteenth century, the pro-papal Guelphs had driven the pro-imperial Ghibellines out of Florence. The Guelphs of Florence, in turn, divided into the Black Guelphs, who favored aristocratic rule and were aided by the pope, and the White Guelphs, who favored Florence's republican government and resented Pope Boniface VIII's increasing interference in local affairs. Dante was a member of the White Guelphs, and when Charles of Valois, the brother of King Philip IV of France, helped bring the Black Guelphs to power with the support of Boniface, Dante was sent into exile. While in exile, Dante came to hope that an emperor would emerge to restore unity to Italy and to end the papacy's involvement in temporal affairs. This is the immediate context of Dante's *Monarchia*, although he touches on themes of universal importance.

In *Monarchia*, Dante concludes that temporal well-being, including peace, could best be brought about by a universal monarch ruling the whole earth.

Dante argues that just as a city or a kingdom is left in chaos if power is divided, so too the whole of humanity must be guided by one ruler.[84] When two equal rulers come into conflict, they turn to a superior to act as judge; therefore, in order for there to be justice in the world, there must be one supreme ruler to whom lower rulers can turn to render judgment between them.[85] Dante has few qualms about the possibility that a universal emperor would become a tyrant; the emperor would be just because, since his jurisdiction is universal, he would not covet the possessions of others as lesser rulers do.[86] Dante argued that the Holy Roman Emperor, as the successor of the ancient Romans, was the best candidate for supreme ruler.[87]

Pierre Dubois (c. 1250–c. 1312), Dante's contemporary, was a proponent of French royal power in its struggle against the papacy. Dubois was a lawyer and pamphleteer, part of the emerging legal bureaucracy in France that was fiercely loyal to the king. Dubois supported King Philip IV of France against Pope Boniface VIII when the king began to heavily tax French churches without the pope's permission in order to fund his war with England. Taxes on churches were typically to be used to fund a crusade, and Boniface objected to the use of these funds for fighting fellow Christians. Eventually Philip had a council declare Boniface a heretic and a French force briefly imprisoned the pope. Upon Boniface's death soon after, the Frenchman Clement V was elected pope, and in a few years he moved the papacy to Avignon in France, where it was effectively under French control. Dubois' writings on the unification of Europe were shaped by his support for Philip's policies.

In *The Recovery of the Holy Land*, Dubois outlines a plan for the unification of Christian Europe in order to establish peace. He, however, seeks peace in Europe to better fight the Muslims in a crusade. Conflicts among Christians are detrimental to a crusade, according to Dubois, because they distract Christians' attention from retaking the Holy Land. Therefore Christians should seek to form a single commonwealth.[88] According to Dubois, "Now if all Catholics are at peace with one another, warriors will stream from every direction toward the Holy Land and will in all probability be able to recover and defend it."[89] Echoing the holy war language of the Bible, Dubois writes that Christians must pray to God, who "is the God and Lord of armies, who alone is the cause of peace and victory. The Holy Land can never be regained and held if the war leaders and the warriors under them rely on their own strength and consider that sufficient to gain so great a victory and preserve its fruits in perpetuity."[90] When the Saracens hear that Europe has united in peace, out of fear they may simply give up the Holy Land without a fight.[91]

Dubois' plan for the unification of Europe is a council dedicated to collective security. The council should be made up of Europe's political and ecclesiastical leaders. If a vassal goes to war, he should be subjected to an economic embargo and his lands devastated by his lord and his allies. Fear of this devastation and the pleadings of his people will convince the vassal not to go to war.[92]

Conflicts between rulers without superiors should be adjudicated by three impartial judges.[93] In contrast to Dante, Dubois has no faith in the possibility of a universal monarch. He writes, "If there were a tendency in this direction there would be wars, rebellions, and dissensions without end. There would be no one who could quell these disturbances because of the multitude of people and the distant areas involved, local differences, and the natural inclination of men toward strife."[94] Nevertheless, Dubois is clear that France should play a leading role in the council.

Dubois does mention a demonic influence on war. He writes that often the victims of war are encouraged by demons to seek revenge through further war. The Saracens are also inspired by the demons who aid them in battle.[95] Dubois adds that those who illegally resort to war should be sent to the front lines of a crusade, and "since they voluntarily welcomed illicit war at Satan's instigation, they should be compelled involuntarily to fight in the vanguard for the destruction of the idol worshippers, the enemies of peace, by withstanding the very ones who [previously] urged them on."[96] Dubois' account of the demonic influence in war is barely a caricature of that of the fathers, however, and his overall plan suggests that the main cause of war is the lack of an institution for conflict resolution among kingdoms.

Although their writings are distinct, both Dante and Dubois find the origins of war in the lack of an overarching political institution to promote justice among nations. According to Dante, war exists because there is no ruler superior to the kingdoms of the world able to adjudicate conflicts between them. Although Dubois is skeptical about the possibility of such a universal monarch, he, too, envisions an institution superior to individual rulers. For Dubois, this institution would be a council of princes and bishops, preferably led by France, that would adjudicate conflicts among individual kingdoms. The purpose of this council would be to promote peace in Europe, but only for the greater goal of recovering the Holy Land from the Muslims. That Dante and Dubois began to think of such institutions in the fourteenth century is paradoxical, given that it was around this time that the medieval notion of Christendom was dissolving and the modern nation-states of Europe were beginning to form, particularly in France and England. This is reflected in the tension in Dubois' work between his internationalism and his French nationalism. The conflicts between temporal rulers and the papacy also show that the Catholic Church was losing its status as the unifier of Europe, even before Christendom was permanently split by the Protestant Reformation. Christians were beginning to conclude that some other form of unification was necessary. Dante and Dubois' early reflections on what we would call international institutions mark the beginning of an idea that would become increasingly important in both Catholic thought and modern political thought: The lack of an authority above the states contributes to conflicts among them, and therefore international institutions have the potential to contribute to international peace.

CONCLUSION

The biblical and patristic writers provided the foundations for a way of thinking about war's origins and the medieval period saw important developments in that way of thinking. The fathers of the church found the origins of war in cultural practices, particularly pagan religious practices, and Augustine extended the notion of idolatry to all forms of wickedness, including unjust wars. In the Middle Ages these two types of reflection on war became separated in the works of John of Salisbury and Thomas Aquinas. John of Salisbury described the temptations to vice in life at court that could turn a good ruler into a tyrant. Aquinas developed a detailed account of politics and the law, as well as moral concepts such as the natural law and the virtues necessary for moral reflection on war. Also during the medieval period, Dante Alighieri and Pierre Dubois began thinking about the lack of international institutions as a factor in the outbreak of war.

The Middle Ages also saw the development of a synthesis of the philosophical with the moral, and the natural with the supernatural, in Christian political thought, particularly in the work of Thomas Aquinas. According to Aquinas, human nature can only be understood in relation to God, and human nature, as it is created by God, is the source of morality. Because humanity is fulfilled only by the supernatural destiny of communion with God, a good that is beyond our powers to achieve, we must be transformed by grace to be truly fulfilled. And because political life is natural to humanity, this means that human political life must be seen through a theological lens. If this is true, then we would expect to find that theological categories are crucial for the task of understanding the origins of war. But the synthesis behind this claim already showed signs of breaking down in the Middle Ages, and it continued to dissolve as the centuries progressed. Modernity in political thought could be characterized as the total breakdown of this synthesis.

NOTES

1. Bainton, *Christian Attitudes*; Lisa Sowle Cahill, *Love Your Enemies*.

2. Wood, *Perspectives on War*, 12–17. Susan Niditch describes sacrificial elements in the cultic aspects of the holy war in *War in the Hebrew Bible*, 29–37.

3. Von Rad, *Holy War*, 54–57; see also McDonald, *God and Violence*, 128–32. T. R. Hobbs describes the various theories about the historical events behind Joshua in *A Time for War*, 30–33.

4. Von Rad, *Holy War*, 74.

5. Hobbs, *A Time for War*, 19.

6. Von Rad, *Holy War*, 117–18, 124–27; Hobbs, *A Time for War*, 150–51; Niditch, *War in the Hebrew Bible*, 56–57.

7. Hobbs, *A Time for War*, 184–85; McDonald, *God and Violence*, 152–53.

8. McDonald, *God and Violence*, 36–38.

9. Ibid., 83.

10. Hobbs, *A Time for War*, 193–97.

11. Von Rad, *Holy War*, 104–6; McDonald, *God and Violence*, 182–89.

12. Wood, *Perspectives on War*, 75.

13. Ibid., 43.

14. Hobbs, *A Time for War*, 219–22.

15. Swaim, *War, Peace, and the Bible*, 11.

16. McDonald, *God and Violence*, 179.

17. For commentaries on some of the most contested passages, see: Humphrey, "Matthew 5:9," 62–63, 70; Wink, "Neither Passivity nor Violence," 102–25; Horsley, "Ethics and Exegesis," 81–83, 86–87; Klassen, "'Love Your Enemies,'" 10–11.

18. When speaking of the knowledge of God, it is important to recognize that in many cases the biblical concept of knowledge means more than adherence to true beliefs; rather, knowledge of a person means an intimate relationship with that person. Therefore knowledge of God means having a relationship with God and living a life of faith, not just believing the right things; a person could hold true beliefs about God and still be far from knowing him.

19. Swaim, *War, Peace, and the Bible*, 41.

20. Ibid., 48–49.

21. Tambasco, "Principalities, Powers and Peace," 119–20.

22. Ibid., 123–24.

23. Zerbe, "Nonretaliation and Peace," 181.

24. Bainton, *Christian Attitudes*, 71–72; Helgeland, Daly, and Burns, *Christians and the Military*, 54; Hunter, "Early Christians and Military Service," 88; Ryan, "The Rejection of Military Service," 225–27; Swift, *Early Fathers on War*, 26–27, 228–29, 242–43.

25. Justin Martyr, *The First Apology*, 5, 14.

26. Tertullian, *Apology*, 10–12, 23.

27. Ibid., 22.6–7.

28. Irenaeus of Lyons, *Against Heresies*, 5.24.3.

29. Justin Martyr, *The First Apology*, 5, 46.

30. Origen, *Against Celsus*, 8.44.

31. Justin Martyr, *The Second Apology*, 5.

32. Origen, *Against Celsus*, 8.73–4.

33. Justin Martyr, *The First Apology*, 14.

34. Justin Martyr, *Dialogue with Trypho*, 110.

35. Irenaeus of Lyons, *Against Heresies*, 5.24.1.

36. Tertullian, *Apology*, 30; see also Tertullian, *To Scapula*, 2.

37. Tertullian, *Apology*, 33.1–2.

38. Ibid., 26.1.

39. Origen, *Against Celsus*, 6.68–70; Origen, *Commentary on Romans*, 9.26–7.

40. Tertullian, *Apology*, 21.24: "And the Caesars, too, would have believed about Christ, had Caesars not been necessary for the world, or if Christians could have been Caesars"; Origen, *Against Celsus*, 8.75.

41. Augustine, *City of God*, 7.18.

42. Ibid., 2.10.

43. Ibid., 2.25.

44. Ibid., 4.28.

45. Ibid., 18.49.

46. Ibid., 7.33.

47. Ibid., 19.17.

48. Ibid., 19.5, 7.

49. Ibid., 2.22–25.

50. Ibid., 2.19.

51. Paulus Orosius, *Against the Pagans*, 1.1.

52. Augustine, *Free Choice*, 1.1.1.

53. Ibid., 2.14.40.

54. Ibid., 2.15.43.

55. Ibid., 1.16.34–35.

56. Ibid., 1.15.33.

57. Augustine, *The Confessions*, 2.6.

58. Augustine, "Letter 189"; Augustine, *Reply to Faustus*, 22.74–75.

59. I am not denying the doctrine of original sin; original sin is not something intrinsically evil in human nature, but rather a privation or lack in human nature.

60. John of Salisbury, *Policraticus*, 4.1.

61. Ibid., 4.2, 6.1.

62. Ibid., 6.19.

63. Ibid., 8.17.

64. Ibid., 8.18.

65. Ibid., 3.15. John adds, "But 'receives [the sword]' is to be understood to pertain to he who has rashly usurped that which is not his, not to he who receives what he uses from the power of God."

66. Ibid., 5.10.

67. Ibid., 3.2.

68. Ibid., 1.1.

69. Ibid., 3.1.

70. Ibid., 6.29.

71. Aquinas, *Summa Theologica*, I-II, q. 91, a. 2.

72. Ibid., I-II, q. 94, a. 2.

73. Ibid., I-II, q. 91, a. 4.

74. Ibid., I-II, q. 95, a. 2.

75. Ibid., I-II, q. 95, a. 4.

76. Ibid., I-II, q. 95, a. 4, ad 2.

77. Aquinas, *On Kingship*, 1.1.

78. Ibid., 2.3–4.

79. Aquinas, *Summa Theologica*, II-II, q. 40, a. 1, 3.

80. Ibid., I-II, q. 49, a. 3; q. 51, a. 2.

81. Ibid., I-II, q. 50, a. 1–5.

82. Ibid., I-II, q. 62, a. 1; q. 63, a. 3.

83. Ibid., III, q. 62, aa. 1–2.

84. Dante, *Monarchia*, 1.5.

85. Ibid., 1.10.

86. Ibid., 1.11, 14.

87. Ibid., 2.5.

88. Dubois, *Recovery of the Holy Land*, 1.2.

89. Ibid., 1.9.
90. Ibid., 1.27.
91. Ibid., 1.104.
92. Ibid., 1.3–5, 8.
93. Ibid., 1.12.
94. Ibid., 1.63.
95. Ibid., 1.2.
96. Ibid., 1.7.

Chapter Two

·····················

The Emergence of Modernity

IN THE MODERN period, political thought underwent radical changes that transformed the way the origins of war were understood.[1] The first of these changes was an increasing emphasis on the limitless desire of the human will. The second was the severing of any connection between the state and humanity's ultimate, transcendent end. The third change was the emerging view of politics as a supposedly objective science independent of metaphysical or religious claims. These three changes came about, at least in part, through the intentional repudiation of the preceding Christian political tradition, and therefore not surprisingly contributed to ways of understanding the origins of war quite different from those found in the Christian tradition. Despite this conscious distancing from the Christian past, modern political thought itself had roots dating back to the Middle Ages.

PRECURSORS OF MODERNITY

The writers Marsilius of Padua (1290–1342) and William of Ockham (c. 1285–c. 1349) were fourteenth-century contemporaries who each had a profound influence on the future shape of political thought. Both Marsilius and Ockham challenged the papacy's assertion of temporal authority over political rulers, and both sought refuge with Louis of Bavaria, whose claim to the Holy Roman Empire was denied by Popes Clement V and John XXII. Marsilius and Ockham believed that the pretensions of these popes were the cause of the conflicts of their day, but both placed their contemporary situation within a broader political framework. For both writers, this political framework included an increased emphasis on the will, rather than on reason—an emphasis on the will of the ruler, and in Ockham's case, an emphasis on the will of God as well. These writers had little to say about the interaction of states in general, or war in particular, but their ideas about the nature of the human person and the state would influence later theories of international relations.

Marsilius of Padua

In his major work, the *Defensor Pacis*, Marsilius developed the notion that has come to be called "popular sovereignty." The people of a commonwealth have the primary responsibility for creating its laws, and therefore Marsilius calls the people "the Legislator." The people are also responsible for electing their ruler.[2] Even when the ruler makes the law, the people do so indirectly through him. It is better, however, for the greater part of the people to be involved in the making of laws because they have a better sense of what will be for the common benefit and will be more likely to obey a law created with popular input than one imposed on them.[3] None of this was unusual for a medieval account of the state; where Marsilius departs from the tradition is in his treatment of the law. Whereas Aquinas had argued that human law has authority to the extent that it reflects and makes concrete the natural law, Marsilius finds the law's authority primarily in the command of the Legislator and in its coercive power, and only secondarily in its morality.[4] Thus he introduces a new emphasis on the will of the ruler and the people.

Marsilius also promotes the idea of the state as a unitary power, that is, the only authority of any kind within its territory. The government ought to be unitary, according to Marsilius, because overlapping authorities lead to chaos and conflict.[5] Therefore all of the other parts of the state ought to be subordinated to the ruler, who is responsible for the maintenance of the others. In Marsilius's view, the ruler must be especially careful to subordinate priests and soldiers to his power. The authority of the civil ruler is concerned with the present life, whereas priests should be concerned only with the life to come; in this life, the Legislator, that is, the people, should have authority over the church.[6] Thus Marsilius overturns the earlier view that in light of humanity's ultimate end, the church has authority over the state, even if not direct political authority. In Marsilius's thought, the end or purpose of the state becomes independent of humanity's ultimate, supernatural end.

William of Ockham

Like his contemporary Marsilius, William of Ockham also emphasizes the role of the will in ethics and politics, an emphasis rooted in his philosophy. He was a leading exponent of nominalism, the belief that the universal categories with which we describe things do not exist either separately from things, as Platonists held, or in the things themselves, as realists held; these categories are only names that we give to similar things because of their shared characteristics. Because Ockham denies the existence of universals or natures, he claims that the will of God, rather than human nature, is the source of morality. Aquinas also understood the good in terms of the will of God, but, in contrast to Ockham, he held that the will of God is reflected in the rational order of creation. For Ockham, on the other hand, there is no such order; God is absolutely free, and whatever God wills is just, simply because God wills it.[7]

When Ockham turns to political matters, he focuses primarily on the human will rather than God's will. Whereas for Aquinas the human will is naturally ordained to God as its final end, for Ockham, the fundamental characteristic of the will is the freedom to choose good or evil without any interior or exterior compulsion.[8] Because there is no immutable human nature tending toward an end, the will is indeterminate or aimless in its orientation. This leads Ockham to emphasize the power of the will, that is, its ability to impose itself on an object by choosing that object as its end, an emphasis that is essential to his political thought. Ockham states that before the Fall of Adam and Eve, property and government were not necessary, but after the Fall, humans have both the need and the power to appropriate temporal things by imposing their will on them and the power to establish a government.[9] Upon establishing a government, the people transfer their power to the ruler, who then exercises power over the people, in essence imposing his will on them.[10]

Ockham clearly distinguishes this power possessed by the government from the power of the church. He interprets Jesus's command to his followers not to rule like the rulers of the nations, who lord it over others, to mean that church leaders should not possess temporal power.[11] The temporal ruler can legitimately impose coercive limitations on the exercise of the will, whereas the church cannot.[12] The church does exercise an authority distinct from that of the state; however, Ockham's understanding of this authority is quite different from that of both the proponents of the pope's temporal power and Marsilius.[13] Ockham's assertion of the aimlessness of the human will would be taken up and transformed by later modern philosophers, and his characterization of government primarily in terms of power would likewise prove influential. Although neither Marsilius nor Ockham devoted much attention to the question of war, their innovations in political thought would have a significant impact on later thinking about war.

THE RENAISSANCE AND REFORMATION

The early modern period of the Renaissance and Protestant Reformation saw a sharp departure from the Western Christian tradition of thought on the origins of war, even as this period's major figures looked back to medieval thinkers for inspiration. Niccolò Machiavelli, in some ways influenced by Marsilius and Ockham, attempted to create a scientific account of politics, which he saw as governed by limitless desire and the quest for power. The Renaissance humanists Desiderius Erasmus and Juan Luis Vives built on John of Salisbury's concern for the virtues and vices of rulers, but they began to divorce faith and reason as they found the source of the virtues in humanistic study rather than religious faith and practice. Catholic and Protestant natural law jurists inherited the moral and political synthesis of Thomas Aquinas but pushed it in ways that created cracks in its foundations.

Niccolò Machiavelli

The Florentine writer Niccolò Machiavelli (1469–1527) took Marsilius and Ockham's political ideas to extremes and in the process inaugurated the truly modern era in political thought. Machiavelli attempted to give an account of political life independent of transcendent, religious concerns. This led him to promote the expediency of the state as the ultimate goal of politics. Machiavelli also transformed William of Ockham's assertion of the aimlessness of the will into a claim about the limitlessness of human desire, which he saw as the origin of conflict and war.

Machiavelli deepens Marsilius's emphasis on the commanding and coercive element of the law, rather than the moral element, arguing that the actions of a ruler should be governed by expediency rather than moral scruples. In the *Discourses on Livy*, he writes: "Where one deliberates entirely on the safety of his fatherland, there ought not to enter any consideration of either just or unjust, merciful or cruel, praiseworthy or ignominious; indeed every other concern put aside, one ought to follow entirely the policy that saves its life and maintains its liberty."[14]

Likewise, he writes in *The Prince* that a ruler "should not deviate from what is good, if that is possible, but he should know how to do evil, if that is necessary."[15] Machiavelli subverts the traditional Christian notion of virtue. He claims that half of life is governed by fortune, half by our free will, and virtue (or rather, *virtù*) consists in bending fortune to one's will for the sake of the state.[16] This is a far cry from John of Salisbury's support for virtue among rulers.

For Machiavelli, the security of the state should be the ruler's primary concern. A state's foreign policy should be guided by the pursuit of power; for example, when a state's neighbors war with each other, that state should take a side in the conflict with the aim of enhancing its power rather than remaining neutral.[17] According to David Boucher, for Machiavelli there is no universal common good; the only common good is that of the state, which comes at the expense of other states.[18] This constant quest for power originates in the people, because "nature has created men so that they are able to desire everything and are unable to attain everything."[19] This is surely a development of Ockham's claim about the will's lack of an ultimate end, transformed to mean that ultimately nothing can satisfy human desires. For Machiavelli, these desires are the source of conflict, including war among states.

The state also lacks a transcendent end. As Warren Winiarski correctly notes, "Whereas the tradition taught that the crucial political considerations must ultimately be seen in light of the 'end,' for man and for society, Machiavelli wishes to understand all political things in light of the 'beginning.'"[20] In the early chapters of *The Prince*, Machiavelli claims that establishing a new state, or a new regime within an existing state, is the most difficult task for a ruler, and therefore only the greatest rulers are capable of this feat, exercising great force and cruelty in the process.[21] The founder of a state in a way infuses his own virtue into the state through his choice of location and the laws he establishes, and all future rulers of the state must imitate him.[22] Over time the state must renew itself by returning to its beginnings, "Because in the process of time that goodness is corrupted, [and] unless something intervenes to lead it back to the mark, it of necessity kills that body [i.e., the state]."[23] The state's health depends on periodically returning to its origins, and because the state lacks any real end or purpose, its health, measured in terms of security, becomes an end in itself.

Religion plays an important role in the foundation and maintenance of the state, according to Machiavelli. He claims that the founders of states supplement their authority through religion, which gives their laws a divine mandate. Religion is crucial for the well-being of the state because it unites the nation, and the ruler should maintain his nation's religion even if he believes it to be false.[24] Despite religion's general benefit to the state, Machiavelli believes that the religion promoted by the Catholic Church of his day was harmful because it "placed the highest good in humility, abjectness, and contempt of things human."[25] By subordinating religion to the well-being of the state, Machiavelli, like Marsilius, suggests that political life has little need for religious ends beyond itself.

Machiavelli's subordination of religion to the expediency of the state is connected with his search for a scientific understanding of statecraft. He argues that the ruler should not be concerned with issues of justice and injustice, and therefore he rejects those accounts of politics that emphasize the normative rather than the descriptive. He writes, "Since my intention is to say something that will prove of practical use to the inquirer, I have thought it proper to represent things as they are in a real truth, rather than as they are imagined."[26] A complete account of politics can be given without reference to religious or any other beliefs beyond what can be observed in human behavior. Machiavelli believes a scientific account of politics is possible, because "whoever considers present and ancient things easily knows that in all cities and in all peoples there are the same desires and the same humors, and there always have been." Examining the past will help us to understand the present and to shape the future.[27] By attempting to develop an account of politics in purely earthly terms, Machiavelli clearly inaugurated the era of modern political thought.

The Renaissance Humanists

The Renaissance humanists Desiderius Erasmus (c. 1466–1536) and Juan Luis Vives (1492–1540) also demonstrate the emergence of the modern out of the medieval. Erasmus and Vives inherited the early Christian notion that the

virtues and vices of rulers are key in matters of peace and war, but they believed the virtues were better established through humanistic study than through
Christian faith and practice. They were harsh critics of the wars of their age,
claiming that these arose out of the vices of supposedly Christian rulers. Both
Erasmus and Vives wrote during the reigns of the three great monarchs Henry
VIII of England, Francis I of France, and the Holy Roman Emperor Charles V,
who often warred with each other in struggles for power. Although the rulers
claimed that these wars were just, for Erasmus and Vives, the monarchs' wars
really arose out of their vices. The best hope for peace was the cultivation of
virtue through humanistic education.

Vives speaks directly about virtue and vice in his short work *Introduction to
Wisdom*, a collection of proverbs. He writes, "The queen and principal mistress
of this world is Virtue. All other things serve her as handmaids do their mistress,
if they wish to fulfill their ends." Virtue consists in "reverence toward God and
man, a right service of God and a love for man, all joined to a willingness to
do good."[28] Training in the virtues ought to begin in childhood.[29] One should
be careful that one's friends are virtuous so that they are not a bad influence.
Vives adds, "Flee from the company of evil men as from men infected with the
plague; contagion from the one is to be feared no less than from the other."[30]

In *The Education of a Christian Prince*, written for the young Holy Roman
Emperor Charles V, Erasmus applies the humanists' teaching on virtue to the
life of a ruler. According to Erasmus, a prince should be trained in the virtues
from childhood so that he will be virtuous when he begins to rule. He adds, "If
as boys they did nothing but play at tyrants, what (I ask you) are they to work at
as adults except tyranny?"[31] The prince should be taught correct ideas as well as
good behavior "by parents, nurses, and tutor."[32] The teachings of Christ should
be central in the prince's education.[33]

Once the prince has become an adult ruler, he must be diligent in maintaining the virtues and avoiding the vices. He must resist flattery because flattery
leads to tyranny.[34] The prince must be able to know the truth from falsehood:
"For it is not true happiness when a people is given over to idle luxury, nor is
it true freedom when people can do what they like. Nor is it servitude to live
according to what is prescribed by just laws."[35] When the ruler lives according
to the virtues, he deserves the title of prince, but if he rules for himself, he is a
tyrant.[36] The ruler's behavior influences his people, for good or ill.[37] Erasmus's
linkage of the vices with tyranny is clearly in the tradition of John of Salisbury
and directly contrary to the advice of Machiavelli.

The vices of rulers are the primary cause of wars, according to both Erasmus
and Vives. Erasmus writes, "When a tyrant sees that affairs of state are flourishing he stirs up a war, having invented some pretext or even invited an enemy in,
so as to reduce thereby the strength of his own people."[38] A just prince, on the
other hand, seeks "that the devices of war may never be needed."[39] The prince
must seek to be on friendly relations with his neighbors and to avoid contact

with countries that are distant or have different cultures.[40] Conflicts between nations should not lead to war; they should be arbitrated by a bishop or abbot.[41] It is easy for a ruler to find a pretext for a "just war," but most are hardly worth the cost, and in most cases, "evil cupidities and desires do engender these debates and tumults."[42] Vives writes that many rulers enjoy turning disputes into pretexts for war, and often enough they have the support of the people; victory in war is "the most powerful advancer of men, so foolish is the madness of the mob."[43] The Christian prince, according to Erasmus, should always think long and hard before going to war, considering the destruction it causes, and "in the end, if so pernicious a thing cannot be avoided, the prince's first concern should be to fight with the least possible harm to his subjects, at the lowest cost in Christian blood, and to end it as quickly as possible."[44]

Erasmus is particularly scandalized by war between Christian princes. He argues that peace is desirable because humans are social by nature, but if that is not sufficient, their shared Christian faith should be enough to keep Christians from fighting one another.[45] Christians are united by baptism and by the Eucharist, so where do the divisions that lead to war come from?[46] It is absurd that priests accompany both sides in a war; he adds, "Still more absurd, Christ is present in both camps, as if fighting against himself."[47] Unlike Pierre Dubois, Erasmus does not seek peace among Christians in order to better subdue Muslims. A war to spread Christianity among the Ottoman Turks would be self-defeating; Christianity spreads best through peaceful means.[48]

Like Aquinas, Erasmus and Vives believe that the virtues necessary for peace must be fostered by good practices, but for the humanists, the practices of the scholar become more important than religious practices. Erasmus's attitude toward religious practices is ambiguous. Although not rejecting them outright, he believes that visible ceremonies must be supplemented by a change of heart and "invisible worship."[49] It is better to imitate the saints and follow their teachings than to perform ceremonies and venerate relics.[50] Vives writes that it is not through our own actions alone, but only with God's aid that we can achieve virtue, so we must pray for God's assistance. He adds, "Nothing greater or more excellent can be given to man than religion, which is the knowledge, love, and veneration of the Prince and Father of this world."[51] The true worship of God involves purging ourselves of vices and imitating God.[52] Yet the practice by which "we may more easily know sin and avoid it, and know virtue and attain to it, holding all other things to be superfluous," is humanistic study.[53] Here humanistic study almost seems to take the place that the sacraments hold in Aquinas's theology. This shift perhaps already reflects a break in the synthesis developed by Aquinas between our earthly life and our supernatural destiny: The sacraments, supernatural means of grace, are no longer necessary for attaining the goods of virtue and peace. Therefore, despite holding values directly contrary to those of Machiavelli, Erasmus and Vives are like him in that they draw from the earlier Christian tradition in their reflections on the origins of war, while also demonstrating a breakdown in at least one aspect of the earlier synthesis. The natural law jurists of the following centuries would also adopt themes from the earlier Christian tradition and move these in new directions.

The Natural Law Jurists

Whereas Erasmus and Vives continued in the tradition of John of Salisbury by reflecting on the virtues and vices of rulers, the Spanish Catholic theologians Francisco de Vitoria (c. 1480–1546) and Francisco Suarez (1548–1617) took up the scholastic tradition of Thomas Aquinas. Writing principally in the sixteenth century, Vitoria and Suarez faced a rapidly changing world. In 1492 Christopher Columbus had opened up the New World to European explorers, and the Spanish quickly came to dominate much of the Americas. Vitoria tackled the ethical issues involved in the conquest of the New World in his *On the American Indians*, coming to view the subjugation of the Native Americans as unjust. In the early sixteenth century, Christendom was split by the Protestant Reformation. Suarez was among the theologians who defended the Catholic faith against the Protestant reformers. Finally, as Bernice Hamilton notes, the sixteenth-century wars between France and the Habsburgs "scandalized Christendom and aroused a new interest in the ethics of warfare," an interest reflected in Vitoria and Suarez's writings on the just war.[54]

The Spanish scholastics were followed by several Protestant natural law jurists. The first were the Italian Alberico Gentili (1552–1608) in the late sixteenth century and the Dutch Hugo Grotius (1583–1645) in the early seventeenth century.[55] Both Gentili and Grotius were personally familiar with war. Gentili fled from Italy because of his Protestant beliefs and served as a lawyer for England under Queen Elizabeth in its conflicts with Spain. Grotius lived through most of the Thirty Years' War and himself was given a life sentence for his part in a religious civil war in the Netherlands between Arminians and orthodox Calvinists; after three years, he escaped prison by being smuggled out in a book chest. In the seventeenth century the German Samuel von Pufendorf (1632–94) developed a modern account of the natural law, including the law of nations. Pufendorf was one of the first to philosophize about international politics after the Peace of Westphalia ended the Thirty Years' War in 1648. That war had an impact on his academic career—his native Saxony was ravaged by the war, which led him to take up academic posts in Sweden and Denmark. Finally, in the eighteenth century the German philosopher Christian von Wolff (1679–1754) and the Swiss jurist Emer (or Emerich) de Vattel (1714–67) created impressive systems of international law. Although both the Catholic and Protestant natural law jurists were inheritors of the medieval synthesis concerning politics and war, their innovations show the influence of the patterns of thinking characteristic of modernity.

In their major writings, Vitoria and Suarez greatly expand upon Thomas Aquinas's considerations of a just cause for war and also adapt the norms of just conduct to developments in weaponry, such as gunpowder. Their contributions to a better understanding of the origins of war, however, are found in their discussion of problems concerning the legitimate authority to wage war, in which they consider the possibility of international institutions meant to resolve conflicts between kingdoms. Reflecting the vestiges of the feudal order, Vitoria argues that a subordinate ruler who nevertheless has total authority over his lands can legitimately wage war, while a subordinate ruler without that authority cannot. Still, this second sort of ruler can wage war when his superior does not respond to an attack upon the former's land in a timely manner.[56] Suarez concludes similarly, but adds that the subordinate can legitimately go to war only "when it would be the wish of the sovereign to do so, but an immediate response is needed, and when aggressors have already entered the imperfect state's [i.e., the subordinate's] territory." Normally, however, a subordinate ruler must defer to his superior.[57]

The same is not true for rulers without a superior. There is no international authority that can act as judge between states that come into conflict, and therefore a state must act as the judge of its own cause, both judging and punishing those it believes have treated it unjustly. Suarez recognizes that this is a precarious situation and that it would probably be better if there were some sort of international authority that could resolve disputes, but he concludes that, for practical reasons, it is not likely that such an institution could ever exist.[58] Therefore, Suarez shows greater skepticism than Dante Aligheri and Pierre Dubois about the possibilities of international institutions playing an important role in establishing peace, but shares their perception that in some way the absence of such an authority contributes to the presence of war. The Protestant jurists Pufendorf, Wolff, and Vattel, on the other hand, suggest that international order and peace may be possible even without such an authority by reinterpreting the law of nations as the law of nature applied to states as moral persons, a law that all states can recognize and to which all are bound.[59]

In addition to developing the just war theory, Suarez also modified Aquinas's natural law theory—particularly the relationship between the natural law and humanity's supernatural end, and the relationship between the natural law and God's authority—and in the process created cracks in Aquinas's synthesis. Concerning the first issue, Suarez writes that the natural law can be divided into two parts: one part concerning humanity as "pure nature," the other pertaining to humanity's supernatural end.[60] This is somewhat similar to Aquinas's claim that the natural law pertains to what humans are inclined toward by nature, whereas divine law pertains to our supernatural end. Where Suarez departs from Aquinas is in claiming that grace is not necessary for the fulfillment of the natural law (or the first part of it, in Suarez's terms). According to Aquinas, human nature is ordained to a supernatural end, and because of this, human nature is in a way oriented toward this supernatural end such that grace is necessary even to fulfill the natural law.[61] For Suarez, on the other hand, the human person seems to be divided in two: human nature on the one hand, humanity's supernatural end, which is "superadded" to that nature, on the other. Grace pertains only to the latter, and therefore is not necessary for the fulfillment of the natural law, which pertains to the former.[62]

Suarez deals with the second issue, the relationship between the natural law and God's authority, while criticizing the ethical theories of the medieval theologians Gregory of Rimini and William of Ockham. According to Suarez, Gregory of Rimini held that the natural law resides in our rational nature itself independently of the will of God, and would exist even if God did not exist; William of Ockham, on the other hand, held that natural law derives solely from the command of God, not from our nature.[63] Suarez splits the difference by claiming that by a distinct act of his will, God prescribes or prohibits acts that are good or evil by nature.[64] Here again Suarez departs from the thought of Thomas Aquinas. Even though he rejects Gregory of Rimini's ethical theory, Suarez accepts his presupposition that human nature can be conceived apart from God, whereas for Aquinas this would be nonsense. For Aquinas, all things necessarily have their being through participation in God's being.[65] Suarez reflects a growing tendency to think of human nature, both in terms of its fulfillment and end and the sources of morality, as independent of any relationship with God.

The Protestant natural law jurists also reflect this tendency. Grotius takes a view similar to the one Suarez attributes to Gregory of Rimini, saying that the law of nature includes those laws that are "in conformity with rational nature." He continues, "What we have been saying would have a degree of validity even if we should concede that which cannot be conceded without the utmost wickedness, that there is no God, or that the affairs of men are of no concern to Him."[66] Pufendorf disagrees with Grotius, instead claiming, in terms similar to Suarez's, that the will of God alone determines what is right or wrong, even if God binds himself to will the natural law in accord with the inclinations of human nature.[67] Both Grotius and Pufendorf, however, show the growing influence of the idea that human nature and political life can be understood without reference to God.

Pufendorf and Wolff also contribute to the development of politics as a supposedly objective science. Against Aristotle, Pufendorf argues that moral science, including politics, can be as exact as the physical sciences.[68] As Boucher points out, Pufendorf seeks clear principles that no sane person could reject despite differences of faith, reflecting the Westphalian religious and political settlement.[69] Wolff also attempts to make morality and politics comparable to the natural sciences. Pufendorf and Wolff limit themselves to the claim that the morality of politics can be studied objectively, not that scientific laws could predict the actual behavior of states; yet as natural law theories of morality were increasingly challenged, the latter idea, already proposed by Machiavelli, gained plausibility.

The growing separation between humanity and God and between politics and religious faith in the thought of the natural law jurists is only indirectly related to the origins of war, but is nevertheless important in understanding how Catholic thinking on war's origins developed. These developments in natural law theory are symptomatic of broader changes in political thought of the time. Political thinkers were beginning to conceive of politics as a realm of human existence cut off from any relationship with God and therefore supposedly capable of being studied and explained without reference to larger philosophical claims about God, human nature, and so forth. This shift is important for thinking about the origins of war because it means that humanity's response to God, whether it is one of love or of rejection and sin, is no longer understood as influencing the behavior of states. Obviously the natural law jurists did not go this far. Nevertheless, their thinking about both the natural law and the morality of war has been highly influential on subsequent Catholic thought. The natural law jurists' adoption of certain features of modern political thought has brought ways of thinking about politics that are alien to the Catholic tradition into the church's own teaching, making it harder for later Catholics to avoid some of the modern conclusions about war and its origins.

THE SEVENTEENTH CENTURY AND THE SOCIAL CONTRACT

The seventeenth-century English philosophers Thomas Hobbes (1588–1679) and John Locke (1632–1704) continued the shift toward modernity hinted at by the Renaissance humanists and the natural law jurists and inaugurated by Machiavelli. Hobbes and Locke provided classic accounts of the origin and nature of the state. Both imagined a state of nature in which individuals exist prior to the creation of the state. Individuals enter into a social contract and establish the state in order to avoid the hardships of life in the state of nature. Both Hobbes and Locke also considered the state of affairs among independent states as analogous to this original state of nature. This analogy served as the basis for their theories on the origins of war. The two differed in important respects, particularly over the severity of the state of nature and the authority of the sovereign over his subjects, perhaps reflecting Hobbes's having lived through the chaos of the English Civil War in the middle of the seventeenth century, and Locke's having lived under the later tyranny of James II and Charles II. Both, however, demonstrated similar departures from the preceding Christian tradition.

Thomas Hobbes

Hobbes is clearly indebted to William of Ockham.[70] According to Hobbes, when we perceive, we perceive only sense perceptions and not "intelligible species," or universals.[71] There is no knowable human nature, and no final end that brings us happiness. Hobbes writes, "Felicity is a continuall progresse of the desire, from one object to another; the attaining of the former, being still but the way to the latter." Like Machiavelli, Hobbes claims that this insatiable desire is what causes rulers to seek greater power and go to war.[72] Because he rejects the notions of a universal human nature and a final end, Hobbes, like Ockham, also emphasizes the power of the will. He defines freedom as "the absence of Opposition; (by Opposition, I mean externall Impediments of motion;)," and power as the ability to exercise freedom in order to obtain some good.[73]

Hobbes imagines a state of nature in which individuals live on their own prior to the establishment of society, coming into frequent conflict with one another because of their boundless desires and leading to a state of war. Humans are equal enough in strength and cunning that all must live in fear, "And the life of man [is] solitary, poore, nasty, brutish, and short."[74] Because of the intolerability of this state, individuals band together and consent to give up their right to govern themselves to one man or an assembly of men, creating the Leviathan, the "Artificiall Man" and "Mortall God."[75] Because of this consent, the sovereign possesses sufficient power to control the wills of the subjects, limiting the freedom they possessed in the state of nature.[76] Hobbes admits that the pure state of nature never actually existed, but it is a useful hypothesis for understanding the nature of the sovereign.[77] Even so, he does believe that what Boucher calls a "modified state of nature" preceded the establishment of the sovereign, a state of clashing families, tribes, and temporary confederations.[78]

For Hobbes, life is not governed by a universal moral order. Rather, humans have both the obligation to preserve themselves ("the law of nature") and the ability to obtain their well-being for themselves ("the right of nature"). The formation of the commonwealth fulfills the law of nature precisely by placing limits on the right of nature, that is, by imposing the will of the sovereign on his subjects through the civil law.[79] Beyond the law of self-preservation, however, there is no standard of justice by which the civil laws can be judged, because the civil laws establish what is just and unjust, and the sovereign himself is not subject to the laws.[80]

Most importantly for understanding the origins of war, Hobbes also uses the idea of the state of nature to describe the relations between states. States exist in a state of nature with each other, which is also a state of war, because each is independent without a superior to command it.[81] Because this state is not as intolerable as the state of nature among individuals, Hobbes does not believe that sovereigns will consent to form a worldwide state. The condition of relations among the states for Hobbes is actually more like the "modified state of nature," according to Boucher, because states create imbalances of power through constantly shifting alliances and federations.[82] Even though ultimately Hobbes traces the origins of conflict to humanity's boundless desires, in another sense conflict between states occurs because there is no world sovereign powerful enough to force states to obey it.

John Locke

John Locke also uses the concept of the state of nature to give an account of the state, although his theory differs from Hobbes's in important respects. Like Hobbes, Locke believes that in the state of nature, individuals are at perfect liberty to do as they please with themselves and their possessions.[83] Unlike Hobbes, however, he holds that the law of nature gives individuals not only the duty of self-preservation, but also that of treating others as equals, and "no one ought to harm another in his Life, Health, Liberty, or Possessions." Because in the state of nature there is no government, when someone injures another, everyone has the right to punish the violator and seek restitution for the victim.[84] Also unlike Hobbes, Locke asserts that the state of nature actually existed, even if it was short lived because of its inconveniences.[85] In the state of nature people lived in uncertainty because there was neither any clear standard of right and wrong nor any impartial judge of disputes, and often one did not possess adequate power to defend one's property.[86] For Locke, this uncertainty did not amount to a state of war, but a state of uncertain peace in which war might break out whenever one person violated the rights of another.[87]

Even if the state of nature was a state of uneasy peace, the people formed civil governments by means of contract to avoid war and the other inconveniences of the state of nature. The formation of the state resolved the conflicts of the state of nature because it created a superior who could resolve disputes without recourse to violence.[88] Later Locke defines this contract as the transfer of individuals' right to punish wrongdoing to the government.[89] Whereas in the state of nature individuals possessed natural liberty, with the state they possess the "liberty of men under society," or a common rule of government and the freedom to do everything not contrary to that rule.[90] The civil state is superior to the state of nature because it preserves and enlarges the freedom that was limited by the will of others in the state of nature.[91]

Locke, like Hobbes, considers the states to exist in a state of nature in relation to each other because there is no superior to adjudicate their disputes.[92] Just as in the state of nature individuals had the right to defend themselves and others from violations of their life, liberty, and property, states have the right to defend themselves and others from violations of their political independence and territorial integrity.[93] Like the original state of nature, the state of nature existing among states is not a state of war, but "is fraught with 'inconveniences' that provoke even just states into war."[94] Just as the original state of nature was characterized by a lack of clear standards of right and wrong, a lack of impartial judges, and the inability to defend one's possessions, so the state of nature existing among nations is characterized by bias and ignorance, partiality, and weakness and fear. These are, for Locke, the primary causes of war. Peace requires overcoming these irrational passions and limitations through the use of reason. Michael W. Doyle argues that the logical conclusion of Locke's line of thinking is the establishment of a world state, a conclusion that Locke himself did not draw, even if later thinkers did.[95]

Despite their differences, Hobbes and Locke shared many conclusions central to their understandings of war's origins. Both considered society an artificial creation rather than a natural feature of human existence, made necessary by the inconveniences created by human beings pursuing their limitless desires. Even though governments put limits on individuals' freedom, both Hobbes and Locke believed government created a superior state of living for humankind. Both also drew analogies between the state of nature and international politics. Hobbes and Locke both considered international politics a state of nature, although only Hobbes also considered it a state of war. For both philosophers, humanity's limitless desires and the lack of an international sovereign are the primary sources of war.

THE LIBERAL ATTACK ON NATURAL LAW

The liberal political philosophies of the utilitarians and Immanuel Kant were all attacks on the natural law approach to understanding politics, that of both the natural law jurists and earlier medieval theologians. Thomas Hobbes and John Locke had already departed significantly from the natural law tradition, drawing on the voluntarism originating with William of Ockham. The utilitarians and Kant, however, directly attacked the natural law approach. The utilitarians claimed that morality is derived from subjective experiences of pleasure and pain, not from an objective human nature. Kant also denied the intelligibility of human nature and claimed that morality should be based on duties established by the will alone. These new philosophical approaches led to new directions in understanding the origins of war.

Utilitarianism

One attack on the natural law tradition came from the eighteenth- and nineteenth-century school of philosophy known as utilitarianism. According to Jeremy Bentham, the founder of utilitarianism, the goodness of actions is measured by the pleasure and pain they cause for oneself and for others. According to Bentham, the purpose of government is to increase the pleasure and diminish the pain of the greatest number. War causes enormous amounts of suffering, and through the rational organization of international politics, it can be avoided. Bentham also joined Adam Smith in pointing out the peaceful effects of free trade and economic interdependence. John Stuart Mill, in contrast, developed a utilitarian and liberal justification for imperialism.

In his writings, Jeremy Bentham (1748–1832) develops a distinctive approach to politics based on his utilitarian philosophy. Drawing on a long line of empiricism, including that of Ockham, Hobbes, and Locke, Bentham denies that we can know anything about human nature or that it can form the basis for morality. Therefore natural law and natural rights do not exist: "*Natural rights is simply nonsense: natural and imprescriptible rights, rhetorical nonsense— nonsense upon stilts.*"[96] We do know about pleasure and pain as measures of human happiness, however, and these form the basis of our judgments about right and wrong. According to Bentham, "it is the greatest happiness of the greatest number that is the measure of right and wrong."[97] In *A Fragment on Government*, he applies this principle to the law. He argues that actions that on balance are harmful to society ought to be forbidden by law, and laws themselves should be judged by their utility for society, rather than their conformity to some nonexistent natural law.[98]

Bentham interprets international politics and war in terms of his utilitarianism, arguing that true international government is possible and would serve the utility of all states.[99] He provides descriptions of the various institutions such a government might include, and, according to Doyle, in so doing he provides solutions for the inconveniences of international life that Locke left unsolved: Collective security and disarmament will overcome weakness and fear. An international congress and a "Common Court of Judicature" will put an end to partiality. A "Pacific or Philharmonic Society" that educates the public about its true interests will conquer ignorance and bias.[100] Bentham shares Locke's beliefs about the origins of war and brings to a logical conclusion the latter's ideas on how to prevent it.

Bentham also reflects a strand of thought emphasizing the pacific influence of economic liberalism. The economist Adam Smith rejects mercantilism, an economic system in which one state's gain is another's loss, leading states inevitably into conflict with one another as they seek after wealth. On the other hand, free trade among states would contribute to peace. One state would be less likely to attack another if the two were engaged in mutually beneficial trade.[101] Similarly, Bentham argues that mutual trade is beneficial to all, whereas economic protectionism leads to conflict and war, which is "in its essence ruinous."[102]

More so than Bentham, his nineteenth-century disciple John Stuart Mill (1806–73) develops a utilitarian defense of political liberty and rights. Like Bentham, Mill denies that there is a natural law from which abstract rights could be derived: "It is proper to state that I forego any advantage which could be derived to my argument from the idea of abstract right, as a thing independent of utility. I regard utility as the ultimate appeal on all ethical questions."[103] According to Mill, however, even if we possess no natural rights, the greater good of society is promoted if a private sphere of liberty is protected. He concludes that "the only purpose for which power can be rightfully exercised over any member of a civilized community, against his will, is to prevent harm to others."[104]

Mill also claims, however, that not all nations are capable of living in liberty, and with this argument he justifies a form of liberal imperialism. Like Bentham,

Mill is generally opposed to aggressive wars and believes that peace could be established through trade and international institutions. Also like Bentham, he believes there is a natural harmony of interests among societies, and therefore conflict is not inevitable.[105] This is only true, however, when societies are governed by a spirit of liberty. Mill argues that the primary hindrance to the establishment of liberty in a society is the prevalence of "custom": "The despotism of custom is everywhere the standing hindrance to human advancement, being in unceasing antagonism to that disposition to aim at something better than customary, which is called, according to circumstances, the spirit of liberty, or that of progress or improvement."[106] Mill therefore draws on a typical modern dichotomy between reason and tradition. War is primarily caused by societies' backward customs and their despotic forms of government. Mill is generally opposed to intervention in the affairs of another state, but colonial intervention in the affairs of backward societies is justified in order to accelerate their social development.[107] Therefore Mill finds the origins of conflict in attachment to custom and tradition, which foster bias and ignorance, and yet the persistence of custom in backward countries itself serves as a justification for intervention, including military intervention, by more civilized states.

Immanuel Kant

The German philosopher Immanuel Kant (1724–1804) develops a liberal account of international politics and the possibilities of peace distinct from that developed by the utilitarians. Like Bentham, Kant is skeptical about our ability to know human nature, but he claims that duty, rather than pleasure or utility, is the basis of morality. According to Kant, we do not know things as they are in themselves, but know only our perceptions of things filtered through the categories of the mind, such as cause and effect, or necessity and contingency. Thus Kant, like Bentham, denies the ability to derive morals from human nature.[108] Rather than turning to subjective experiences of pleasure and pain, however, Kant turns to the will and duty as the sources of morality.[109] Morality cannot be guided by utility because we cannot know all of the consequences of an action. Instead, we must be guided by the formula: "Act in such a way that you can wish your maxim to become a universal law (irrespective of what the end in view may be)."[110]

Kant's moral philosophy has political implications. His universal maxim will preserve the freedom of others by establishing "the right," that is, "the sum total of those conditions within which the will of one person can be reconciled with the will of another in accordance with a universal law of freedom." The right, in turn, is protected by "the public right," the sum of the laws necessary to bring about the right.[111]

According to Kant, all societies are gradually evolving toward republicanism, the name that he gives to a society governed by right.[112] Through the clash of human wills, a lawful, republican society will emerge, and eventually a lawful society will emerge at the international level, as well.[113] The emergence of a just government at the national level does not depend on the people themselves being just, because "although the citizens are opposed to one another in their private attitudes, these opposing views may inhibit one another in such a way that the public conduct of the citizens will be the same as if they did not have such evil attitudes."[114]

The establishment of a peaceful federation of states will require a much more conscious effort than the establishment of republican government. Whereas individuals seeking their own private interests could establish the republican state, states must consciously seek the moral good that a peaceful federation of states promises.[115] The very nature of republican states makes this possible, though: Republican states are less likely to go to war than monarchies, because the people who bear the burdens of war are those making the decisions.[116] This is why Kant believes that the federation will begin with one or more republics and gradually expand to include other states.[117]

Kant gives a detailed account of how such a federation might come to be. The world must prepare for such a federation by preliminary articles of peace that eliminate practices likely to lead to war, such as maintaining a standing army and the use of assassins.[118] Once these conditions have been established, the three definitive articles of peace can be enacted. The first of these is that every state ought to be republican. The second is that the federation ought to be established among republican states and spread to other republican states. The third article is that strangers in foreign lands ought to be shown hospitality, and strangers should show hospitality in foreign lands. These three definitive articles correspond to the three levels of right: the *ius civitatis* among individuals within the state, the *ius gentium* among states, and the *ius cosmopoliticum* of individuals and states in relation to the universal community.[119] The federation of states meant to preserve peace is not a world state, nor is it a temporary congress of states; Kant claims that the best analogy is the federal structure of the (early) United States.[120]

Kant's account of the establishment of republican states and the peaceful federation of such states sheds light on his views on the nature and origins of war. War arises from the conflicting wills of humans not governed in such a way that their wills can exercise freedom harmoniously. Kant sees conflict and war as necessary for the development of republican government and the peaceful federation, and even as positive phenomena, because they create the desire among republics to form the peaceful federation. Nevertheless, the ultimate purpose of the development of human society is the establishment of worldwide peace. Developing institutions in which humans are able to exercise their freedom harmoniously is therefore the sure means of establishing peace. Oddly, Kant shares with Hobbes the belief that war originates from both clashing human wills and the absence of international political institutions. He shares with

Bentham, however, an optimism about the ability of international institutions to establish peace.

MARXISM

Karl Marx (1818–83) developed a unique theory of international relations that has had continued influence on later views on the origins of war. Early in his career, Marx was influenced by the German philosopher Georg Wilhelm Friedrich Hegel, who argued that history is the gradual coming to self-awareness of Spirit, an almost God-like entity immanent in the world and expressed in human consciousness. Spirit's self-awareness is reflected in human freedom. Like Hegel, Marx believes that history is a process in which true freedom gradually emerges, but unlike Hegel, he concludes that history is not a spiritual process, but rather a material process. According to Marx, history is a succession of economic systems characterized by class conflict. Capitalism, the last stage prior to communism, is characterized by a conflict between the bourgeoisie and the proletariat. Within a society, all human endeavors, such as art, religion, and politics, emerge out of and reinforce that society's economic system. Marx clearly accepts modern philosophy's divorce of political life from transcendent ends, even if politics itself is subordinated to or explained by economics. He also claims to describe history by means of a scientific approach that not only does not rely on religious truths, but even denies the existence of spiritual realities.

Marx's view of the state and its relation to class conflict is essential to his theory of international relations. According to Marx and his associate Friedrich Engels (1820–95), the behavior of states depends on their historical situation, described in economic terms. They claim that the behavior of states depends on their stage of economic development and which class is in control of the government. The modern state is simply the political expression of the domination of the working class by the bourgeois class and will disappear under communism. They do admit some variety among modern states: Capitalist states that were incompletely bourgeois, such as Napoleon III's France and Bismarck's Germany, would be aggressive, whereas fully bourgeois states would have peaceful relations with one another.[121] They do not consider the nature of relations between capitalist and socialist states because they believe that the socialist revolution would be worldwide, or at least encompass the entire capitalist world.[122]

Marx and Engels do consider the relations of capitalist and socialist states with precapitalist states, however. Despite later Marxist attacks on imperialism, Marx and Engels believe that imperialism and colonialism have positive aspects. They acknowledge that imperialism had existed long before the development of capitalism, and they argue that imperialism is not a necessary feature of capitalism, even if it was a likely one. Capitalist states benefit from colonial markets, and at the same time colonialism helps capitalism to develop in nations where it previously did not exist.[123] In fact, in countries characterized by what Marx calls "Asiatic" economies, or economies that are static and stagnant, imperialism is necessary for economic development.[124] Later Marxist theorists, including Vladimir Lenin, would radically alter Marx's appraisal of imperialism, however. The important point, though, is that for Marx and Engels, conflict among states, whether it is war between capitalist states or the imperial domination of a capitalist state over an "Asiatic" one, is the result of the dynamics of the economic systems of those states. Later Marxists would more clearly articulate a Marxist theory of international relations and war's origins, which is discussed in the next chapter.

CONCLUSION

Modern political philosophy tended to depart from the Western Christian tradition of the past in three important, interrelated ways, even if these changes had roots in the Middle Ages. The first departure began with William of Ockham's claim that freedom of the will is best understood in terms of indifference, or the ability to choose this or that object, rather than in terms of an orientation toward the ultimate good, God. Later thinkers such as Machiavelli and Hobbes eventually transformed that claim into an assertion that human desire is aimless and limitless. This departure, connected as it is with a denial of our ability to know human nature, also contributed to the decline of natural law approaches to morality, despite the contributions of thinkers such as Suarez, Grotius, and Pufendorf.

The second departure began with Marsilius of Padua's subordination of the church to the state and continued with various thinkers' claims that the purposes of the state can be understood without reference to ultimate, transcendent ends. Even though the church fathers, Thomas Aquinas, and others had argued that the state was not primarily concerned with people's relationship with God, it was still inconceivable to them that the state be understood apart from the transcendent. Yet Machiavelli claimed that religion ought to further the independent purposes of the state, and even Grotius believed that the natural law governing individuals and states could be conceived independently of God. The Renaissance humanists, although not rejecting religion, believed that the virtues necessary for governing could be gained through humanistic study rather than through religious practice. Marx went so far as to claim that belief in God contributes to the alienation of the working class and therefore hinders the establishment of a just society. This departure created a tendency not only to downplay the moral purpose of the state, but also to downplay the transcendent dimension of human activity, as well. In some cases, human political aspirations were limited to self-preservation or the pursuit of pleasure and the avoidance of pain.

The third departure is the attempt to develop a science of politics supposedly independent of transcendent or metaphysical claims. This is reflected not only in Machiavelli's claim to describe politics as it really is rather than as it is imagined, but also in Pufendorf and Wolff's attempts to develop a politics as clear and precise as the natural sciences, and therefore acceptable to all regardless of their diverse metaphysical beliefs. Marx claimed to have developed a science of history, politics, and economics understood completely in material terms, although he denied that social analysis can ever be objective, instead arguing that it either reflects the interests of the status quo or of revolution. This departure contributed to the development of the notion of international relations as an objective science whose practitioners could temporarily put aside their own ultimate commitments and ends.

From a Christian perspective, these developments in political thought were not entirely negative. Modern political thought's recognition of the role of power in politics is an advance over classical and medieval thought, and its emphasis on the human will has contributed to the political freedoms valued today. Modern political thought also contributed to a greater distinction between state and church power that most today would find necessary. Finally, the development of political science as a discipline has contributed greatly to our understanding of political life. Nevertheless, for Christians these advances came at a cost, the undermining of some of the essential elements of the earlier Christian outlook.

The development of modern political thought also led to views on the origins of war quite different from those found in the previous Christian tradition. What began with William of Ockham as a rejection of the notion that the human will is oriented to God, and was transformed by Machiavelli and Hobbes into purposeless and limitless desire, eventually led modern thinkers to understand conflict and war in terms of the opposition of wills in pursuit of power. The separation of the political from the transcendent tended to lead philosophers to understand human political motivations in terms of material interests rather than transcendent beliefs; some, such as Hobbes, Hegel, and Marx, believed that conflicts over such interests were inevitable, whereas others, such as Locke, the utilitarians, and Kant, believed that material interests could be ultimately harmonized through the elimination of limitations such as weakness, bias, and ignorance. If transcendent beliefs do enter the picture, they are typically a cause of conflict that must be tempered by reason, fostered by the objective and scientific study of international politics. These modern departures from the political thought of the Christian past were carried over into the twentieth-century theories of international relations that have developed the most well-known accounts of the origins of war.

NOTES

1. I use the terms "modern" and "modernity" primarily to describe a way of thinking, and only secondarily a time period. For these purposes, modernity can be understood as a way of thought characterized by the changes in political philosophy

described in this chapter, although it could be described in other ways. These ideas developed during a general period of time, but it would be futile to try to pinpoint the precise beginning (and end) of modernity.

2. Marsilius of Padua, *Defensor Pacis*, 1.15.

3. Ibid., 1.12.

4. Ibid., 1.10.

5. Ibid., 1.17.

6. Ibid., 2.8–9, 15.

7. Freppert, *Basis of Morality*, 127–28.

8. Ibid, 33–35.

9. William of Ockham, *Short Discourse on Tyrannical Government*, 3.8. Ockham's emphasis on the power of the will coalesced with a development in medieval jurisprudence in which jurists, beginning with Accursius in the thirteenth century and culminating with Bartolus of Sassoferrato in the fourteenth, began to refer to *ius*, or right, as *dominium*, or a possession, leading later nominalists to develop a subjective theory of rights. Tuck, *Natural Rights Theories*, 15–31.

10. William of Ockham, *Short Discourse on Tyrannical Government*, 4.2–6.

11. Ibid., 2.19; William of Ockham, *On the Powers*, 1.

12. Ockham, *On the Powers*, 8.

13. McGrade, *Political Thought of William of Ockham*, 78–172.

14. Machiavelli, *Discourses on Livy*, 3.41.

15. Machiavelli, *The Prince*, 18.

16. Ibid., 25; see also ibid., 22, where, like John of Salisbury and Erasmus, Machiavelli warns the ruler against flatterers; this is not because they are harmful to the ruler's virtue, though, but rather because they will deceive the prince about his status with the people and with neighboring states, leading him to make foolish decisions.

17. Ibid., 21.

18. Boucher, *Political Theories*, 94.

19. Machiavelli, *Discourses*, 1.37; see also ibid., 1.3.

20. Winiarski, "Niccolo Machiavelli," 267.

21. Machiavelli, *The Prince*, 5, 8; Machiavelli, *Discourses on Livy*, 1.9.

22. Machiavelli, *Discourses on Livy*, 1.1.

23. Ibid., 3.1.

24. Ibid., 1.11–2.

25. Ibid., 2.2.

26. Machiavelli, *The Prince*, 14–15.

27. Machiavelli, *Discourses on Livy*, 1.39; see also Boucher, *Political Theories*, 92.

28. Vives, *Introduction to Wisdom*, 17–19. The numbers listed refer to Vives's proverbs rather than pages.

29. Ibid., 9–10.

30. Ibid., 517, 526.

31. Erasmus, *Christian Prince*, 5, 9.

32. Ibid., 53–54.

33. Ibid., 13.

34. Ibid., 54.

35. Ibid., 72.

36. Ibid., 25.

37. Ibid., 21.

38. Ibid., 28.

39. Ibid., 65.

40. Ibid., 94–95.

41. Erasmus, *The Complaint of Peace*, 39, 43–44.

42. Ibid., 40, 50; Erasmus, *Christian Prince*, 104.

43. Vives, "Commentaries on Saint Augustine," 19.13; Vives, *Introduction to Wisdom*, 57.

44. Erasmus, *Christian Prince*, 102–3.

45. Erasmus, *The Complaint of Peace*, 11–13.

46. Ibid., 26–28.

47. Erasmus, *Christian Prince*, 108.

48. Ibid., 108–9; Erasmus, *Enchiridion*, 8–10.

49. Erasmus, *Enchiridion*, 130; Erasmus, *Christian Prince*, 18.

50. Erasmus, *Enchiridion*, 114–17.

51. Vives, *Introduction to Wisdom*, 202–3, 255.

52. Ibid., 290.

53. Ibid., 35.

54. Hamilton, *Political Thought*, 5.

55. Tuck argues, however, that Gentili and Grotius represent a humanist tradition drawing on the literary and rhetorical writings of the ancient world, in contrast to Vitoria and Suarez, who belong to a scholastic tradition drawing on ancient philosophy and medieval sources. *Rights of War and Peace*, 16–17, 108.

56. Vitoria, *Law of War*, 1.2.

57. Suarez, *Faith, Hope, and Charity*, 13.2.1–3.

58. Ibid., 13.4.5–7; Hamilton, *Political Thought*, 144–45.

59. Pufendorf, *De Jure Naturae*, 226–29; Wolff, *Jus Gentium*, 5; Vattel, *Le Droit de Gens*, 3–4.

60. Suarez, *Law and God the Lawgiver*, 1.3.11, 2.8.1.

61. Aquinas, *Summa Theologica*, I-II, q. 109, a. 4.

62. Suarez, *Law and God the Lawgiver*, 2.11.6–8.

63. Ibid., 2.6.3–4.

64. Ibid., 2.6.11.

65. Aquinas, *Summa Theologica*, I, q. 44, a. 1.

66. Hugo Grotius, *De Jure Belli*, 13–14, 38–39.

67. Pufendorf, *De Jure Naturae*, 27–31, 183–85.

68. Ibid., 22.

69. Boucher, *Political Theories*, 225–26.

70. Ibid., 146.

71. Thomas Hobbes, *Leviathan*, 13–14.

72. Ibid., 70.

73. Ibid., 145, 62.

74. Ibid., 86–89. The idea of a state of nature had emerged among Renaissance humanists, drawing on Cicero's account of such a state in his *De Inventione* and on the Roman jurists' distinction between the *ius naturale* that humans have in common with animals and the *ius gentium* that is particular to humans. Tuck, *Natural Rights Theories*, 31–45.

75. Hobbes, *Leviathan*, 9, 120–21.

76. Ibid., 147–48.

77. Ibid., 89–90.

78. Boucher, *Political Theories*, 152–57.

79. Hobbes, *Leviathan*, 91–92, 185.

80. Ibid., 239, 184.

81. Ibid., 90, 149. Tuck points out that a generation earlier, Hugo Grotius had argued that the autonomy of individuals is comparable to that of states, and that in general modern political thought is better characterized as applying the perceived qualities of states to individuals rather than the other way around. *Rights of War and Peace*, 81–83.

82. Boucher, *Political Theories*, 157–62.

83. Locke, *Second Treatise*, 269.

84. Ibid., 271–73; see also Doyle, *Ways of War and Peace*, 216–17.

85. Locke, *Second Treatise*, 334.

86. Ibid., 350–52.

87. Ibid., 278–81; see also Doyle, *Ways of War and Peace*, 217–18.

88. Locke, *Second Treatise*, 282.

89. Ibid., 323–25, 352–53.

90. Ibid., 283–84.

91. Ibid., 306.

92. Ibid., 276.

93. Doyle, *Ways of War and Peace*, 220.

94. Ibid., 223.

95. Ibid., 223–25.

96. Bentham, "Anarchical Fallacies," 90. Emphasis in original.

97. Bentham, *Fragment on Government*, 93.

98. Ibid., 118–21, 128.

99. Bentham, *Universal and Perpetual Peace*, 11.

100. Doyle, *Ways of War and Peace*, 226–28.

101. Ibid., 231–41.

102. Bentham, *Universal and Perpetual Peace*, 25.

103. Mill, *On Liberty*, 81.

104. Ibid., 80.

105. Miller, "Mill's Theory," 497–504.

106. Mill, *On Liberty*, 134.

107. Miller, "Mill's Theory," 505–9.

108. Boucher, *Political Theories*, 270.

109. Immanuel Kant, *Perpetual Peace*, 112.

110. Ibid., 116–25.

111. Kant, *Metaphysics of Morals*, 132–37.

112. Ibid., 162–63.

113. Kant, *Universal History*, 42–53.

114. Kant, *Perpetual Peace*, 108–14.

115. Boucher, *Political Theories*, 278.

116. Doyle, *Ways of War and Peace*, 280–81.

117. Kant, *Perpetual Peace*, 104.

118. Ibid., 93–97.

119. Ibid., 98–108.

120. Kant, *Metaphysics of Morals*, 171. Therefore Doyle seems mistaken when he writes that Kant "does not find institutionalization [of the federation] necessary. He appears to have in mind a mutual nonaggression pact, perhaps a collective security agreement, and the cosmopolitan law set forth in the third definitive article." *Ways of War and Peace*, 258.

121. Doyle, *Ways of War and Peace*, 334–38.

122. Kubálková and Cruickshank, *Marxism and International Relations*, 36–37.

123. Ibid., 331–34.

124. Boucher, *Political Theories*, 366–69.

CHAPTER THREE

· ·

CONTEMPORARY INTERNATIONAL
RELATIONS THEORY

THE MAJOR APPROACHES to international relations theory that emerged
in the twentieth century developed directly out of the thought of the political
philosophers described in the previous chapter. Michael W. Doyle divides this
thought into three strands that have shaped international relations theory in
the twentieth century: realism, liberalism, and socialism (or Marxism). Doyle
associates Machiavelli and Hobbes (along with Jean-Jacques Rousseau) with
realism; Locke, commercial pacifists like Adam Smith and Jeremy Bentham,
and Kant with liberalism; and Marx with socialism.[1] In the twentieth century,
each of these strands developed more systematic approaches to understanding
international relations, including the origins of war.

CLASSICAL REALISM

Proponents of the school of international relations theory known as realism tend
to think of states as self-interested seekers of power and are relatively pessimistic
about the possibilities of overcoming conflict among states. Realism developed
in the middle of the twentieth century, in part as a reaction against forms of
liberalism, described later in this chapter, that were inspired by Locke, Kant, and
the utilitarians. It drew on a tradition going back to the ancient Greek historian
Thucydides and looked to modern thinkers such as Machiavelli and Hobbes for
inspiration. Liberals such as United States President Woodrow Wilson and the
writers Norman Angell, Alfred Zimmern, and G. Lowe Dickinson were generally confident in the possibility of bringing about peace through education and
believed that history was inevitably progressing toward peace, manifested in
the creation of the League of Nations.[2] In contrast, the first generation of realists, sometimes called the classical realists, argued that human nature is flawed
and therefore not perfectible, and that politics inevitably involves a struggle
for power. International politics is characterized by conflict, and although that
conflict can be moderated, it can never be pacified.[3] The events leading up to
the Second World War and the inability of liberal leaders and institutions to
prevent that war, and then the beginning of the cold war, greatly increased the

plausibility of realism, to such an extent that today, "Realism is widely regarded as the most influential theoretical tradition in International Relations, even by its harshest critics."[4] Government figures such as George Kennan and Henry Kissinger were influential realists, but two of the most important realist thinkers were Reinhold Niebuhr and Hans J. Morgenthau.

Reinhold Niebuhr

The American Protestant theologian Reinhold Niebuhr (1892–1971) developed a Christian realism that was rooted in his account of human nature. According to Michael Joseph Smith, "Niebuhr without question [was] the most profound thinker of the modern realist school."[5] The movement known as Christian realism began with the publication of Niebuhr's *Moral Man and Immoral Society* in 1932. By the late 1940s and early 1950s, Christian realism had become a major force in Christian theology, dominating the thinking of the Protestant ecumenical group the World Council of Churches, but it also had an important influence on the field of international relations theory.[6] The fact that Niebuhr's was a *Christian* realism was something of an exception to the general trend of modern political thought to explain politics in nonreligious terms; nonetheless, Niebuhr's thought still exhibits many of the same characteristics as that of other modern thinkers.

In *Moral Man and Immoral Society*, Niebuhr writes that the defining characteristic of human nature is our self-awareness of our finitude. The human mind rebels against this finitude, transforming the natural desire for self-preservation into a desire to make one's finite perspective universal by imposing it on others.[7] This extension of desire applies to groups as well as individuals: "Every group, as every individual, has expansive desires which are rooted in the instinct of survival and soon extend beyond it. The will-to-live becomes the will-to-power."[8] Niebuhr at times refers to the attempt to make a particular and partial point of view universal as "idolatry," and elsewhere calls it "original sin."[9] Human persons vary greatly in time and culture, but this underlying aspect of human nature is universal.[10]

Niebuhr argues that because of this universal desire for self-aggrandizement, politics is primarily a struggle for power. The tendency to make one's partial point of view universal leads individuals and groups to confuse their own political interests with moral ideals, leading to hypocrisy and self-deception, so that even the most virtuous political actions are mixed with self-interest.[11] Religious idealists and rationalists are wrong to think that selfishness can be eliminated from society by religious conversion or education, respectively. Limited improvement is possible for individuals, but it is not likely for the social groups engaged in politics.[12] Echoing Hobbes, Niebuhr claims that both domestic and international society are in a state of war because of the inevitable clashes of self-interest, and therefore any sort of social cooperation requires a certain amount of coercion.[13] Reason can expose the ways in which the interests of the powerful are masked by ideology, but it cannot eliminate conflict. The best that can be hoped for is a rational system of justice in which power is carefully balanced.[14] Like Kant, Niebuhr believes that this balancing comes about through the interaction of opposing forces in history rather than through conscious planning.[15]

Niebuhr describes justice as the balancing of self-interested powers, but he also states that justice requires more than self-interest. He writes, "Any justice which is only justice soon degenerates into something less than justice. It must be saved by something which is more than justice."[16] This something more is religious morality, which Niebuhr defines as disinterestedness toward one's self-interest. Religious disinterestedness has positive effects on society, although those effects diminish on larger social bodies.[17] Religious disinterestedness may be necessary for true justice, but political society cannot be arranged as if all people were disinterested.[18] Nevertheless, Niebuhr claims there can be limited progress toward justice in society, a view that sets him apart from many other realists.[19]

According to Niebuhr, international politics, no less than domestic politics, consists in a struggle for power. Colm McKeogh writes: "For Niebuhr, the problems of international politics are the problems of humanity writ large. The perennial characteristics of human historical existence manifest themselves more clearly in international politics than elsewhere, and all aspects of our historical problems appear more vividly and in more discernible proportions in the large field of international relations."[20] Niebuhr argues that just as human individuals vary greatly yet possess a common nature, "the structure of political organization on both the parochial and the imperial level is fairly constant—while the ideological pretensions, which furnish the prestige which is one part of the structure, vary endlessly."[21] Like individuals, states confuse their national interest with universal values, which inevitably leads to conflict.[22] A central authority at the international level with coercive power could moderate conflicts, but such an authority does not exist at the international level and is unlikely to exist for a long time.[23]

Like other classical realists, Niebuhr finds the ultimate origins of war in the human desire for self-aggrandizement, which characterizes social groups such as states just as it does individuals. He seems to suggest ideology as one cause of war through his claim that conflicts among states tend to arise from states seeking to impose their values on others. For Niebuhr, however, it is not so much the content of ideologies that matters, but rather the universal human desire to impose those ideologies on others. Unlike other realists, though, Niebuhr claims that both individuals and social groups can and must seek to move beyond their limited perspectives in order to seek relative justice, even if it is impossible to completely overcome one's limitations.

Hans J. Morgenthau

Unlike Niebuhr, Hans J. Morgenthau (1904–90), who for most of his career was a professor of political science at the University of Chicago and the City University of New York, clearly separates power and morality. In his *Politics among Nations: The Struggle for Power and Peace*, Morgenthau distinguishes between idealism, which believes in "the essential goodness and infinite malleability of human nature, and blames the failure of the social order to measure up to the rational standards on lack of knowledge and understanding, obsolescent social institutions, or the depravity of certain isolated individuals or groups," and realism, which believes that by nature humans seek power and that conflict is inevitable.[24] Morgenthau claims that the origins of the pursuit of power and the ensuing conflict are found in human biology, not in any particular social arrangement.[25] Society puts limits on the individual's drive for power, but individuals transfer this desire to the state, where it becomes virtually limitless.[26]

Morgenthau attempts to develop politics as a science of power. He defines power as "man's control over the minds and actions of other men," and political power as "the mutual relations of control among the holders of public authority and between the latter and the people at large." Influenced by the sociologist Max Weber, Morgenthau claims that politics is the sphere of power, and political science is the science of power.[27] States have ultimate ends other than power, such as freedom and prosperity, yet these are extrapolitical goals that can be distinguished from the purely political pursuit of power.[28] Like Niebuhr, Morgenthau describes the desire to make one nation's national interest into a universal value as idolatrous, but unlike Niebuhr, he does not believe that individuals or states can ever move beyond the pursuit of self-interest.[29]

Morgenthau attempts to make international relations a science, and some consider him the father of twentieth-century scientific international relations theory.[30] Scott Burchill notes: "From the tone and style of [*Politics among Nations*] it is possible to sense the extent to which the U.S. academic community was influenced, if not enthralled by developments in the natural sciences during [the 1950s]."[31] During this period, American political scientists attempted to model their discipline on the natural sciences, partly to meet the demands of New Deal government programs that sought to bring about desired outcomes through the precise study and management of social forces, and partly to try to find ways of managing American foreign policy that could avoid igniting the ideological passions of the cold war.[32]

Morgenthau sought to develop a science of international politics, but as he noted in his earlier work *Scientific Man vs. Power Politics*, that effort should not be interpreted to mean that international politics is a series of problems to be solved, and he continues to make this point in *Politics among Nations*. For example, he takes issue with the false scientific accounts of international politics that seek to find a single cause of conflict and war so that, once discovered, it can be eliminated. This is the flaw of liberalism, which believes that "since all men partake of reason, they must sooner or later meet on that common ground, discovering that their conflicts are apparent rather than real and can all be solved by a rational formula acceptable to all."[33] The science of politics tells us the way things are, but does not necessarily give us the power to change them.

According to Morgenthau, states pursue power in various ways, resulting in a balance of power among states. The three general strategies that states pursue are policies of the status quo, policies of imperialism, and policies of prestige; that is, policies of keeping power, increasing power, and demonstrating power.[34] States' pursuit of these various strategies "leads of necessity to a configuration that is called the balance of power and to policies that aim at preserving it."[35] These balance-of-power configurations, or systems, exist at the regional level (e.g., Europe, East Asia, etc.), and these regional systems interlock to form an international balance-of-power system.[36]

The balance of power inevitably arises in international politics, but it alone is not sufficient to reduce conflict. Morgenthau claims that in the eighteenth and nineteenth centuries, with the exception of the Napoleonic Wars, the balance of power helped to limit war in Europe, but only because of two additional factors: shared morality, mores, and laws among policymakers, and the supranational loyalties of the aristocrats responsible for diplomacy.[37] In the eighteenth and nineteenth centuries, diplomacy was carried out by members of the aristocracy, who not only shared morality, mores, and laws because of their shared European culture, but also were often related to one another and at times would even represent nations other than their own. Because of these two phenomena, there was usually less at stake in international conflicts, and therefore war was limited.

Morgenthau traces the end of this state of affairs to the development of modern democracy. With the transition of states to democracy, diplomats no longer had supranational loyalties, but rather were loyal to their nation alone. The shared morality dissolved, and states pursued ethical systems of national origin as if they were universal claims. "Compromise, the virtue of the old diplomacy, becomes the treason of the new," Morgenthau explains, "for the mutual accommodation of conflicting claims, possible or legitimate within a common framework of moral standards, amounts to surrender when the moral standards themselves are the stakes of the conflict."[38] Therefore the prudent diplomat must always struggle against the passions of democracy. Morgenthau's realism takes on a moral dimension, then, since adherence to realist principles will lead to the pursuit of a modest national interest and the diminishment of conflict.[39]

For Morgenthau, like other classical realists, the origins of war lay in an innate human desire for self-aggrandizement, but in his reflections on diplomacy, Morgenthau adds something of a cultural component as well. Humans possess a biological desire for power that is then transferred to the state, which inevitably comes into conflict with other states in the pursuit of power. This is a permanent feature of human existence, not a problem to be solved. Like Niebuhr,

Morgenthau believes that ideologies are typically just masks for self-interest. Ideologies play a role in conflict not because of their specific content, but because they foster self-deception and recklessness. Interestingly, though, Morgenthau seems to suggest that the dangers of ideology are best tempered by a culture of diplomacy in which the pursuit of the national interest is recognized for what it is. Yet this implies that the pursuit of power is not the autonomous realm that Morgenthau elsewhere described, and that cultural practices and values shape the way power is understood and pursued. By the end of the 1970s, however, neorealism would sweep away these concerns with the ways that individual states form their foreign policies.

NEOREALISM

Neorealism emerged as an approach to international relations theory in the late 1970s and quickly became the dominant paradigm in the field. In the 1970s realism had become less compelling, as the economic interdependence among countries seemed to have as much importance as the balance of military power, whether through the ability of relatively weak states to cripple the world economy with the OPEC oil embargo or through the integration of western Europe into the European Economic Community. A resurgent liberalism, described later in this chapter, sought to give an account of these developments. Neorealism emerged as a challenge to the new liberalism, claiming that despite these changes in international relations, the underlying reality of power politics remained unchanged. Neorealism seemed to be vindicated by the resumption of a confrontational attitude between the United States and the Soviet Union in the late 1970s and early 1980s.

Neorealism, sometimes called structural realism, shares with classical realism the claim that international politics is inherently conflictual, but finds the source of this conflict in the anarchical nature of the international system rather than in the nature of individuals or states. According to Robert G. Gilpin, classical realists and neorealists share the following premises: that the international system is anarchical and conflictual; that in understanding international politics, social groups have priority over individuals; and that the quest for security and power is the most important human motivation. Both schools also share a commitment to scientific rigor.[40] In fact, neorealism shares the scientific approach to international politics that is found in Morgenthau's work.[41] Despite these similarities, neorealists such as Kenneth Waltz and John J. Mearsheimer have used this scientific approach in a way distinct from that of earlier realists.

A Structural Theory of International Politics

Kenneth Waltz, the leading neorealist, has attempted to define the scientific nature of international relations theory. According to Waltz, theories seek to explain facts but also necessarily involve abstraction. Neorealism abstracts the international system from the whole reality of international politics, while recognizing that in real life "everything is related to everything else."[42] Theorists also make assumptions about state behavior, even though states do not always behave according to those assumptions, and an international relations theory does not seek to predict specific outcomes, but rather a broad pattern of behaviors and outcomes.[43] Other neorealists, such as John J. Mearsheimer, are more ambitious, claiming that theories can be used to make "predictions of events soon to unfold."[44]

In his *Man, the State, and War*, Waltz divides theories on the causes of war into three "images": first-image theories find the cause of war in human nature; second-image theories find it within the structure of individual states; and third-image theories find it in the international system, by which Waltz means all states considered together and the relations among them.[45] First-image explanations, according to Waltz, are inadequate because human nature is constant, whereas the behavior of states varies and must be explained by some other factor.[46] Second-image accounts of war fail for a similar reason: states with similar structures behave in diverse ways, so some other variable must come into play.[47] Waltz believes that the crucial variable is the international system. In his best-known work, *Theory of International Politics*, he writes that a theory of international relations must begin by describing how the international system constrains and shapes state behavior, and only then fill in the details of domestic factors.[48]

Waltz believes that the most important feature of the international system is its anarchical nature, meaning that, unlike in domestic society, there is no governing authority with a monopoly on the legitimate use of force, leading states to accumulate power for the sake of survival.[49] States are faced with a security dilemma: All states must be prepared to use force, even if they would rather not, because they face potential threats from other states. Waltz writes, "The state among states . . . conducts its affairs in the brooding shadow of violence."[50] States do not so much pursue power as pursue security, even though the latter requires power.[51] He concludes that even though states pursue power, they do not in fact seek to maximize their power, since this would lead other states to attack them; Mearsheimer, however, argues the contrary, because the most secure situation is to be a hegemon, or dominant power.[52]

The Balance of Power

Besides its anarchical nature, the second most important attribute of the international system is its structure, or the distribution of power among states. Neorealists are particularly concerned with "great powers," or those states with significantly more power than others; they classify the distribution of power among the great powers as unipolar, bipolar, or multipolar. For example, Waltz characterizes the structure of the international system during the cold war as bipolar; that is, having two great powers, the United States and the Soviet Union. The distribution of power shapes how states respond to the anarchical international system.[53] States' pursuit of survival and security leads them to pursue policies that promote the balance of power, even if that is not the intended purpose of their policies.[54]

Many neorealists argue that the balance of power is best secured in a bipolar system, and that instability, and therefore conflict, is more likely in a multipolar system. Waltz asserts that bipolar systems are inherently more stable than multipolar systems, because in a multipolar system, great powers are more willing to pass the buck to others when a threat emerges, whereas in a bipolar system the great powers must rely on themselves and respond to the threat.[55] Mearsheimer makes a similar argument, although some neorealists, such as Robert Gilpin, argue that a unipolar world with a single hegemon is the most stable international structure, and that major wars are less likely in such a state of affairs.[56] Many neorealists are also skeptical of the possibilities for peace provided by international institutions, because typically those institutions merely reflect the balance of power and are powerless to overcome states' drive for security and power.[57]

Neorealists generally agree that the anarchical nature of the international system is the primary cause of state behavior, and therefore of conflict among states. This idea goes back to at least Thomas Hobbes, who thought that international politics exists in a "state of war" because there is no sovereign to govern the different states. The neorealists consider theories of human nature unhelpful in understanding conflict among states. They also find little role for ideology in understanding state behavior, because they claim that ideologically diverse states behave similarly in similar strategic situations. The most important variable determining state behavior is the distribution and balance of power among the great powers. In an anarchical system, according to the neorealists, conflict is most likely when states feel insecure, and states are most insecure when there is an imbalance of power.

LIBERALISM

Although realism was the dominant school of thought in the field of international relations theory in the twentieth century, the origins of the discipline are associated with liberalism. Twentieth-century liberalism had its roots in the thought of utilitarians such as Bentham and Mill, that of Immanuel Kant, and even the progressive idealism of G. W. F. Hegel. The liberals of the early twentieth century tended to believe that international institutions such as the League of Nations embodied a new spirit of humanity that made war practically impossible. The events of the 1930s through the 1950s demolished this idealism and contributed to the preeminence of realism in international relations theory, and liberalism's influence greatly diminished. Nevertheless, liberal theorists studied the integration of western Europe after World War II, which seemed to demonstrate the cooperation liberals had always claimed was possible, and eventually developed more universal theories of international relations. Two forms of liberalism in particular became influential in the last decades of the twentieth century: neoliberalism and the democratic peace theory.[58]

Early Twentieth-Century Liberalism

Early twentieth-century liberalism has sometimes been called idealism or idealist liberalism because of its strong faith in progress toward peace and the protection of human rights. Robert Jackson and Georg Sørensen describe three characteristic assumptions of liberal international relations theorists: a positive view of human nature, a belief that international politics can be cooperative rather than conflictual, and a belief in progress. These beliefs were reflected in the thought of early liberals such as United States President Woodrow Wilson and the English writer Norman Angell. Although liberalism lost much of its idealism after World War II, postwar liberals continued to be guided by more guarded versions of these assumptions.

The origins of liberalism as a school of international relations theory are to be found in the seemingly senseless destruction of World War I. The discipline of international relations theory itself began when scholars began to ask questions such as why the war had happened and what could be done in the future to prevent such a war from happening again. There were several reasons why early international relations theory took a liberal direction. First of all, the idea that the problems of war could be solved by science was consistent with the liberal belief that education was necessary for the establishment of peace. Second, it became commonplace to claim that the origins of World War I could be found in the balance-of-power system that had governed European international affairs for the preceding two centuries, and the shifting alliances that came with it, as well as in the undemocratic governments of many European states. Finally, as Jackson and Sørensen note, the primary beneficiaries in the aftermath of World War I were the United States and Great Britain, both of which were liberal democracies, and therefore it was inevitable that questions concerning the war would be interpreted through a liberal lens.[59]

This latter point is particularly reflected in the important role of U.S. President Woodrow Wilson (1856–1924, president 1913–21) in promoting liberalism as an approach to international relations. Earlier in his life Wilson had been a political scientist, and in the aftermath of World War I he promoted his liberal ideas on world order, many of which were implemented in the Paris Peace Conference of 1919. According to Jackson and Sørensen, the key conviction of Wilsonian idealism is that a rationally designed international institution could put an end to war, even without abolishing states and statecraft.[60] Although World War I had shattered any illusions that progress in human affairs would be automatic, it did not dampen Wilson's belief in progress itself. As Tim Dunne writes, "The First World War shifted liberal thinking towards a recognition that peace is not a natural condition but is one which must be constructed."[61] Peace was to be constructed by means of an international political authority such as the League of Nations, which was established in 1920. Wilson also believed that the nondemocratic governments of the European powers had played an important role in leading Europe to war, and therefore that promoting democracy was necessary for peace. This was reflected in the inclusion of national self-determination as one of the features of the peace settlement Wilson designed.

If Wilson focused on the political aspect of liberalism with his emphasis on international institutions and democratic government, the English writer Norman Angell (1872–1967) continued the tradition of economic liberalism founded by Adam Smith and Jeremy Bentham. Angell's most important work, *The Great Illusion*, was written in 1909, before World War I, but he continued to promote his ideas in the 1920s and 1930s.[62] According to Angell, the increasing economic interdependence of the world means that war will be more costly than peace, and therefore ought to be inconceivable. When political leaders claim that a war will benefit their nation, they are either mistaken or misleading their people for their own benefit. Angell argues that people are basically rational, and therefore the best strategy for promoting peace is to educate people about the costs of war.[63] Angell's ideas therefore demonstrate typical liberal themes: that peace and cooperation among states are possible; that one cause of war is the lack of adequate information; and that another cause of war is nondemocratic governments that are unresponsive to the well-being of their people.

The events of the 1920s and 1930s proved fatal to this early idealist liberalism. The League of Nations, the source of hope for many liberals who believed that a strong international institution would provide peace, was hampered from the beginning by the failure of the United States to sign on as a member and by the lack of real commitment to the institution on the part of Great Britain and France. The League was further weakened by its failure to stop the Japanese invasion of Manchuria in 1931 and the Italian invasion of Ethiopia in 1935, and it was totally discredited by the outbreak of World War II in 1939. Angell's optimism about the development of economic interdependence and its beneficial effects was severely challenged by the Great Depression of 1929, in which interdependence seemed to spread economic misery rather than mutual benefit. These events contributed to the rise of realism as the dominant school of international relations theory. Nevertheless, liberal ideas continued to have adherents after World War II, even if in a chastened form.

The growing cooperation among the states of western Europe after World War II provided an object of study for thinkers outside the realist school. Beginning in the 1930s, David Mitrany claimed that increasing transnational relations, that is, connections between groups within societies rather than between governments, among the countries of western Europe would lead to greater integration and peace.[64] In the 1950s, Ernst B. Haas further developed Mitrany's ideas, arguing that Mitrany had not given sufficient attention to the role of political authorities in the process of integration. According to Haas, political leaders must play an active role in the integration of states, and an important part of the process of integration is the shifting of these leaders' allegiances from their own states to institutions with jurisdiction over them.[65]

Karl W. Deutsch mirrors Mitrany and Haas's focus on transnational relations, looking not at their effects on integration, but rather on security. According to Deutsch, the increasing transnational relations among the states of western Europe and the United States after World War II led to a "pluralistic security community" that had seemingly overcome the insecurity that realists claimed was inevitable. Increasing contacts among the peoples of western Europe and the United States had led them to realize that they could resolve their conflicts without resorting to force.[66] Therefore Deutsch demonstrates the liberal emphasis not only on the possibility of cooperation, but also on people's ability to learn. Despite these important developments, liberalism faced an important weakness in comparison with realism: its explanatory power was limited to western Europe and the United States.

Liberal international relations theory had an important breakthrough in the 1970s. In that decade, economic interdependence and international institutions seemed to become increasingly important worldwide, not just in Europe, as the OPEC countries demonstrated the vulnerability of much more militarily powerful countries through disruptions in oil supply and price, and several third world countries made a serious effort, with OPEC's backing and through the United Nations, to promote an initiative known as the New International Economic Order. In their book *Power and Interdependence*, Robert O. Keohane and Joseph S. Nye Jr. restored liberalism as a major force in international relations theory by trying to account for these changes in international politics.

In *Power and Interdependence*, Keohane and Nye describe interdependence as a reality that complicates the realist picture of international relations. Contrary to the realists, Keohane and Nye argue that some states have relationships of complex interdependence, which includes growing ties between nondiplomatic governmental agencies and nongovernmental organizations, the absence of a clear hierarchy among issues, and the decreased importance of military force.[67] International institutions are more likely to develop in situations of complex interdependence, and these institutions, or regimes, can change the nature of the international system, making greater cooperation among states possible.[68] Although complex interdependence is increasing globally, it will continue to coexist with the realist world of military power; nevertheless, a theory more complex than realism is needed to account for complex interdependence.[69] Other liberal international relations theorists have also focused on the importance of transnational relations and economic interdependence.[70] Significantly, unlike earlier liberals, these more recent liberals have tried to show how states can cooperate with one another and live in peace even without an overarching political authority.

Neoliberalism

In his later work, Keohane has sought to explain complex interdependence in terms of the basic assumptions of neorealism, an approach that has come to define neoliberalism. His onetime collaborator Nye has increasingly emphasized the transnational connections brought about by complex interdependence and their potential for changing the norms and institutions of international politics, which has led him toward views similar to those of the constructivists, described in the next chapter.[71] Keohane, on the other hand, has downplayed this element, adopting the state-centric, systemic model of the neorealists, thus demonstrating the great influence of Waltz's work.[72] In *After Hegemony*, Keohane sought to show how international institutions established during the period of American hegemony, and the cooperation that they fostered in the 1970s and 1980s, could persist during a period of decline in American power, therefore undermining neorealist claims about international politics.[73]

Keohane argues that states can learn to cooperate and that the institutions they establish for this purpose provide them with clear benefits. He uses utilitarian-inspired game theory to show that cooperation is possible among states.[74] The international institutions, or regimes, that states create when they cooperate can make states more accountable for the violation of rules, reduce the costs of interactions between states, and provide states with more information for decision making.[75] Here Keohane echoes the claims of Locke, Bentham, and Kant that international institutions can lessen the effects of bias, fear, and ignorance. Because international institutions are decentralized, they do not change the essential nature of the anarchical international system, even if they do change the way that that system shapes state behavior.[76]

The significant difference between neorealism and neoliberalism when it comes to considering the origins of war is that neoliberals are more optimistic about the possibility of establishing cooperation among states, and therefore of minimizing conflict. Significantly, neoliberals share with neorealists the belief that the anarchical nature of the international system is the primary cause of conflict among states as they seek to protect their security. For neoliberals, like neorealists, this is a much more significant cause of conflict than human nature or ideology. Where neoliberals differ from neorealists is in their belief that states can begin to cooperate and form institutions that alter the landscape of the international system, decreasing the chances of conflict by making states feel more secure. Because of the neoliberals' focus on cooperation, however, explaining war has not been one of their primary concerns.

Democratic Peace Theory

Unlike neoliberals, proponents of the democratic peace theory are quite concerned with questions of war and peace, connecting these questions with the roots of liberal international relations theory in the aftermath of World War I. According to the democratic peace theory, whose most prominent exponents have been Michael W. Doyle and Bruce Russett, democratic states rarely if ever go to war with one another. Because of its emphasis on regime type, the democratic peace theory is often considered a competitor to structural theories of international relations, particularly neorealism; as Russett claims, "The theoretical edifice of [neo]realism will collapse if attributes of states' political systems are shown to have a major influence on which states do or do not fight each other."[77] The democratic peace theory gained plausibility because of the security community that emerged in western Europe, but it fully developed as a theory during what has been called the third wave of democratization in Latin America, Eastern Europe, and Asia of the 1980 and 1990s, when a zone of peace seemed to be emerging among the world's democracies.[78]

The central assertion of the democratic peace theory is that democracies never or very rarely go to war with one another. Doyle writes: "Even though liberal states have become involved in numerous wars with nonliberal states, constitutionally secure liberal states have yet to engage in war with one another."[79] It is not true, as Kant thought, that democracies are in general more peaceful because the citizens bear the costs of war, since they continue to war with nondemocratic states.[80] The democratic peace suggests, according to Russett, that democracies have found means of resolving conflicts *among themselves* without war, and possibly that they believe they should not fight wars with one another.[81] Neorealists have challenged this conclusion, but not without reply.[82]

Democratic peace theorists have given various accounts of why democracies rarely if ever war with one another. Some of these accounts are institutional, finding the causes of the democratic peace in the domestic structure of democratic states.[83] Other accounts of the democratic peace are normative. According to Russett, democracies seek to resolve conflicts with one another in ways consistent with the cultural values that shape their domestic democratic decision making, while they see autocracies as illegitimate.[84] John M. Owen argues for a model that incorporates both normative and institutional elements: "Liberal ideas are the source—the independent variable—behind the distinctive foreign policies of liberal democracies. These ideas give rise to two intervening variables, liberal ideology and domestic democratic institutions, which shape foreign policy."[85]

In *Triangulating Peace*, Russett and Oneal seek to extend the democratic peace theory to encompass the pacific effects of international trade and international organizations. Mearsheimer criticizes the traditional liberal claim that increasing economic interdependence will contribute to peace by arguing that economic interdependence can lead to conflict just as easily as to peace.[86] Russett and Oneal show through a statistical analysis, however, that both increased bilateral trade and greater economic openness between two states contribute to greater peace between those two states.[87] Shared membership in international organizations also contributes to peace.[88] Russett and Oneal argue that these three elements of a "Kantian triangle"—democratic governance, international trade, and international institutions—tend to reinforce one another and are themselves reinforced by peaceful relations among states.[89]

Unlike neorealism and neoliberalism, the democratic peace theory focuses on the characteristics of individual states that make war more or less likely, not on the characteristics of the international system. Institutional versions of the theory hearken back to the older liberal theories of Locke, Smith, and Kant, and therefore suggest the traditional liberal answers to the question of war's origins: ignorance, bias, and weakness. Normative versions of the theory point forward to constructivism, discussed in the next chapter, an approach to international relations that emphasizes the importance of culture and identity in world politics and that suggests that war has its origins in clashing values and identities. Before moving on to constructivism, however, it is important to note that theorists inspired by Karl Marx have also continued to play an important role in international relations theory, providing a distinct perspective on the origins of war.

MARXIST THOUGHT ON THE ORIGINS OF WAR

Thinkers following in the line of Karl Marx in the nineteenth century have developed theories that find the origins of war in economic relations, whether within the state or among states. I have already described how Marx and his associate Friedrich Engels viewed class conflict as the primary engine of history; in this view, the affairs of states and the relations among them, including war, reflect this underlying economic conflict. Marx's Russian disciple Vladimir Lenin transformed Marx's thought in his theory of imperialism. World-systems theory, developed in the 1960s and 1970s, took Marxism in new directions, suggesting that interstate conflict results from features of the global economic system rather than the economic systems of individual states.

Lenin and Imperialism

The Soviet leader Vladimir Lenin (1870–1924) developed the first significant variant of Marx's theory of international relations. Nevertheless, Lenin heavily drew on the work of others in his pamphlet *Imperialism, the Highest Stage of Capitalism*. Anthony Brewer argues that Lenin contributed very little to the actual development of Marxist thought on imperialism, but still, his pamphlet is the classic statement.[90] Lenin describes how in the last decades of the nineteenth century, industries were reduced to only a few firms, that is, they were cartelized or monopolized. This was true in both protectionist and free-trading states, and, according to Lenin, it was an inevitable development of capitalism. Banks also became cartelized, and therefore a small number of individuals were able to control the investment of capital in industries, giving them virtual control of those industries.[91] He also writes that because of monopolization, capitalist countries suffered from underconsumption, and therefore finance capitalists sought colonies for new investments and new markets.[92] The finance capitalists divided the world among themselves but often came into conflict with one another, which led to wars.[93] Therefore, for Lenin, wars, whether between a capitalist state and a potential colony or between capitalist states themselves, are primarily caused by economic factors, namely capitalist states' demand for new markets because of their own faltering economics.

Lenin believes that imperialism divided the worldwide working class, making it necessary for the revolution to begin in the colonized countries. He argues that imperialism led to economic stagnation in the home country, as more and more of the country's income derived from investments and loans rather than production. A portion of the working class was given some of this wealth, creating a group of workers bound to the imperialist system that Lenin calls the "labor aristocracy."[94] According to Lenin, it was the labor aristocracy that led the workers to subordinate class loyalty to national loyalty in World War I.[95] Members of the labor aristocracy gave up on revolution, instead concluding that socialism can be brought about through democratic reform. Because the socialists in the imperialist countries have therefore become corrupt and complacent, the socialist revolution will begin in the "colonies," such as Russia.[96]

World-Systems Theory

World-systems theory looks at international relations from the perspective of the global economic system. In the 1960s, Marxist-inspired dependency theory originated the insight that the study of class conflict cannot be limited to the domestic level, but rather must examine the entire international economy as a whole. World-systems theory developed this insight into a broader perspective on international relations. Like traditional Marxist theories, world-systems theory focuses on modes of production and class relations, but according to Immanuel Wallerstein, one of the most prominent world-systems theorists, the mode of production and class relations in an individual state cannot be understood in isolation from the "world-system," the worldwide network of economic interrelations.[97] This is because the different actors within the world-system, such as states and economic classes, are products of that system rather than "primordial atomic elements" that pre-exist the system. Although these actors have freedom of action, that freedom is constrained by the world-system and their role within it.[98] When one studies international politics, the world-system should be the primary unit of analysis, not the individual nation-state.[99]

Wallerstein argues that the present world-system can be characterized as a capitalist world-economy. World systems come in two varieties: world economies and world empires. In the former, multiple cultures interact with each other and are linked economically, whereas in the latter they are also united under a single political authority. The modern capitalist world-economy, which had its origins in sixteenth-century Europe and has gradually spread to cover the whole world, is unique because of its ability to persist as a world-economy without becoming a world-empire. Previous world economies have become world empires as dominant political units within the system expanded their authority through conquest.[100]

The capitalist world-economy is characterized by two types of firms: core firms that have achieved monopoly or near-monopoly status, and peripheral firms that exist in a more competitive market. The terms "core" and "periphery" can also be applied to states, because core firms tend to be concentrated in powerful states capable of maintaining their monopoly status, whereas peripheral firms tend to be concentrated in weak states; nevertheless, the firms themselves are the primary forces in the world-system. The behavior of states in the world-system is determined by what type of firms are concentrated in each state: core states act to protect the monopolies of the core firms; peripheral states tend to be acted upon rather than act; and semi-peripheral states, which contain both types of firms, attempt to move into the core and resist falling into the periphery.[101]

The position of states within the capitalist world-economy also determines their relations with one another. Strong states seek to dominate weak states in order to keep the economic channels of the weak states open, pressuring them, sometimes through military force, to conform to the preferences of the strong states. Strong states relate to each other as competitors because their firms compete with one another; this competition among strong states sometimes erupts into war, but these states also cooperate to maintain the world-economy. This competition creates a rough balance of power among the strong states, although sometimes one state acquires hegemony over the world-system. This hegemony is never consolidated into an empire, however, because a unified political authority is contrary to the interests of the core firms who dominate the world-economy.[102] Although Wallerstein, like Marx, finds an economic basis for war among states, for the former it lies in the worldwide economic system as a whole, not in the economic systems of particular states; the behavior of states is determined by their role within the world-system.

Like Marx, Wallerstein also believes that historical change inevitably takes place through conflict. World systems collapse because of their own internal contradictions. Despite the ability of the capitalist world-economy to maintain itself, Wallerstein believes that the same fate awaits it, and that the system has been in a state of crisis since about the year 1968. He believes that the world-system emerging from its ashes will be either unilateral political domination by the United States or a world-system guided by worldwide radical social movements.[103]

The diverse Marxist theories of international relations all find the origins of war in economic conflict. Marx did not believe that there is one universally valid cause of war; rather, the causes of war depend on the historical moment, particularly the nature of the economic system and its conflictual relations. Marx himself saw the capitalist period as one of increasing peace, albeit a peace that masked the increasing conflict within states between the bourgeoisie and the proletariat. Lenin, on the other hand, saw imperialism as the particular source of war in the epoch of late capitalism. The world-systems theory of Immanuel Wallerstein, in particular, claims that international conflicts are caused by the desire of core states, dominated by core firms, to maintain their domination of the weaker peripheral states through the free flow of the goods produced in peripheral production processes. Despite their differences, then, theories of international relations inspired by Marxism find the ultimate origins of international conflict in the clashing economic forces of economic systems, whether within a single state or in the world economy as a whole.

CONCLUSION

The primary schools of international relations theory that arose in the twentieth century—realism, liberalism, and Marxism—developed sophisticated accounts of international politics, including the origins of war. But because these schools emerged out of earlier strands of modern political thought, they shared the presuppositions that distinguished that thought from the earlier Christian tradition. Those presuppositions shaped the way these theories describe the origins of war.

The various twentieth-century international relations theories continued to think of the desires of the human will as limitless and having no transcendent end. The classical realists were clearly in the tradition of Machiavelli and Hobbes in understanding the human will as limitless in its desires. For the classical realists, international politics is the realm of the pursuit of power cut off from any other human ends. Institutional versions of the democratic peace theory instead use a utilitarian model of understanding individual behavior, but in this model, too, human desires are limitless and have no real purpose. Proponents of neorealism and neoliberalism are not concerned with describing human nature, but the theme of the limitless will is still reflected in their emphasis on states' power- and utility-maximization, respectively, absent any connection to other ends. Marxist theories also deny that humans have an innate, transcendent end, instead arguing that individuals' and groups' desires are determined by their status within an economic system.

These theories consequently do not see any connection between political life and transcendent or religious values. For the realists and neorealists, political life is concerned with power and survival. Questions about the purposes for which power should be used are considered to be outside the realm of politics, or are ignored altogether, and so, as for Machiavelli, survival becomes an end in itself. The neoliberals and institutional democratic peace theorists, on the other hand, consider utility-maximization to be the primary purpose of political life, and therefore, as for the earlier utilitarians, politics seems to be bound by worldly concerns. Marxist theories most clearly sever political life from the transcendent, explicitly supporting a materialist philosophy in which everything can be explained in material, and specifically economic, terms.

Finally, most of the major theories of the twentieth century claimed to be the result of objective science, based on observation of facts and absent any religious or metaphysical assumptions. Hans Morgenthau saw realism as the development of a truly scientific international relations theory, concerning itself with the way things are rather than the way we might wish them to be. Both neorealism and neoliberalism self-consciously try to model their approaches on other social sciences, especially economics. Like Marx, later Marxist theories deny that a description of human society can be neutral or value-free; it either reinforces the status quo or seeks to change it. Nevertheless, they also believe, like Marx, that a transformative vision of the international system, understood in economic terms, could still be considered rigorously scientific.

These theories' understandings of the origins of war reflect the influence of modern political thought. Classical realists, neorealists, and neoliberals have all continued, in different ways, to think of conflict among states as the result of clashing wills, whether rooted in human nature or the nature of the anarchical international system. These conflicting wills are motivated primarily by material interests, however, whether expressed in terms of power and security by the realists and neorealists, or in terms of utility by the neoliberals. Marxist-inspired theories such as world-systems theory have also understood war as having its origins in clashes of material interests; for such theorists, war is the product of necessary contradictions within an economic system. Cultural and ideological factors play a minor role, whether they are understood as masks for the interests of the powerful by realists and Marxists, or largely ignored by neorealists and neoliberals. These ways of understanding war's origins are quite different from those developed in the earlier Christian tradition. An approach to international relations that has developed in the last thirty years, constructivism, offers a critique of these modern theories that, besides having merit in its own right, also provides resources for developing a Catholic understanding of the origins of war that is consistent with the Christian tradition.

NOTES

1. Doyle, *Ways of War and Peace*, 15–40.
2. Smith, *Realist Thought*, 58.

3. Ibid., 1.

4. Burchill, "Realism and Neo-realism," 70.

5. Smith, *Realist Thought*, 99.

6. Patterson, "Niebuhr and His Contemporaries," 3–6.

7. Niebuhr, *Moral Man*, 41–42.

8. Ibid., 18.

9. Niebuhr, "Church in a Secular Age," 204–7; Niebuhr, *Structure of Nations*, 135–36.

10. Niebuhr, "Modern Utopians," 154–55.

11. Niebuhr, *Moral Man*, 44–45, 95.

12. Ibid., 23–25.

13. Ibid., 3–4, 19–20.

14. Ibid., 30–31.

15. Niebuhr, *Structure of Nations*, 293–94.

16. Niebuhr, *Moral Man*, 258.

17. Ibid., 263–68.

18. Ibid., 73.

19. Niebuhr, *Structure of Nations*, 144; McKeogh, *Political Realism*, 137–40.

20. McKeogh, *Political Realism*, 8.

21. Niebuhr, *Structure of Nations*, 22.

22. Niebuhr, "Ideology and Pretense," 108–9.

23. Niebuhr, *Structure of Nations*, 31, 262–66.

24. Morgenthau, *Politics among Nations*, 3.

25. Ibid., 35–38.

26. Ibid., 114–15.

27. Ibid., 13–16; see also Smith, *Realist Thought*, 24–27.

28. Morgenthau, *Politics among Nations*, 29.

29. Ibid., 12–13; Smith, *Realist Thought*, 136–37.

30. Keohane, "Realism, Neorealism," 10.

31. Burchill, "Realism and Neo-realism," 77.

32. Jackson and Sørensen, *International Relations*, 45–48.

33. Morgenthau, *Politics among Nations*, 41–49.

34. Ibid., 50–51.

35. Ibid., 179–84.

36. Ibid., 209.

37. Ibid., 224–31.

38. Ibid., 251–65.

39. Thompson and Clinton, "Foreword," xxviii–xxxiii.

40. Gilpin, "Tradition of Political Realism," 304–8.

41. Epp, "Ironies of Christian Realism," 201–7.

42. Waltz, "Realist Thought," 67–70; Waltz, "Origins of War," 615–16.

43. Waltz, "Reflections on *Theory of International Politics*," 344; Waltz, *Theory of International Politics*, 91–92.

44. Mearsheimer, "Back to the Future," 9.

45. Waltz, *Man, the State, and War*, 12–15.

46. Ibid., 80–81.

47. Ibid., 122–23.

48. Waltz, *Theory of International Politics*, 65.

49. Ibid., 88–91.

50. Ibid., 102–7; Waltz, *Man, the State, and War*, 160.

51. Waltz, "Origins of War," 616.

52. Waltz, *Theory of International Politics*, 126–27; Mearsheimer, "False Promise," 10–12; Mearsheimer, *Tragedy*, 2–3, 30–36.

53. Waltz, *Theory of International Politics*, 79–81.

54. Ibid., 128; Waltz, *Man, the State, and War*, 208.

55. Waltz, *Theory of International Politics*, 161–70.

56. Mearsheimer, "Back to the Future," 13–18; Gilpin, *War and Change*; Gilpin, *Political Economy*.

57. Mearsheimer, "False Promise," 12–14; Mearsheimer, *Tragedy*, 46–48.

58. For a description of all of the strands of liberal international relations theory since the end of World War II, see Zacher and Matthew, "Liberal International Theory," 120–37.

59. Jackson and Sørensen, *Introduction to International Relations*, 35–38; see also Dunne, "Liberalism," 192.

60. Ibid., 38.

61. Dunne, "Liberalism," 191.

62. Angell, *Great Illusion*.

63. Jackson and Sørensen, *Introduction to International Relations*, 39.

64. Mitrany, *Working Peace System*; Mitrany, *Functional Theory of Politics*.

65. Haas, *Uniting of Europe*; Haas, *Beyond the Nation-State*.

66. Deutsch et al., *Political Community*.

67. Keohane and Nye, *Power and Interdependence*, 21–25.

68. Ibid., 18, 30–31.

69. Ibid., 33–52, 197–200.

70. Rosenau, *Global Interdependence*; Rosenau, *Turbulence in World Politics*; Rosenau, "Citizenship," 272–94; Rosecrance, *Trading State*; Rosecrance, *Virtual State*.

71. Nye, *Understanding International Conflicts*, 36–39, 60–61, 164; Nye, *Soft Power*.

72. Keohane, *After Hegemony*, 25–26.

73. Ibid., 7–10, 31–32.

74. Ibid., 64–85.

75. Ibid., 85–98.

76. Ibid., 237–38.

77. Russett, "Democratic Peace," 337; see also Doyle, "Kant, Liberal Legacies," 218–24.

78. Jackson and Sørensen, *Introduction to International Relations*, 50; Huntington, *Third Wave*.

79. Doyle, "Kant, Liberal Legacies," 213–15.

80. Ibid., 225.

81. Russett, *Grasping the Democratic Peace*, 4.

82. Mearsheimer, "Back to the Future," 48–51; Farber and Gowa, "Polities and Peace," 244–62; Russett and Oneal, *Triangulating Peace*, 60, 111–14.

83. Russett, *Grasping the Democratic Peace*, 38–42; Bueno de Mesquita, Morrow, Siverson, and Smith, "Institutional Explanation," 791.

84. Russett, *Grasping the Democratic Peace*, 30–38.

85. Owen, "Liberalism," 122.

86. Mearsheimer, "Back to the Future," 42–48.

87. Russett and Oneal, *Triangulating Peace*, 145–51.

88. Ibid., 171–74.

89. Ibid., 212–28.

90. Brewer, *Marxist Theories*, 116.

91. Lenin, *Imperialism*, 16–46.

92. Ibid., 62–67.

93. Ibid., 68–87.

94. Ibid., 88–108.

95. Brewer, *Marxist Theories*, 123–28.

96. Kubálková and Cruickshank, *Marxism and International Relations*, 51–53.

97. Wallerstein, *World-Systems Analysis*, 20.

98. Ibid., 21–22.

99. Ibid., 16–17.

100. Ibid., 23–24.

101. Ibid., 28–30. Wallerstein is unclear why semi-peripheral states have interests of their own independent of the interests of the firms concentrated within them.

102. Ibid., 55 59.

103. Ibid., 76–90.

CHAPTER FOUR

·····················

CONSTRUCTIVISM

IN THE 1980s and 1990s, a handful of international relations scholars calling themselves constructivists began to challenge the then-dominant theories of international relations, particularly neorealism and neoliberalism. They argued that earlier theories had presented too limited views of state behavior, ignoring the important role of culture. In reality, the constructivists claim, the identities, interests, and norms that shape state behavior are formed by states' relations with one another as well as by domestic social forces, and states are motivated by a wide variety of interests. I will argue that the constructivists' main claims suggest that war results from clashing socially constructed identities, interests, and norms. Constructivism challenges some of the presuppositions of modern thinking about international politics and can contribute to a new Catholic perspective on the origins of war.

CONSTRUCTIVISM, CRITICAL THEORY, AND POSTMODERNISM

Constructivism is in part a response to an empirical crisis in the field of international relations theory. There had already been dissatisfaction with the approaches of neorealism and neoliberalism in the 1980s, but the end of the cold war in 1989 created a sense of crisis because neither neorealists nor neoliberals predicted it, and neither could adequately explain it or the historical events that followed.[1] Events of the 1990s, including the resurgence of religious and ethnic violence and the increasing willingness of states to engage in humanitarian intervention, reinforced the need for an approach to international relations centered on identity and norms.[2]

Constructivism's criticisms of the major theories of international relations went beyond the empirical to the theoretical, however, and reflected a broader crisis within the social sciences.[3] This crisis emerged because of dissatisfaction with the supposedly scientific, positivist approach to the social sciences developed in the 1940s and 1950s, and because of the influence of philosophical currents that challenged the objectivity of our knowledge about social reality. The field of international relations theory was not immune to this crisis. As

Mark Hoffman writes, "The problem the discipline faces is that . . . there is no longer any clear sense of what the discipline is about, what its core concepts are, what its methodology should be, what central issues and questions it should be addressing."[4] Like other movements in the social sciences that have sprung up as a result of this crisis, constructivism has drawn on such diverse influences as neo-Kantian philosophy and the sociology of knowledge; philosophers such as Martin Heidegger, Hans-Georg Gadamer, Ludwig Wittgenstein, Jacques Derrida, and Michel Foucault; the critical theory of the Frankfurt School; and pragmatism.[5] Constructivists have not sought to refine the older theories of international relations but rather to create a new approach. They therefore make not only empirical criticisms of neorealism and neoliberalism, but also theoretical challenges, focusing on two points: the presumption that states are atomistic and rationally self-interested, and the presumption that the international relations theorist is an objective observer of world events.

The first criticism is that both neorealism and neoliberalism assume the identity and interests of states as givens. Alexander Wendt, a leading constructivist, argues that although the neorealist Kenneth Waltz claims to show the effects of the international system on states, in what he considers a "systemic" approach to international relations, his theory assumes that states have a particular nature that will be affected in a certain way by that system. Ontologically speaking, states are imagined prior to the system and only subsequently placed within the system.[6] This is true of neoliberalism as well, since it consciously accepts the basic presuppositions of neorealism.[7] Neorealism and neoliberalism consider the identities and interests of states to be given, rather than formed over time through social interaction. Therefore they consider states to be atomistic, or understandable apart from their relations with other states. This atomistic view of states has also led neorealists and neoliberals to a very narrow understanding of the rationality of state behavior.

Many have criticized neorealists and neoliberals for their narrow view of the rationality of states, arguing that state behavior is much more complex. Neorealists and neoliberals assume that states seek power, security, and wealth in a rational way, but as Martha Finnemore writes, "It is all fine and well to assume that states want power, security, and wealth, but what kind of power? Power for what ends? What kind of security? What does security mean? How do you ensure or obtain it? Similarly, what kind of wealth? Wealth for whom? How do you obtain it?"[8] According to rational-choice theory, actors are fundamentally self-interested, and despite their differences, both neorealism and neoliberalism share this rationalist perspective, typically expressed in microeconomic terms.[9] Because of this, both Richard K. Ashley and John Gerard Ruggie argue that neorealism and neoliberalism are at root utilitarian theories.[10] Elsewhere Ashley writes that neorealists and neoliberals are trapped by a "logic of economy," understanding states as motivated only by technical reason and economic efficiency.[11] Although Ashley compares the neorealists unfavorably to the classical realists in this regard, even the latter saw power as unaffected by the ends for which power is pursued, and so in this way were very close to the neorealists.[12] The critics of neoliberalism and neorealism, on the other hand, claim that states are motivated by a wide variety of interests developed in a social context: "We cannot understand what states want without understanding the international social structure of which they are a part. States are embedded in dense networks of transnational and international social relations that shape their perceptions of the world and their role in that world. States are *socialized* to want certain things by the international society in which they and the people in them live."[13]

Neorealists and neoliberals have also been criticized for their claims to present an objective analysis of international politics; this criticism could also be leveled at most modern international relations theories. Ashley lists five typical presuppositions of this positivism in the social sciences: that science seeks to know objective reality independently of human subjectivity; that the goal of science is to produce technically useful knowledge; that knowledge is value neutral; that truth claims can be tested by their correspondence to objective reality; and that human subjectivity does not cause problems for the scientific endeavor.[14] The critics of neorealism and neoliberalism argue that international theorists cannot help but approach the field with metaphysical, epistemological, and political positions that shape the way they see the world. Some also criticize the supposed value-neutrality of international relations theory. Robert W. Cox writes, "Theory is always for someone and for some purpose."[15] Ashley argues that by thinking of state interests as given rather than created, neorealists and neoliberals privilege the interests of those who are actually in control of states by hiding the ways their interests have become equated with the "national interest."[16] Critics of the neorealists and neoliberals largely agree that this supposedly objective, value-neutral positivism is flawed, but they differ in their proposed alternatives.

Constructivists represent only one school among those who are critical of mainstream international relations theories. There is a wide variety of classifications of constructivists in relation to similar schools of thought, and there is no consensus on the boundaries of the school. Yosef Lapid writes that postpositivism, one term for this group of related approaches "presents itself as a rather loosely patched-up umbrella for a confusing array of only remotely related philosophical articulations."[17] Despite this confusion, constructivists can most usefully be distinguished from critical theorists and postmodernists, primarily in regards to the question of whether objective knowledge of international relations is attainable. Critical theorists argue that the description of social reality always reflects interests, whether they are the interests of those seeking to preserve "cultural hegemony" or those resisting that hegemony. Postmodernists claim that descriptions of social reality are always exercises of power that must be constantly questioned.

Constructivists share with the critical theorists and postmodernists the belief that reality is socially constructed, but depart from them by claiming that it is nevertheless possible to provide a relatively objective account of reality.[18] Wendt writes: "All observation is theory-*laden* in the sense that what we see is mediated by our existing theories, and to that extent knowledge is inherently problematic. But this does not mean that observation, let alone reality, is theory-*determined*. The world is still out there constraining our beliefs, and may punish us for incorrect ones. Montezuma had a theory that the Spanish were gods, but it was wrong, with disastrous consequences. We do not have unmediated access to the world, but this does not preclude understanding how it works."[19] The question of objectivity arises, according to Ruggie, because "social facts" are distinct from "natural facts": Social facts, such as "money, property rights, sovereignty, marriage, football, and Valentine's Day," unlike natural facts, "depend on human agreement that they exist and typically require human institutions for their existence."[20] Many theorists often make the false assumption that this means that social facts are either unreal or unknowable: positivists do not believe they exist because they cannot be observed through the senses, critical theorists and postmodernists believe that because they are socially constructed, they are purely the expressions of power relations. Wendt argues that even though our way of seeing the world is socially constructed, social facts are indeed objectively knowable, even though our knowledge of them only approximates the truth.[21] This pair of premises, that social reality is socially constructed and that we can know it objectively, is generally what distinguishes constructivists from mainstream theorists like the neorealists and neoliberals on the one hand, and critical theorists and postmodernists on the other.

THE CONSTRUCTIVIST APPROACH TO INTERNATIONAL RELATIONS

Identities, interests, and norms of behavior are three characteristics of states that are central to the constructivist approach to international relations. Identities are facts that tell us something about an actor—whether an individual, a state, or some other social group—that is relevant for understanding its behavior or others' behavior towards it. Interests refer to the reasons why an actor acts. Despite the difficulties in understanding human motivation, the interests of an individual person are relatively straightforward compared to the interests of social groups such as states, which are made up of many individuals with conflicting interests. Nevertheless, a state, as an organized grouping of persons, can have interests of its own; I will discuss what that might mean later. Finally, norms of behavior refer to the rules that an actor follows in pursuing its interests, wherever those rules may come from.

Identities, interests, and norms of behavior are all closely related. Friedrich V. Kratochwil argues that identities and interests can themselves be considered types of norms.[22] For example, the rules of chess are a set of norms: some determine what the different pieces are capable of doing (identities), some determine the purposes of the game (interests). Kratochwil's claim makes intuitive sense, because often an identity can be expressed as "I'm the sort of person who does *A* and *B*, but not *C* and *D*." Likewise, an interest in the form of "*x* is good for me" can be formulated as the norm "I ought to pursue *x*," and vice versa. Negative norms, or prohibitions, simply show when the pursuit of one interest should not be followed at the expense of another. The connection between identities and interests is perhaps even clearer. As Alexander Wendt writes, "Interests presuppose identities because an actor cannot know what it wants until it knows who it is."[23] Thus identities, interests, and norms of behavior can be understood as three ways of thinking about the same realities. It also seems reasonable to conclude that, as Audie Klotz argues, changes in norms are likely to produce changes in identities and interests, and changes in interests and the emergence of new identities lead to changes in norms.[24]

The identities, interests, and norms that shape state behavior are part of what Wendt calls "common knowledge" and "collective knowledge." Common knowledge consists in the beliefs shared by all of the members of a community that they are aware of sharing, and collective knowledge consists in ideas or values that transcend the beliefs of the individuals in a community but are only manifest in the beliefs of those individuals. For example, the idea of "Canada" is a community identity that has persisted over time even as the individuals who have made up that community have changed, and is therefore a form of collective knowledge; nevertheless, the idea of "Canada" only exists in the beliefs of those who currently make up the community, and is therefore manifest in that community's common knowledge. Common knowledge and collective knowledge together make up culture, which has the central role in determining the identities, interests, and norms of behavior of individuals and the institutions they form.[25] Constructivists claim that the collective knowledge of the society within a state shapes the identities, interests, and norms of that state, and the international system itself is a form of collective knowledge that also helps to shape states' identities, interests, and norms of behavior.

Constructivists primarily focus on describing the ways in which the identities, interests, and norms of states are shaped by the international system and by domestic forces, and how at the same time states continuously shape the international system through their own actions. According to Wendt, any social theory, including a theory of international relations, must explain the relationship between a social structure and the actors who make it up. Wendt believes that the most adequate social theory is the structurationist theory of Anthony Giddens, which claims that any social structure constitutes the actors or agents who make it up, while at the same time the agents constitute the structure through their practices.[26] In international relations this would mean that the international system of states, in addition to constraining the behavior of states with given identities and interests, as neorealists and neoliberals claim, also shapes the very identities, interests, and norms of those states (as do forces internal to each state). At the same time, states are continuously maintaining and transforming the international system through their actions.[27] The behavior of states is not mechanically determined by the international system; their identities and interests present them with a variety of options for action. These options are what allow states to change the international system.[28]

Wendt uses structuration theory to critique the dominant theories of international relations, neorealism and neoliberalism. Neorealists such as Waltz claim to present a structuralist theory; that is, a theory that shows the way the social structure, the anarchical international system, constitutes the interests and behaviors of states. Wendt argues that neorealism in fact does no such thing; it only describes the effects of the international system on states whose interests are presupposed, and the effects of the international system themselves depend on these presuppositions about the interests of states. Despite neorealists' claims to the contrary, in neorealism, the international system plays no constitutive role in determining the interests or identities of states. Therefore neorealism is better characterized as an "individualist" social theory, according to Wendt, that leaves unexplained both how state identities and interests are formed and what role the international system plays in that process. The same criticisms could be made of neoliberalism, which borrows many of the presuppositions of neorealism.

Wendt also challenges the neorealists' understanding of the anarchical international system, based on his understanding of how states shape that international system. Neorealists such as Waltz and Mearsheimer argue that the anarchical nature of the international system leads to the competitive and "self-help" behavior of states, the quest for power and security that lies at the origins of war. Wendt, on the other hand, argues that: "There is no 'logic' of anarchy apart from the practices that create and instantiate one structure of identities and interests rather than another; structure has no existence or causal powers apart from process. Self-help and power politics are institutions, not essential features of anarchy. *Anarchy is what states make of it.*"[29] The competitive behavior of states helps to create the competitive environment that neorealists see as the cause of such behavior. Even though competitive state behavior is socially constructed and not inevitable, this does not mean it would be easy to change, since the current socially constructed identities and norms reinforce such behavior.[30]

Wendt also criticizes alternative approaches to international relations such as world-systems theory and postmodernism. The world-systems theory of Immanuel Wallerstein, unlike neorealism, is truly structuralist because in that theory, actors in the international system only have identities as part of the system, the capitalist world-economy. Because in this case international actors play no role in constituting the international system, world-systems theory can give no account of why the international system has the nature that it does or how change in the system could come about. Wendt also believes that a structuration-ist approach to international relations can avoid the relativism characteristic of postmodernism: The individual actor *is* constituted by the surrounding social structure, as postmodernists claim, but the fact that actors also shape the social structure ensures that the actor exists as a distinct reality and is not dissolved into a morass of social construction.[31]

Moving from the abstract to the concrete, constructivists have offered examples of how the international system plays a role in constituting states' identities, interests, and norms. Perhaps the most important way that the international system constitutes states is through establishing the principle by which political units are differentiated from one another. John Gerard Ruggie writes that Waltz's neorealism fails to describe *"the principles on the basis of which the constituent units are separated* from one another. If anarchy tells us *that* the political system is a segmented realm, differentiation tells us *on what basis* the segmentation is determined."* In other words, we must try to understand the different ways that political boundaries, both physical and conceptual, have been drawn over time. These principles of differentiation cannot be simply understood as qualities of the political units, but rather as attributes of the international system itself, since they only become defined through the interaction of the political units.[32] There have been various principles of differentiation throughout history: primitive communities based on kinship; nomadic societies with territorial cycles of migration; the "heteronomous" medieval system of overlapping fealties; and the demarcated territories of modern sovereign states.[33] Clearly the way that states distinguish themselves from one another plays an important role in constituting their identities.

Christian Reus-Smit describes the key ways—what he calls "constitutional structures"—that the international system shapes states, besides the principle of differentiation described by Ruggie. In addition to the principle of differentiation, the other constitutional structures are beliefs about the moral purpose of the state and the prevalent norms of procedural justice.[34] Among other examples, Reus-Smit describes how the city-states of Renaissance Italy saw their purpose as the pursuit of civic glory and understood justice in terms of the ritual enactment of a patronage system, whereas the absolutist states of eighteenth-century Europe understood their purpose as the preservation of divine order and understood justice as obedience to legitimate authority. According to Reus-Smit, constitutional structures such as these define the identities of state actors, their interests, and what they would consider right action.[35] Again, these are not just characteristics of the states, but shared understandings among states that arise from and shape their interactions with one another. These constitutional structures underlie what Reus-Smit calls "fundamental institutions," or "the elementary rules of practice that states formulate to solve the coordination and collaboration problems associated with coexistence under anarchy."[36] To continue the previous examples, Reus-Smit finds the constitutional structures of Renaissance Italy expressed in the "oratorical diplomacy" of the period, and the constitutional structures of absolutist Europe expressed in the natural law

theories of thinkers like Emmerich de Vattel and in the balance-of-power diplomacy of the age.[37]

The individuals and groups within a state also play an important role in
constituting the state's identity, interests, and norms of behavior, perhaps a role
even more significant than that played by the international system. Despite his
emphasis on the international system, Wendt himself believes that domestic
factors play the more decisive role.[38] This domestic process works in a manner
similar to the international process: individuals and groups within a state shape
its identities, interests, and norms of behavior; and the identities, interests, and
norms of behavior of the individuals and groups are at least partly formed by
their membership in the state and their interactions with one another. The domestic and international processes through which a state's identities, interests,
and norms of behavior are formed, moreover, are closely interconnected. Forces
within a state, depending on the nature of its political institutions, shape the
state's identities, interests, and norms of behavior "from below"; those forces
within the international system that shape a state's identities, interests, and
norms of behavior "from above" must do so by means of the forces within the
state.[39] For example, within the current international system, states are encouraged to adopt democratic forms of government, but such a change could only
take place through the efforts of democratic reformers within the state itself.
Therefore, "international and domestic politics are not hermetically sealed
within their own spheres."[40]

THE FORMATION OF INTERESTS AND NORMS

A handful of constructivists have described in more detail what the interests of
states might be and how their norms of behavior are formed. Alexander Wendt
provides one of the best accounts of the national interest. According to Wendt,
the "national interest" consists of those things necessary for the maintenance
of a state's identities, including the physical survival of the state, autonomy in
governing its affairs, economic well-being, and the "collective self-esteem" of
the community.[41] Some interests, such as physical survival, exist relatively independently of a state's interactions with other states, but others "depend on a
particular construction of self-identity in relation to the conceived identity of
others."[42] For example, the United States understands preserving its democratic
way of life as part of its national interest. The national interest also includes those
conditions necessary for individuals within a society, whether all or some, to
pursue their own interests.[43] Thus the material well-being of a state is at least
in part defined by the material well-being of its citizens, and a state that has an
interest in preserving its democracy does so because its citizens value democracy. The precise ways that states pursue their national interests vary according
to cultural factors.

This complex understanding of the national interest contrasts sharply with that of the neorealists and neoliberals. Proponents of these latter views tend to focus on states' material capabilities, especially military power and wealth. Those aspects of the national interest that pertain to constructed self-identities are either seen as unimportant or are understood simply as means of acquiring material capabilities. Constructivists have claimed, however, that it is mistaken to assume that military power and wealth have self-evident meaning for states. As Finnemore argues, "Material facts acquire meaning only through human cognition and social interaction."[44] In other words, states usually pursue material capabilities in ways consistent with their identity and for purposes consistent with that identity. States also perceive the accumulation of material capabilities by other states in the light of their own identities and those of the other states. For example, Great Britain's nuclear weapons mean something different to the United States than do nuclear weapons in the hands of North Korea. This is not to say that the significance of a state's material capabilities can be reduced to socially constructed meanings: Material factors can have a constraining influence on state behavior, and if there is a significant gap between a state's beliefs and material reality, this can lead to either cognitive dissonance and a change in beliefs, or, perhaps more commonly, miscalculations and failure.[45]

If, as I argued earlier, interests and norms are closely related, then a state's national interests can also be expressed in terms of norms. For example, Wendt sensibly claims that maintaining its physical security is one of a state's most fundamental national interests, and this could be expressed as: "It is good that we maintain our physical security." In turn, this could be translated into a norm as: "We ought to preserve our physical security." Any other national interest, whether it is maintaining access to the resources necessary for the state's auto industry, preserving the state's culture from foreign influence, or obeying international law, could be expressed as a norm in the same way. Therefore, there is some truth in the neorealist claim that states rationally pursue their interests, but if those interests are much richer than merely military power and wealth, then their rational pursuit is governed by a complex set of norms, rather than simplistic utilitarian calculus.

A potential problem with the idea that a state's norms simply express its national interests is that some norms seem to deal with the way a state treats other states or groups, rather than with its own national interest—for example, the current international agreement that states will intervene to prevent another state from committing genocide against its people. Such a norm seems to promote the interests of another people, not those of the states that intervene. Of course, one could give a cynical explanation, that states follow such norms when doing so promotes their own interests and ignore them when it does not, and this is undoubtedly true in some cases. But another way of looking at the problem is that through such norms, states express an interest in preserving a certain identity for themselves: "We are not the sort of state that tolerates genocide."

Or yet another way of thinking about it is that an actor's identity includes its relationships with other actors, and therefore a state might have an interest in preserving a certain sort of relationship with other states or social groups according to its conception of justice: "We ought to maintain a just relationship with the people of x, which includes protecting them from genocide." In such cases the good of others and the national interest can be understood as two sides of the same coin.

The constructivist account of norms differs from that developed by some neoliberals. Even though neorealists and neoliberals consider state identities and interests as given, some neoliberals have made a place for norms in their account of international politics. They understand norms, however, as coming about through the "rational self-interest" of states.[46] In other words, states may adopt altruistic or cooperative behavior, but only because they perceive following such norms as the most efficient way of achieving their self-interest, not because of any intrinsic value assigned to altruism or cooperation themselves. Constructivists see norms in a different way, as governed by a "logic of appropriateness" rather than a "logic of consequences": "Actors may ask themselves, 'What kind of situation is this?' and 'What am I supposed to do now?' rather than 'How do I get what I want?'"[47] In brief, neoliberals understand norms as means that states develop to pursue their self-interest through cooperation, whereas constructivists see norms as establishing what a state's interests are in the first place.

There can be exceptions to this rule, however. Even though states may internalize norms, they may also adopt them because it fulfills some other interest or because they are coerced into doing so.[48] For example, it is unlikely that China takes part in the relatively democratic procedures of the United Nations because it values democracy or believes that international affairs should be governed by democratic norms, but rather because given the state of affairs in the current international system, participating in those procedures is the best way of achieving China's interests. Therefore norms *can* be simply the means for achieving a state's interests, but this should not be understood as a general rule about *all* norms, as neoliberals suggest; states use norms as means to an end only in order to fulfill other norms and only if doing so does not violate other norms.

Constructivists such as Martha Finnemore and Kathryn Sikkink have studied the ways in which norms emerge out of a state's interests and then spread from that state to others. Finnemore and Sikkink describe a typical "life cycle" of a successful international norm. First is the stage of "norm emergence," in which "norm entrepreneurs," individuals or groups that seek to see a norm adopted, succeed in having a handful of states adopt a particular norm. When a norm has spread to a certain number of states, there is a tipping point, and in a "norm cascade," the norm quickly spreads to other states. Once a norm has been widely established, it is internalized and becomes a seemingly natural form of behavior.[49] Many international norms begin as domestic norms, and even when they spread internationally—a process that can take many forms—they must do so "through the filter of domestic structures and domestic norms, which can produce important variations in compliance and interpretation of these norms."[50]

NORMS ABOUT WAR, WARS ABOUT NORMS

Some of the most striking examples of evolving international norms that have been studied by constructivists are norms about the conduct of war. As Finnemore writes: "War engages some of the most fundamental issues of morality and conscience. It raises questions about treatment of other human beings at the most fundamental level, for it involves killing large numbers of them. War-making is permeated by norms and social structure."[51] Richard Price and Nina Tannenwald, for example, have studied the emergence of taboos against the use of chemical and nuclear weapons. Neorealists and neoliberals, who tend to see international norms and institutions as the product of the rational self-interest of states, have argued that states are reluctant to use chemical and nuclear weapons because of a self-interested fear of retaliation. As Price and Tannenwald point out, however, this theory does not explain why these weapons have not been used when there was no threat of retaliation from the other side, why there is no comparable taboo against the use of conventional methods of warfare at least as destructive as some falling under the taboo, or why nonnuclear states have felt secure enough to engage in military action against nuclear states. Chemical and nuclear weapons are taboo, Price and Tannenwald suggest, because they have come to be seen as illegitimate and as contrary to the identity that states hold of themselves.[52]

Finnemore provides another example of norms about the conduct of war. She traces the development of international norms concerning the treatment of the wounded in battle in the middle of the nineteenth century under the influence of the International Committee of the Red Cross, leading to the signing of the First Geneva Convention in 1866. Finnemore argues that the adoption of these norms runs counter to the state behavior that traditional international relations theories would predict, since these norms place limits on the exercise of state sovereignty, particularly the essential element of sovereignty, the monopoly on the use of violence within a given territory.[53]

So far constructivists have not sought to explain why states resort to military violence in general, but Finnemore has studied the changing norms of military intervention in the affairs of other states. She argues that the purposes of military intervention, which have changed over time, are closely related to the norms prevalent in international politics. Military intervention reflects and reinforces international norms by seeking to enforce them, but is also shaped by norms concerning when intervention is permissible.[54] For example, Finnemore notes that at the turn of the twentieth century it was accepted practice for states to intervene militarily in order to collect debts from debtor nations, but an international treaty banned this practice in 1907 because of the work of "norm entrepreneurs."[55] In the 1990s, humanitarian intervention, or military intervention to stop massive violations of human rights, became an integral part of maintaining international order because of growing acceptance of protecting human rights as an international norm.[56] Finnemore's work on military intervention demonstrates that states are governed by norms not only in the conduct of warfare, such as those concerning the use of chemical and nuclear weapons and the treatment of the wounded in battle, but also in the purposes for which they are willing to use military force.

Given the general constructivist approach to international relations and the insights into national interests and norms outlined above, it should be possible to sketch an account of the origins of war superior to those provided by the dominant twentieth-century theories of international relations.[57] Marxists of various stripes (and one might add proponents of economic liberalism) have found war's origins in economic factors. Liberals (of both the utilitarian and Kantian varieties), realists, neorealists, and neoliberals have found the origins of war in the self-interested behavior of states in a world without adequate international institutions for resolving conflicts peacefully, although these schools differ in their beliefs about the possibilities for such institutions. Each of these theories, however, seeks to find the origins of war in a single explanatory factor. Yet the causes of war are highly variable. Kalevi J. Holsti writes that the causes of war in the nineteenth and twentieth centuries alone have included territorial disputes, the creation of new nation-states, ideology, economic interests, sympathy (ethnic, religious, etc.), and the desire to destroy another state, and these causes have varied in prominence over time.[58] The insights of the constructivists suggest a general approach to understanding the origins of war that respects this diversity.

War is best understood as originating in a clash of the identities, interests, and norms of states (and certain nonstate actors), all of which are socially constructed by both domestic and international factors. As Finnemore writes, "It is social values that give war a purpose, that define its meaning and make it worth fighting."[59] Norms govern state behavior when states conflict with one another, not only when they cooperate, as many neoliberals suggest.[60] Nevertheless, war is not a practice governed by a single norm, a practice that might eventually be abolished, like slavery, through a change in that norm.[61] Rather, war is governed by a whole network of norms, including not only norms governing which interests a state pursues, but norms about in which cases, if any, war is justified in the pursuit of those interests; who counts as friend or foe; what it means to be at war and how that should affect domestic society; how war is fought; when war is over; and what should be done when war is over. Alistair Iain Johnston calls the network of beliefs "about the role of war in human affairs . . . , about the nature of the adversary and the threat it poses . . . , and about the efficacy of the use of force," as well as the norms governing behavior during war, a state's "strategic culture."[62]

By thinking of war as a clash of identities, interests, and norms that is itself governed by norms, one can distinguish different types of conflict. There are some clashes of interest between states or between a nonstate actor and a state that have potential for compromise because fundamental values are not at stake; in these cases, it is possible that the conflict could be resolved by international institutions or some other form of mediation. Fundamental clashes, however, occur when the identities, interests, and norms of states and nonstate actors are such that compromise would involve an unthinkable violation of cherished values. In such a situation, war is much more likely: "It is . . . difficult to fashion compromises between fundamentally incompatible belief systems. Conflict and war historically have been seemingly inevitable results of the clash of two or more *Weltanschauungen* [comprehensive worldviews]."[63]

Some concrete examples will illustrate these points. In 1981 a border dispute between Ecuador and Peru was resolved after five days of light fighting once the Organization of American States intervened as a forum for arbitration, because little was at stake ideologically: the patch of land was only minimally related to either state's identity, and its relevance to their national interests was small. The conflict between Israelis and Palestinian Arabs, on the other hand, has lasted for years and involved horrific violence because the land is highly charged with value for both sides; it is a key part of each side's self-identity. Finnemore describes the American Civil War as another example of a war in which fundamental values were involved and compromise was impossible.[64]

It is not that having different identities, interests, and norms necessarily leads to conflict, and having the same identities, interests, and norms leads to peace. Rather, it is the particular content of the identities, interests, and norms that matters. As the democratic peace theorists have pointed out, after World War II, the democracies of western Europe and the United States created a peaceful alliance that has lasted to the present day, but this cooperation has come about because of the particular content of their shared democratic values, not simply because they shared the same values. After all, it is highly unlikely that a peaceful confederation of fascist states would have come about had the Axis powers won the war, precisely because of the centrality of competition, conflict, and violence to fascist identity.

The perspective on the origins of war that I have been describing can incorporate realist and neorealist insights about the origins of war and at the same time overcome the weaknesses of these approaches. The classical realists argued that the anarchical nature of international politics is rooted in the will-to-power found in every human person and social group. As Kenneth Waltz points out, however, this account could never explain why peace between states exists most of the time, or even at all.[65] Yet neorealism also cannot explain why states go to war with certain states and not others. Even if states are governed by a will-to-power or feel a general sense of insecurity in an anarchical system, they perceive threats in terms of their own identities, interests, and norms, and the identities, interests, and norms of others. As Reus-Smit writes, "Canada and Cuba are both medium powers existing alongside the United States, yet the simple balance of military power cannot explain the fact that the former is a close American ally, the latter a sworn enemy."[66] According to a constructivist perspective, classical realists are correct that states must seek power to accomplish their goals, and neorealists are correct that in an anarchical international system, states must preserve their own security; both are correct that these demands often contribute to conflict among states. Where the classical realists go astray is in believing that power and its pursuit can be understood apart from the other ends that states pursue: The reasons a state pursues power shape the ways that the state pursues it. Where the neorealists go astray is in ignoring the fact that socially constructed identities, interests, and norms shape a state's perceptions of threats to its security and help to create a conception of "security" that goes beyond mere physical survival to include the survival of certain values and ways of life.

My account of the origins of war also demonstrates some of the weaknesses of the approach of world-systems theory. I have already described Wendt's criticism of world-systems theory; namely, that it ignores the role that states play in constituting the international system, and therefore has trouble explaining how there can be change in that system. World-systems theory also overemphasizes the material and economic factors in determining state behavior, downplaying the way that a state's material interests are understood by that state within the context of cultural values. World-systems theorists are right to claim that economic factors play an important role in determining state behavior, because material needs are an important part of a state's national interest. Yet even a state's economic interests cannot be understood in purely economic terms; a state pursues material well-being for specific purposes consistent with its identities, interests, and norms of behavior, and those factors shape the ways in which the state pursues material well-being. It may be true, as a world-systems theorist might respond, that often a state's (or other actor's) values simply mask its economic interests, but the influence goes both ways, leading to a thesis world-systems theorists do not accept: A state's (or other actor's) economic interests are shaped by its values.[67] It is also true that states will have economic interests in a war, and some individuals and industries will always stand to benefit from victory, but the causes of war cannot be *reduced* to these interests; a state's behavior can only be fully understood by describing its identities, interests, and norms, which are primarily cultural and not economic.

The account of the origins of war that I have briefly put forward also develops the neoliberal view of international institutions and their role in establishing peace. Neoliberals understand international institutions or regimes as embodying "norms" developed by states so that they can cooperate in order to maximize their utility and avoid conflict with one another. They may be right that states can establish institutions that help them achieve their purposes and avoid conflict with one another, but if, as constructivists claim, states are motivated by interests much more complicated than utility maximization, then it will be more difficult for international institutions to coordinate state interests in a fruitful way. If states do not at a minimum share a commitment to cooperative and deliberative practices, it is likely that international institutions will be subverted by states that have not internalized the norms those institutions are intended to embody, and their ability to promote peace will be compromised.

This perspective on the origins of war, drawing on constructivism, also challenges more traditional forms of liberalism, despite agreeing with them that cultural factors lie at the origins of war. Traditional versions of liberalism generally assert that war is caused by the cultural beliefs and practices of societies, which are expressed in their forms of government and economic systems; this is quite similar to my own claim. Where liberalism differs from my own view is that it contrasts the influence of cultural traditions with that of reason, the former leading to war because they are irrational, the latter leading to peace. According to this view, the cultural forces that shape our identities, interests, and norms of behavior are irrational precisely because we are influenced by them without first rationally examining them and freely choosing them for ourselves. If peace is a rational state of affairs, and international institutions are practical embodiments of reason meant to help states more reasonably relate to one another and prevent conflict, then, in this view, the establishment of international peace and the institutions meant to bring it about do not depend on cultural traditions that promote peace and cooperation (because that is an oxymoron), but rather on the rejection of cultural tradition as irrational.

This liberal point of view is clearly reflected in the thought of the giants of liberalism, Kant and Mill, as well as in more recent institutional versions of democratic peace theory. Immanuel Kant argues that peace can be established when international life is governed by rational principles; as Kant clearly points out in his writings on ethics, rational principles must be chosen free from cultural influences. John Stuart Mill claims that states governed by the rational principles of a "spirit of liberty" live in peace, whereas those who are dominated by "custom" tend to be aggressive.[68] Such a view is also reflected in institutional versions of the democratic peace theory that suggest that peace can be established among democratic states simply because of the rational structure of democratic institutions. Normative versions of the democratic peace theory, on the other hand, that see the democratic peace as the result of shared democratic cultural values, depart in a significant way from traditional versions of liberalism and share a certain affinity with constructivism, as some constructivists have noted.[69]

Where traditional liberalism and its contemporary offshoots fall short is in their failure to recognize that peaceful behavior among states as well as the maintenance of international institutions that can preserve that peace depend on the development of cultures that value those things. There is no sharp contrast between culture and reason; in many cases what is rational depends on the culture. By drawing this sharp contrast, liberals have impoverished the meaning of rationality, reducing it to the pursuit of material well-being. By failing to acknowledge the full range of human goods that individuals and states pursue, and the cultural reasons they pursue them, liberals have unwittingly undermined progress toward their ultimate goal, the establishment of peace.

I would suggest, based on the insights of constructivism, that three elements are necessary for the establishment of peace: first, a certain minimum of shared identity, interests, and norms; second, identities, interests, and norms that value peace, deliberation, and cooperation; and third, institutions that facilitate deliberation and cooperation. Because conflicts between states arise out of clashes of identities, interests, and norms, it seems likely that states must possess at least a certain minimum of shared values if they are to live in peace. As I explained earlier, however, even when states share values, this is unlikely to lead to peace unless those values foster deliberation and cooperation. Finally, and this is where liberals and neoliberals provide a valuable insight, states that share a commitment to deliberation and cooperation do need institutional means for accomplishing those goals. But those institutions are more than just a means for states to pursue their interests, as neoliberals argue, and they do not develop when states reject cultural tradition in favor of reason, as liberals claim; rather, such institutions embody cultural values that promote deliberation and cooperation and discourage conflict.

CONCLUSION

Constructivism, an approach to understanding international relations that has emerged in the past twenty years, can help to provide an account of the origins of war that challenges the predominant modern accounts. Because modern political thought has divorced political life from the full range of human ends, typical contemporary accounts of the origins of war have described states' interests in terms of the pursuit of power- or utility-maximization. War, in this view, arises from the clash of national or class interests that may or may not be able to be reconciled through the establishment of international institutions. In contrast, constructivism argues that states pursue a rich variety of interests, and that the identities, interests, and norms of states are formed both by the interaction of states with each other and by domestic forces. These processes are primarily cultural. War therefore emerges from a clash of the culturally formed identities, interests, and norms of states or nonstate actors. In the next chapter I will show how constructivism provides a fresh way of thinking about some of the Christian tradition's insights into the origins of war that have been downplayed in twentieth-century Catholic thinking, but that are nevertheless compatible with significant trends in recent Catholic theology.

NOTES

1. Koslowksi and Kratochwil, "Understanding Change," 128–34.

2. Jackson and Sørensen, *International Relations*, 59.

3. Lapid, "Third Debate," 235–54.

4. Hoffman, "Critical Theory," 169–85.

5. Adler, "Constructivism and International Relations," 96–97; see also George and Campbell, "Patterns of Dissent," 272–81.

6. Wendt, "Agent-Structure Problem," 335–70; see also Dessler, "What's at Stake," 441–74.

7. Wendt and Duvall, "Institutions and International Order," 55.

8. Finnemore, *National Interests*, 1–2.

9. Wendt, "Anarchy," 391–92.

10. Ashley, "Poverty of Neorealism," 273–79; Ruggie, "What Makes the World," 222–24.

11. Ashley, "Three Modes of Economism," 479–84.

12. Ashley, "Political Realism," 207–21.

13. Finnemore, *National Interests*, 2. Emphasis in original.

14. Ashley, "Poverty of Neorealism," 280–86.

15. Cox, "Social Forces, States and World Orders," 207–10; Cox, "Post-Hegemonic Conceptualization," 133; George and Campbell, "Patterns of Dissent," 287–88.

16. Ashley, "Poverty of Neorealism," 268–72.

17. Lapid, "Third Debate," 239.

18. Adler, "Constructivism and International Relations," 95.

19. Wendt, "Constructing International Politics," 75. Emphasis in original.

20. Ruggie, "What Makes the World," 216. See also Kratochwil, *Rules, Norms, and Decisions*, 21–28.

21. Wendt, *Social Theory*, 47–91.

22. Kratochwil, *Rules, Norms, and Decisions*, 11, 47–53. See also Jepperson, Wendt, and Katzenstein, "Norms, Identity, and Culture," 54; Kowert and Legro, "Norms, Identity, and Their Limits," 453.

23. Wendt, *Social Theory*, 231.

24. Klotz, *Norms in International Relations*, 26–27; Dessler, "What's at Stake," 454–58.

25. Wendt, *Social Theory*, 157–78.

26. Giddens, *Constitution of Society*.

27. Wendt, "Agent-Structure Problem," 335–61; Wendt, *Social Theory*, 23–33; Wendt and Duvall, "Institutions and International Order," 59; Jepperson, Wendt, and Katzenstein, "Norms, Identity, and Culture," 37–42; Koslowski and Kratochwil, "Understanding Change," 128; Reus-Smit, "Beyond Foreign Policy," 175–80.

28. Wendt, "Anarchy," 419; Wendt, *Social Theory*, 188; Kratochwil, *Rules, Norms, and Decisions*, 61.

29. Wendt, "Anarchy," 394–95. Emphasis in original.

30. Ibid., 410–12.

31. Wendt, *Social Theory*, 178–84.

32. Ruggie, "Continuity and Transformation," 141–52. Emphasis in original.

33. Ruggie, "Territoriality and Beyond," 139–74.

34. Reus-Smit, *Moral Purpose*, 26–27.

35. Ibid., 30–31.

36. Ibid., 13–14.

37. Ibid., 77–84, 101–10.

38. Wendt, *Social Theory*, 21.

39. Risse-Kappen, "Ideas Do Not Float Freely," 188. The internal political structure of a state will therefore make a difference in the formation of its interests: Within a pluralist state, different parts of the government with different agendas may have a hand in foreign policy decision making. For example, see R. Kagan, *Twilight Struggle* on how different ideological factions in the United States Congress and President Ronald Reagan's cabinet helped to produce an incoherent policy toward Nicaragua in the 1980s.

40. Koslowski and Kratochwil, "Understanding Change," 134–35.

41. Wendt, *Social Theory*, 231–38.

42. Jepperson, Wendt, and Katzenstein, "Norms, Identity, and Culture," 60.

43. Wendt, *Social Theory*, 130–35.

44. Finnemore, *National Interests*, 6; Finnemore, *Purpose of Intervention*, 93–95; Jepperson, Wendt, and Katzenstein, "Norms, Identity, and Culture," 40; Wendt, "Constructing International Politics," 73; Dessler, "What's at Stake," 451–54.

45. A classic example of the former would be the Soviet "New Thinking" under Mikhail Gorbachev in the face of domestic economic failure and the arms race with the United States; a well-known example of the latter would be Hitler's miscalculation of German capabilities during World War II, particularly on the eastern front against the Soviet Union.

46. Ruggie, "What Makes the World," 231–4; Kowert and Legro, "Norms, Identity, and Their Limits," 458–59; Klotz, *Norms in International Relations*, 21–25.

47. Finnemore, *National Interests*, 28–31; Finnemore and Sikkink, "International Norm Dynamics," 274.

48. Kratochwil, "The Force of Prescriptions," 691–703; Finnemore, "Norms, Culture, and World Politics," 339–40; Reus-Smit, *Moral Purpose*, 35–36.

49. Finnemore and Sikkink, "International Norm Dynamics," 255–65; see also Nadelmann, "Global Prohibition Regimes," 484–86.

50. Ibid., 253; Finnemore, *Purpose of Intervention*, 146–59.

51. Finnemore, *National Interests*, 87.

52. Price and Tannenwald, "Norms and Deterrence," 116–26.

53. Finnemore, *National Interests*, 69–88. One theory explaining the adoption of the First Geneva Convention is that states saw it as in their own interests, since they hoped for reciprocity in the treatment of their own wounded soldiers, but the first signers applied it to themselves without any stipulation of reciprocity from their enemies. Another theory is that the treaty was in states' interests because it allowed them to bring wounded soldiers back to the field, but the convention was put into practice long before military medicine made this feasible. Finally, some have argued that the treaty was in the self-

interest of democratic leaders because it was pleasing to the public, but many of the initial signers were nondemocratic.

54. Finnemore, *Purpose of Intervention*, 2–3.

55. Ibid., 24–26.

56. Ibid., 135–36.

57. It is not implied, of course, that any particular constructivist endorses the account that follows.

58. Holsti, *Peace and War*, 306–34. Holsti is not clear what the desire to destroy another state would mean apart from some other factor, such as ideology or economic interests.

59. Finnemore, *National Interests*, 69.

60. Jepperson, Wendt, and Katzenstein, "Norms, Identity, and Culture," 39; Wendt, "Collective Identity Formation," 389. Likewise, Alastair Iain Johnston writes that constructivists must give an account of the "realpolitik" state behavior that realist theories would predict. Johnston attempts to give such an account of Chinese realpolitik behavior under Mao Zedong. "Cultural Realism," 216–21, 262–68.

61. As suggested by James Lee Ray, "Abolition of Slavery," 405–39.

62. Johnston, "Cultural Realism," 222–23.

63. Holsti, *Peace and War*, 322.

64. Finnemore, *National Interests*, 135 n. 7.

65. Waltz, *Man, the State, and War*, 80–81.

66. Reus-Smit, "Constructivism," 217.

67. For example, whereas some have proposed that many recent civil wars can be understood primarily in terms of economic grievances and poverty, I. William Zartman argues that "need" becomes a source of conflict primarily by being harnessed to "creed," by which he means ethnic, national, or religious identities. He further argues that a prolonged civil war runs the risk of becoming dominated by "greed," the abandonment of ideals in favor of the personal gain of war leaders and their cronies. Zartman, "Need, Creed, and Greed," 256–84.

68. Miller, "Mill's Theory," 505–9.

69. Risse-Kappen, "Collective Identity," 365–71; Hopf, "Promise of Constructivism," 191–92; Wendt, "Anarchy," 392–95.

CHAPTER FIVE

· · · · · · · · · · · · · · · · · · · ·

A CATHOLIC PERSPECTIVE ON THE ORIGINS OF WAR

CATHOLIC THEOLOGIANS AND political scientists concerned with understanding war can use constructivism as a fruitful source for thinking about war's origins. Constructivists are critical of several elements of modern political thought, many of which emerged precisely as a departure from the earlier Christian tradition, as described in chapter 2. Therefore, perhaps surprisingly, a constructivist view on the origins of war shares much in common with that of the earlier Christian tradition. This should be of more than antiquarian interest because, as I will show in this and later chapters, Catholic theologians and official Catholic teaching have consistently challenged central ideas of modern political thought by reaffirming three principles from the premodern Christian tradition: that human existence is oriented toward a relationship with God; that this orientation shapes all areas of human life, including politics, and is not relegated to its own isolated sphere; and that politics must be understood within a broad philosophical and ethical framework. Even if constructivists do not affirm those principles, constructivism could nonetheless be useful to Catholic thinkers in their efforts to articulate and apply those principles. Constructivism can also help to reconceptualize the key points of the earlier Christian understanding of the origins of war that have been downplayed in twentieth-century Catholic thought. In this chapter I will show that developments in Catholic theology in the second half of the twentieth century make such a reconceptualization particularly opportune. Constructivism, therefore, can help Catholics articulate insights from their own tradition in ways consistent with the best contemporary theology.

LINKING CONSTRUCTIVISM AND THE CHRISTIAN TRADITION

As described earlier, modern political thought moved away from the Christian tradition in three ways; constructivism can help Catholics articulate a response to each of them. In the first place, constructivism's concern with how identities, interests, and norms of behavior are formed by cultural traditions opens the way for a renewed discussion of the ends of human existence. As Alasdair

MacIntyre argues, we learn the *telos* or end of a good life through the personal and social narratives, or tradition, of which we are part, and this learning is the very purpose of tradition. The modern rejection of a *telos* for human existence has gone hand in hand with a denial that we are embedded in narratives at all.[1] Therefore a revival of the idea that we are socially constituted can also lead to new reflection on the ends of human life, because it is precisely our culturally formed identities that give our lives purpose. Because it only seeks to describe the way international politics is, rather than to prescribe how it should be, constructivism by itself cannot tell us what the ends of human political activity ought to be, but it at least recognizes that states are motivated by different conceptions of those ends and attempts to describe the processes through which states come to have them.

Constructivism's understanding of politics is compatible with the belief that politics cannot be separated from the transcendent dimension of human existence. Constructivists try to show how political actors' beliefs about the ultimate questions of human existence shape their behavior and therefore influence international politics. Of course, describing how political actors are motivated by beliefs about the transcendent dimension of human existence does not show that there is in fact a connection between political life and the transcendent, and no constructivist would attempt to describe such a relationship. As I will show later in this chapter, however, some important twentieth-century Catholic thinkers have tried to show that the very fact that human beings ask questions about life's ultimate significance means that we do in fact have a relationship with a dimension of reality that transcends this world, namely God. If humanity's responses to these questions play an essential role in understanding political life, then I would argue that it is logical to conclude that ultimately human politics, including international politics, cannot be understood without reference to humanity's relationship with God.

Finally, constructivism rejects the particularly modern way of thinking of politics as an objective science; that is, as understandable apart from metaphysical questions. Modern thinkers have tended to think of politics as an objective science based simply on the observation of facts, whether it is Machiavelli's science of politics, Pufendorf's nonsectarian political morality based on the laws of nature, or Waltz's positivism. Constructivists, as well as critical theorists and postmodernists, argue that despite their claims to the contrary, modern political thinkers' observations have been filtered through the lenses of hidden philosophical presuppositions, and in chapters 2 and 3 I have tried to show how some of these presuppositions developed specifically as a reaction against the Christian past. This conclusion does not mean that constructivists give up on attempting to develop an objective account of international politics; instead, it means that to develop a more objective account of international politics, one needs to ask questions about the most adequate understanding of society, the individual actor, human actions, collective action, and so on. If Christianity has important light to shed on questions like these, as Christians believe, then we might be justified in believing that Christianity can provide significant insights into understanding human politics, including international politics.

Besides articulating criticisms of the ways in which modern political thought departed from the premodern Christian past, constructivism can also help Christians to reformulate the insights of the Christian tradition of reflection on the origins of war, beginning with the biblical concept of "powers" that I described in chapter 1. The powers Paul writes about are in some ways comparable to the collective knowledge, to use Wendt's term, that helps to shape the identities, interests, and norms of states in the international system and of individuals within their own societies. Just as the powers are invisible forces that profoundly influence human existence, collective knowledge is intangible but still has a very real effect on the behavior of individuals, states, and other social groups. The cultural forces that make up collective knowledge also cannot be reduced to the actors who embody them, whether they are the states in the international system or individuals in a society. Just as Christians "are not contending against flesh and blood" (Eph. 6:12) when they struggle against evil, evils such as war have causes that go beyond particular individuals or institutions; as we have seen, these causes include the identities, interests, and norms formed by societies' collective knowledge. Even if in the biblical and patristic view the powers are the source of evils such as war, Paul himself considered the powers to be part of God's creation and therefore in themselves good, just as constructivists consider social structures to be constitutive of human actors rather than constraints from which humans ought to be liberated, as liberals have claimed. And just as the powers have a pernicious influence on humans because they have "rebelled against God," so too a state's identities, interests, and norms that unjustly lead to war can also be considered distorted or corrupted, and perhaps even demonic.

Constructivism also provides insights into how Christians today can understand the traditional Christian claim that a people's cultural beliefs and practices can contribute to evils such as war. Just as the biblical and patristic authors found the origins of war in the pagan practices of the Canaanite and Roman religions, I would argue that constructivism finds them in states' identities, interests, and norms of behavior, which are at least partly formed through cultural practices in domestic society. The international system itself can also be characterized as having a type of culture that both shapes and is shaped by the practices of states. Of course, constructivism does not attempt to make judgments on which cultural beliefs and practices are "wicked," merely to describe how they influence behavior, but constructivism can provide important insights for a Catholic moralist concerned with evaluating the role of cultural beliefs and practices in fostering collective behavior such as war.

A Christian concerned with explaining the origins of war could also turn to constructivism to help understand how wars can be caused by both non-Christians and Christians alike. The patristic notion that war has its origins in pagan religious and cultural practices seemed to imply that Christians would not cause wars. When Christianity had come to dominate Europe in the Middle Ages and yet war continued, Christians could no longer look to pagan religion as the source of war; John of Salisbury in the twelfth century and later the Renaissance humanists Desiderius Erasmus and Juan Luis Vives claimed that war arose among Christians because of their rulers' vices. All people are subject to the vices, and therefore both Christians and non-Christians can be responsible for the outbreak of unjust wars or for the maintenance of cultures that encourage unjust wars. Even though Christianity is a set of practices and beliefs that fosters the virtues, it is possible for Christians to become subject to the vices through the influence of cultural forces contrary to the Gospel. Whether Christian or not, cultural traditions that are likely to produce vicious people are also likely to produce state behavior that could be described as wicked, and cultural traditions that tend to produce virtuous people are likely to produce good state behavior.

Finally, constructivism can help Christians integrate the traditional belief that international institutions must play a role in establishing peace with other Christian insights into war and peace. The Catholic tradition has long held that the establishment of political institutions is a natural part of human activity; the fathers argued that even though it persecuted them, the Roman Empire had its authority from God, and Thomas Aquinas claimed that the making of human laws is a way for humans to consciously participate in the natural law established by God. This led Catholic writers as diverse as Pierre Dubois and Dante Alighieri in the fourteenth century and Francisco de Vitoria and Francisco Suarez in the sixteenth and seventeenth to perceive the need for some type of formal international institutions to promote the common good, because states were no longer able to accomplish this on their own (although Suarez did not believe that such an institution could be established). Constructivism can help contemporary Catholics to understand the important role of international institutions in creating peace without overemphasizing their significance, which, as I will show in later chapters, more recent Catholic writers have done. Thus constructivism not only can help Catholics better understand past insights into the origins of war, but also is consistent with some of the most important trends in recent Catholic theology.

HISTORICITY

In the middle of the twentieth century, a revolution took place in Catholic theology: Catholic theologians who went on to influence the Second Vatican Council challenged the neoscholastic theology that had been dominant in the church for decades. Neoscholasticism was originally developed by Counter-Reformation theologians such as Francisco Suarez, and had a deep influence on

Catholic theology after the neoscholastic revival of the late nineteenth century. Typical neoscholastic tenets such as the idea that the natural law (and hence human political life) can to some extent be rationally understood apart from humankind's relationship with God, and the separation between human nature and humanity's calling to a supernatural destiny, demonstrate the influence of modern political thought on Catholicism. The revolutionary Catholic theologians of the mid-twentieth century criticized neoscholasticism both for its classicist worldview—that is, its reliance on a static view of human nature and its failure to recognize the ways in which a person's historical situation shapes the way he or she thinks and acts—and for its sharp separation between human nature and grace. Their criticisms challenged neoscholasticism at precisely the points where it showed an openness to modern political thought. The increasing importance of historical consciousness in Catholic theology suggested that it was no longer appropriate to think of individuals as rational actors in an unqualified sense, because their thinking was unavoidably influenced by cultural, political, and economic factors. Furthermore, the theologians I draw on here argue that humanity's calling to a supernatural destiny is an integral part of human nature that penetrates all aspects of life, rather than an addition to a nature already complete in itself, putting to rest the idea that human nature as a whole could be understood apart from its relation to God.

Such shifts in Catholic theology should have led to a corresponding shift in thinking about war's origins. For example, given the increasing attention to historicity in Catholic theology, it would make sense for Catholic writers to recognize the ways in which the identities, interests, and norms of states that lead them to make war are culturally formed. Likewise, the more integrated understanding of nature and grace should have led Catholic theologians to consider how the cultural, political, and economic forces shaping state behavior are permeated by both sin and grace, and therefore to acknowledge that theology plays a crucial role in interpreting political phenomena such as war. As I will show in the following chapters, this has not been the case. Before turning to how twentieth- and twenty-first-century Catholics have understood the origins of war, however, I will describe in more detail the two major shifts in twentieth-century Catholic theology—the recognition of historicity and the new understanding of the relationship between nature and grace—and their implications for understanding the origins of war.

The development of awareness of historicity, or historical consciousness, has been a complex process. Historical consciousness had already been developing in premodern Western thought and therefore cannot be considered an exclusively modern phenomenon. The contemporary sense of historicity could be said to have its ultimate origins in the Jewish and Christian religions, particularly in their shared perceptions that history is oriented toward a final messianic goal and that God is actively involved in history. Nevertheless, for much of Christian history, historical consciousness—defined as an awareness of the ways in which one's historical situation shapes one's perceptions—was minimal. Medieval scholars produced massive chronicles, and there was a revival of interest in history during the Renaissance, but in neither period did scholars see the study of history as a way of understanding change over time.[2] During the Enlightenment and its aftermath, the modern sense of historical consciousness emerged as historians began to study history in terms of progress. Then in the nineteenth century, evolutionary and organic modes of thinking that emphasized growth and development transformed and added further justification for such a belief in historical progress.[3] In the twentieth century, critical theorists, sociologists of knowledge, and postmodernists all sought to understand how human communities create the meanings and identities through which the members of that community experience and interpret reality.

The Canadian theologian Bernard J. F. Lonergan, SJ (1904–84), has described the development of historical consciousness in Catholic theology. The neoscholastic theologians of the Renaissance demonstrated an ahistorical view of human nature, or what Lonergan calls a "classicist worldview." Human nature was seen as static and unchanging, and truths were known through eternally valid propositions, unmediated by cultural particularity. As Lonergan writes, "On the whole [classicist Thomism] was unaware of history: of the fact that every act of meaning is embedded in a context, and that over time contexts change subtly, slowly, surely."[4] The classicist worldview of neoscholasticism would make it difficult, but not impossible, for Catholicism to adapt to the increasing awareness of historicity in modern times.

Theologians have long recognized that such an adaptation was necessary, but it has not been self-evident which ideas connected with historical consciousness are compatible with, or even ultimately spring from, the Christian faith, which are mere intellectual fads, and which are harmful to the faith. The recognition of historicity has had a profound influence on Catholic understandings of the interpretation of scripture and of the development of doctrine over time, among other things. Two shifts in twentieth-century theology spurred by the growing awareness of historicity are particularly relevant for developing a Catholic perspective on war's origins: an increasing attention to the subjective dimension of human knowing and acting, and greater sensitivity to historical and cultural diversity in moral theology.

Twentieth-century Catholic theologians have examined the subjective dimension of consciousness and experience, including the response of faith. In the early twentieth century, the French Jesuit Pierre Rousselot criticized neoscholastic attempts to rationally defend the credibility of Christian faith independently of the subjectivity of the believer; Rousselot argued that the neoscholastics ignored the way that faith itself fulfills the subject's inner longing and depends on a transformation of the potential believer's disposition.[5] At around the same time, a Belgian Jesuit, Joseph Maréchal, began to draw on the insights of modern philosophy, particularly German idealism, to present a revised version of Thomism, sometimes called Transcendental Thomism, that also examined human subjectivity; this school was later carried on by thinkers such as Karl Rahner, SJ, and Bernard J. F. Lonergan, SJ.[6]

Rahner (1904–84), in particular, draws on Heidegger's philosophy to develop an account of the human subject as "spirit in the world."[7] According to Rahner, "being-in-the-world," or the fact that we find ourselves in "a world of things and a world of persons, is an intrinsic element of the subject himself." Yet the human person is not only limited by this historical situation, but *experiences* himself or herself as such, which suggests that the human subject in some way transcends those limitations.[8] Rahner concludes that this is because the human subject is also constituted by an openness to infinite Being, which is God.[9]

Although in *Foundations of Christian Faith*, a late work, Rahner notes that the world that partly constitutes the human person includes the community of persons, including culture and language, he has been criticized for presenting a rather ahistorical account of the way in which human persons are historically situated; Rahner's critics assert that he largely ignores the cultural, political, and economic factors that help to shape us.[10] According to Gaspar Martinez, other theologians such as the German Johann Baptist Metz, the Peruvian Gustavo Gutiérrez, and the American David Tracy draw on Rahner's theology while taking into consideration these concrete factors.[11]

Other theologians have examined how human subjectivity is formed by the narrative and practices of Christianity itself. Stanley Hauerwas, a Protestant theologian who has had a profound impact on many younger Catholic theologians, has argued for both a nonfoundationalist account of the truth claims of Christianity—that is, one that does not seek to justify those truth claims in terms of prior principles supposedly agreeable to all regardless of their historical particularities—and also for the importance of the virtues fostered by particular Christian practices.[12] From a very different perspective, the Swiss theologian Hans Urs von Balthasar has emphasized the particularity of God's revelation in Jesus Christ and the human person's innate desire to imitate him and be taken up into the divine drama.[13] Still other theologians have sought to discover the ways in which the Gospel can be expressed within the diversity of cultures of the world without losing its own distinctiveness. Exploring this process of inculturation has become one of the most promising avenues of theological research.[14]

The growing recognition of the way that society and culture shape identities and beliefs has also influenced moral theology. Some theologians have taken the radical step of claiming that morality is relative and that there is no universal human nature that determines morality. For example, Josef Fuchs, SJ, has proposed that objective moral norms may differ from culture to culture.[15] Other theologians have taken a more moderate view, attempting to reconcile a universal human nature with cultural diversity.[16] Liberation theologians in Latin America and elsewhere have examined ethical issues from the perspective of the poor in the developing world. The Argentine Enrique Dussel is particularly noteworthy in this regard.[17]

The focus on human subjectivity and the recognition of the need for sensitivity toward cultural diversity in Catholic theology are especially important themes for a new Catholic perspective on war and its origins. The importance of cultural diversity to moral theology is perhaps the most obviously relevant theme, because it suggests that we need a new way of thinking about the morality of war, one that moves beyond the assumption that the natural law is a universally available form of moral reasoning. But perhaps the renewed emphasis on the subjective dimension of consciousness and experience is ultimately more important because it is the most directly relevant for understanding the ways in which the clashing identities, interests, and norms that are at the origins of war are formed. Before describing how these ideas might influence a Catholic understanding of the origins of war, however, I will examine another important development in twentieth-century Catholic theology that is also crucial for a new Catholic perspective on war and its origins, namely, the retrieval of a more traditional understanding of the relationship between human nature and grace.

NATURE AND GRACE

By the middle of the twentieth century, many Catholic theologians were beginning to realize through historical study that the neoscholastic understanding of the relationship between human nature and grace was a departure from the views of the great Christian theologians of the past; they argued that the neoscholastic opinion was therefore a harmful innovation. The Jesuits Henri de Lubac (1896–1991) and Karl Rahner made the greatest contributions to this argument, though other theologians such as Juan Alfaro, Henri Bouillard, Leopold Malevez, Hans Urs von Balthasar, and Philippe Delhaye were certainly involved in the controversy, to name only those who challenged the neoscholastic view. At first glance, the controversy over nature and grace may seem like an obscure theological debate, but it has serious implications for all of theology, as well as for a Catholic understanding of the origins of war.

Against Pure Nature

Beginning in the sixteenth century, neoscholastic theologians developed the doctrine of pure nature to help account for the gratuity of God's grace in relation to human nature. In response to thinkers such as Michel Baius and Cornelius Jansen, who claimed that because human nature could only be fulfilled by union with God and grace is necessary for that union, grace was therefore "due" to human nature, the neoscholastics defended the view that grace is freely given by God and is not required of him. Believing that they were faithfully interpreting the work of Thomas Aquinas, they defended this view by claiming that God could have created a world in which human nature did not find its fulfillment in union with God, but rather in a natural end of some sort; the neoscholastics called this hypothetical state "pure nature." Human nature as it actually exists is practically the same as this pure nature, except that God has added an orientation to a supernatural destiny rather than a merely natural one. The orientation to a supernatural destiny is not, in itself, part of human nature, and therefore grace is not "due" to us from God. This theory created an extrinsic understanding of grace, in which human nature in itself is left untouched by grace. In most accounts of the theory, original sin also left human nature basically untouched, consisting only in the loss of grace, therefore creating a particularly optimistic view of human potential despite the reality of sin.[18]

In their writings, Henri de Lubac and Karl Rahner challenge this understanding of the relationship between nature and grace. Henri de Lubac's book *Surnaturel*, first published in 1946, marked the opening of the controversy. The neoscholastics claimed to be faithfully presenting the thought of Thomas Aquinas, but de Lubac attempts to show that for Aquinas, in fact, humanity possesses a natural desire for a supernatural end, union with God.[19] According to de Lubac, "In reality, the idea of 'pure nature' did not have the antiquity nor the doctrinal importance that is all too gladly supposed by some modern theologians." The idea really had its origins with the sixteenth-century theologian Cardinal Thomas de Vio Cajetan, one of the early neoscholastics.[20] By claiming that humanity has a natural desire for a supernatural end, though, which he called a paradox, de Lubac opened himself to the charge of denying the gratuity of grace.[21]

Karl Rahner's primary contribution to the debate over nature and grace, the concept of the "supernatural existential," was intended as a way of preserving de Lubac's insight into humanity's supernatural destiny while maintaining the gratuity of grace. The human person's orientation is supernatural because it is not part of human nature as such, but it is also not extrinsic to human nature since this orientation is at the inmost center of human existence (that is, it is an "existential").[22] Nature exists as a distinct reality, but is complete only when it has been transformed by grace: "In the concrete order, then, nature itself can find its way to its own completion only if it realizes that it is actually a factor within the all-embracing reality of grace and redemption. The 'relative autonomy' of the natural physical and cultural spheres never extends, in Catholic teaching, to the implication that they can achieve even the significance which is their own and immanent to them, except through the grace of God in Jesus Christ."[23] Rahner here clearly rejects the neoscholastic understanding of nature.

In his later work *The Mystery of the Supernatural*, de Lubac takes a position similar to Rahner's. The theory of pure nature proves nothing, according to de Lubac, because it only shows that grace is gratuitous in relation to that hypothetical human nature, not to actually existing human beings who have been given a supernatural orientation: "It remains to be shown that the supernatural is absolutely freely given to *me*, in my condition now. Otherwise nothing at all has been said."[24] Like Rahner, de Lubac insists that we can legitimately speak of a natural order within human existence that is distinct from the supernatural but only finds its meaning in the supernatural.[25]

Salvation History

Both de Lubac and Rahner therefore agree that all areas of human existence find their ultimate meaning in Jesus Christ, because human nature itself is oriented toward the supernatural fulfillment that comes through Christ; Rahner in particular explores what this means for our understanding of human history and culture. The human person possesses an orientation toward a supernatural destiny in his or her inmost being, and God's offer of grace affects every aspect of the person's being. Human persons, therefore, either accept God's grace or reject it through sin in their concrete historical existence: "Thus salvation history takes place right in the midst of ordinary history. Man works out his salvation or damnation in everything he does and in everything which impels him. Everything in the history of the world is pregnant with eternity and eternal life or with eternal ruin."[26] Even if salvation takes place in the midst of ordinary, profane history, salvation history and profane history remain conceptually distinct because we are unable to clearly distinguish salvation and damnation within history.[27] The distinction between salvation history and profane history is also revealed by the fact that salvation will not come about in this world, but only after a rupture in which grace is separated from sin.[28] Furthermore, there is a special salvation history, distinct from this more general salvation history, consisting of God's actions in history interpreted by God's word and culminating in the Incarnation of Jesus Christ. This special salvation history provides meaning for history as a whole and helps us to interpret it.[29] As Rahner writes, "For Christianity, the history of this world is a history interpreted in a Christo-centric sense."[30]

Rahner is also clear that this permeation of human existence by grace characterizes not only human history in general but also all of the institutions and spheres of life that play a role in that history. Human institutions and realities from the political and economic down to the biological level have their own natural validity, but "precisely because, and in so far as, the natural order is the presupposed condition for the very possibility of the supernatural order, set apart from itself by the supernatural order itself, natural existence has, within the concrete order of total creation, an inner openness to grace and a real crying need for grace." Therefore these human realities cannot be considered "purely natural."[31] As Rahner explains: "Given a right understanding of our theoretical considerations, it must have become clear that the sanctification of the world does not begin at the point where we take a sound and well-developed world with sound and well-developed structures of its own and then impose a supernatural and religious superstructure upon it. There also has to be an explicit, conscious relating of secular affairs to the supernatural salvation which is in Christ, manifested in morality, in custom, in institutions, in a uniting of secular with explicitly religious matters."[32] Theology therefore plays an important role in interpreting human social life, even if other disciplines are legitimate and necessary.

De Lubac and Rahner's understanding of human existence strongly challenges the presuppositions of much of the modern political thought that I described in chapter 2. Whereas modern political thought assumes that the human will has no end to which it is oriented, de Lubac and Rahner claim that the human person has an intrinsic orientation to union with God. This orientation gives shape to human nature, which in turn provides a basic framework for the organization of political life. Unlike the earlier neoscholastic theologians, de Lubac and Rahner argue that this orientation toward union with God does not exist in a sphere entirely its own, but rather shapes all of the dimensions of human existence, including the political dimension. Therefore political life cannot be understood apart from humanity's relationship with God, although the political realm retains a certain autonomy as well. This last claim also means that theology plays an important role in understanding politics, even if politics cannot be reduced to theology, which certainly challenges the modern notion that politics can be studied as a science free from theological and metaphysical presuppositions. Thus the recovery and renewal of the more traditional understanding of nature and grace has definite implications for a Catholic understanding of the origins of war, to which I now turn.[33]

TWENTIETH-CENTURY THEOLOGY AND THE ORIGINS OF WAR

The two trends in Catholic theology from the second half of the twentieth century that I have been describing—the increasing awareness of historicity and the recovery of the traditional view of the relationship between nature and grace—can provide crucial insights for a Catholic understanding of war and its origins. Catholic descriptions of historicity, particularly of the subjectivity of human experience, point toward a description of social reality similar to that presented by the constructivists: Our identities and values are, in important ways, constituted by the world around us even as we take part in shaping that world. At the same time, the world that creates us and that we create through our practices is permeated by both sin and grace, leading us back to the earlier Christian tradition of reflection on the origins of war.

Political Implications

Keeping in mind Pope John Paul II's statement that to understand society, we must have "a correct view of the human person," an account of the origins of war must begin with the human person.[34] As we have seen, the human person's thoughts, actions, and identities are at least in part formed by his or her historical location, including culture, political identity, and economic status. These social forces are not simply constraints on a potentially autonomous subject who could be free from their limitations; rather, they are constitutive of the very being of the subject. This insight is developed by theologians who recognize that the Gospel must be adapted to the particular cultures that shape the identities of believers and potential believers; by various liberation theologians who claim that the very fact of our being human persons places us within a political and economic context of injustice to which we have no choice but to respond; and by those theologians who have spoken of Christianity itself as a set of constitutive practices.

Still, the Christian cannot accept the view of many postmodernists who proclaim "the death of the subject," or who assert that what we experience as subjectivity is *completely* the product of these social forces. The human person is also constituted by a relationship with God, one in which we receive our very existence as a gift. We are constituted by the world around us, but our consciousness of this reveals that we transcend the world. Consciousness is a reflection of our openness to the infinite, fulfilled only by God. The existence of this transcendent dimension of the human person does not mean that we should seek to become free from the world, since the world is also constitutive of our being; nor does it mean that we experience transcendence in a sphere of existence separate from our experience of the world. It means, rather, that we are not only the passive products of the world, but also the shapers of our own world. That we are constantly shaping our culture accounts for the variety and fluidity existing within even a single culture, and the fact that our subjectivity is constituted by our relationship with God accounts for why human culture is marked by both sin and grace.

The identities, interests, and norms that govern the behavior of social groups, including states, are at least partly constituted by the actions of the persons and groups who compose them. When speaking of states, of course, this process is limited by the size of the state's governing body; for example, the more democratic a state, the more clearly its interests will reflect the values and interests of its people, although even the interests and values of a dictatorial elite will in some way reflect the broader culture.[35] A larger governing body of a state will also reflect more of the variety and fluidity of a culture than a smaller one. In any state, this process of state identity- and interest-formation is also shaped by the structure of the institutions that make up the government.[36] In turn, of course, state identity is one of the constitutive factors of an individual's identity and interests. At the international level, the identities and interests of states, through their relations with one another, constitute the international system. The international system, in turn, partly forms the identities and interests of the states who make it up.[37] Although identities and interests are formed at the cultural level, they are also shaped by more material realities such as military power, wealth, and economic relations with other states. These material realities themselves, though, only have meaning within a cultural context.[38]

Theology enters into this picture because, as theologians such as Karl Rahner have argued, all human activity in the world, and especially activity in which human persons freely create and transform their world, is permeated by sin and grace. Here a theological analysis of international politics must move beyond constructivism, which is rightly concerned only with describing reality, toward the normative dimension: Which identities, interests, and norms in fact reflect the truth about the human person and human flourishing? In other words, Catholic and other Christian theologians and scholars must ask which identities, interests, and norms best reflect human fulfillment in Christ. As a most basic principle of judgment, any set of identities, interests, and norms that denies either the constitutive role the world plays in the existence of the human person or the transcendence of the human person is self-destructive and cannot possibly lead to true human well-being. Such a culture would be denying one of the essential aspects of what it means to be human. Beyond this basic point, if, as the Second Vatican Council teaches, "the truth is that only in the mystery of the incarnate Word does the mystery of man take on light," then Catholic theologians must say that it is only when the Gospel has suffused a culture that it can truly and fully promote human flourishing.[39] A full account of such a Christological and culturally specific ethic is far beyond the scope of this work, but I will elaborate on its specific implications for understanding war and its origins.

The way of life presented in the Gospel and passed on by the church claims to be one that fosters peace, and therefore a culture where the Gospel is present is a culture of peace. Sin is the ultimate cause of violence, and therefore the redemption that frees us from sin is the only possibility for overcoming violence. Sin, however, is not a purely individual and private reality, but rather one that is played out in human history and culture. Sin is fostered by the particular practices of a culture, and those practices shape the forms that sin takes. The sinful actions and attitudes fostered by cultural practices include violence, and therefore a people's cultural practices and beliefs, which constitute their identities, interests, and norms and those of their political community, create the possibility for war. The church fathers were right to claim that war has its origins in demonic forces that transcend particular individuals and institutions, forces that are embodied in religious and cultural practices. As a contemporary example of what I mean, a theological analysis of American culture would recognize consumerism, the confusion of the acquisition of material goods with true happiness, as just such a social sin that shapes the identities of individual Americans and of the United States as a whole. The identities shaped by consumerism, and the corresponding interests and norms, make war more likely both because they make Americans more prone to use violence to maintain access to the material goods they desire, and because, by downplaying the spiritual dimension of the human person that desires fulfillment that material goods cannot deliver, they make Americans more likely to treat others as objects that can be manipulated, including by violence, for their own ends.

Just as sin is not an individual and private reality but rather a force embodied in history and culture, the same is also true of grace, God's remedy for sin and means of uniting himself to us. Grace is present through all of human history and culture because God makes his offer of grace to all human persons, but grace is above all present in the church, in which we learn in concrete form the meaning of God's action in history and how to live the life that fulfills our nature, which is a life of total self-giving love in imitation of and union with Jesus Christ. By learning these practices and attitudes, we can begin to embody them in culture, thereby influencing the political community and creating the possibility for peace. To continue the earlier example, when American Catholics resist consumerism by being self-conscious about their patterns of consumption, in their own small way they help to transform American culture and overcome the ways that consumerism contributes to violence. That such practices can be occasions of grace makes clear that, for example, consumerism cannot be reduced to an economic problem, even if economic analysis is certainly necessary for understanding it; grace, too, is needed to remedy what is ultimately a spiritual problem that requires the transformation of individuals at the deepest level, as well as the transformation of economic and political structures.

The light of theology, then, should guide any Catholic account of international politics, including an understanding of why there is war and why particular wars take place. This should not be taken to mean that we can simply turn to theology for answers to the problems of international politics without examining the concrete reality of the present world. Neither the Bible nor the Christian tradition provides a magic key to understanding current events. In order to understand fully what is going on in the world, we must study the cultural forces and political structures that shape states' identities and interests and norms of behavior, their relations within the international system, as well as the economic and other material factors that provide the basic foundation of their interests. Viewing international politics in the light of theology does not mean doing away with this process of examination, but rather entails adding a further step. It involves seeking the answers to questions like: What sort of persons do these cultural forces create, and are they the sort of people who are able to live in peace? To what extent do these cultural forces foster sinful actions and attitudes, and to what extent do they foster loving and peaceful actions and attitudes? What cultural forces led these conflicting parties to have such a clash of identities, interests, and norms that war seemed the only way to resolve the conflict? How might the Gospel challenge those cultural forces so that people could live in peace?

Ethical Implications

When we begin to look at the world in this new way, it raises three questions about more traditional approaches to analyzing the morality of war. The first question is about the relationship between the presence of sin and grace in the cultural forces that shape the identities, interests, and norms of behavior of states, on the one hand, and the individual person's response to sin or grace, on the other. The second question is about how we should understand the just war theory in light of the recognition that our knowledge and actions are historically conditioned. And the third question is about the relationship between Christian practices and the use of the just war theory.

The relationship between the presence of sin and grace in culture and the individual person's response to them is complex; it pertains to the inner depth of the human heart, which is unknown to others and even to the person himself or herself. The claim that Gospel practices and attitudes are the way to peace seems to suggest that a culture where the Christian faith is not explicitly acknowledged could perhaps never live in peace. And yet has not Catholic teaching and much of theology, at least since the Second Vatican Council, insisted that because God offers his grace to every human being through their concrete historical circumstances, every human person has the possibility of responding to God's grace, regardless of whether or not they explicitly acknowledge the truth of Christianity? Shouldn't that mean that even those without explicit Christian faith should have the possibility of enjoying the fruits of grace, including peace?

This dilemma is more apparent than real. Individuals who have no explicit faith in Jesus Christ live in a historical situation shaped by both sin and grace, and their concrete actions will be shaped by both realities. Their response to God's offer of grace will take shape in the way they respond to the possibilities presented to them by their historical situation. Even if subjectively speaking a person fully responds to God's offer of grace, objectively speaking his or her actions and attitudes may still be affected by sin because of the limitations of his or her knowledge of the truth. This distinction between the subjective and the objective should not be taken to mean that we respond to God's offer of grace at a spiritual level cut off from our concrete actions, because our spiritual lives are always embodied in those concrete actions, and likewise, concrete existence is where spiritual decisions are made; it simply means that our response to God's grace is limited by our historical circumstances, and our actions will therefore be affected at some level by sin.

Even those who explicitly profess Christian faith are limited by their culture. Our knowledge of Christ is always mediated through the forms of our own culture and therefore subject to at least some of the limitations of that culture. This is true even though the Gospel, if it is lived out, over time can purify a culture of these limitations, although never completely so.[40] If the faithful Christian is still subject to the limitations of his or her culture, then this is even truer of the unfaithful Christian, who is tempted by those elements of a culture that depart most completely from the Gospel. This is why the insights of thinkers like John of Salisbury and Desiderius Erasmus are so important for a Catholic theory of the origins of war: They tried to show how cultural practices that foster the vices can contribute to war even within a Christian society.

An example can illustrate this point about our response to grace being formed by our historical situation. Imagine three men in Nicaragua at the time of the civil war in the 1980s. The first lives in the capital city of Managua, having moved there from the countryside in search of work. At first, he has little luck finding work, but eventually finds it with the help of a Sandinista-supported union. He begins to become involved with a local Sandinista Defense Committee, taking part in local governance, and as the civil war with the Contras escalates, he decides to join the Sandinista Popular Army. The second man is a member of the Miskito people of the Atlantic coast. The Sandinistas burned his village to the ground and sent its members to a re-education camp. He escapes and joins a Contra unit, seeking to defend his people against the Sandinistas. The third man lives in the city of Chinandega. In 1984 he is called to serve in the Sandinista Popular Army by the Patriotic Military Service draft, but refuses, claiming that he cannot in good conscience resort to arms, and he is put in prison. It is at least possible that all three were responding to God's offer of grace in their decisions, given their historical situation, even if it is impossible that all three made the objectively right decision based on just war reasoning.

The notion that knowledge, both about morality itself and about our concrete situation, is historically conditioned might appear to challenge the traditional just war theory, which claims to be an objective way of judging the morality of war, but it is in fact entirely consistent with the theory. If we are judged by our historically conditioned response to our concrete situation rather than by objective standards of morality, it is hard to see what use an apparently objective standard such as the just war theory can have. The just war theory is objective in the sense that it encompasses true moral principles, yet it is not objective in the sense that it is a moral standard existing outside of the world that is then brought down and applied to the world in a particular historical situation. We must be trained to judge a situation in just war terms. This is true for both the individual who must make important decisions in war—be it a political leader, a soldier, or a citizen—and for a society as a whole as it decides on its course of action in a time of conflict. This training takes place, or fails to take place, through the cultural practices that shape the identities, interests, and norms of individuals and societies and that are embodiments of sin and grace; therefore the nature of those practices will in large part determine whether a society and its members can rightly make moral decisions about war. The just war theory cannot be applied to a historical situation from the outside, because the ability to think properly in just war terms is itself a part of the historical situation.

To speak of values and practices in connection with a particular faith tradition can be a difficult and delicate task in our pluralistic society. I have no wish to discount many of the positive values and practices associated with other faith traditions and worldviews. From a Christian perspective, however, if it is above all Christian practices that form people in the virtues, then it is above all Christian practices that should enable a society and its members to make proper moral decisions about war. The just war theory, therefore, is not a theory for everybody. This does not mean that objectively speaking it can only be known by revelation and not by reason, or that the just war theory does not arise out of a natural law that reflects an objective and enduring human nature. It does mean that we must be transformed by grace to recognize it as true and to be able to do what it requires.[41] As Joseph E. Capizzi has argued, we must be transformed by grace in order to see that the final goal of a just war is peace, as Augustine had claimed, and that true peace means seeing the possibility of reconciliation and unity with the enemy, particularly the unity that is fulfilled in the church. It is only when we have this intention in mind that we can truly fulfill the other requirements of the just war theory.[42]

Twentieth-century theology's insights into historicity and the relationship between nature and grace do provide a radically different way of looking at international politics, and therefore a radically different way of looking at the origins of war, than that of either mainstream modern political theories or the neoscholasticism that has dominated Catholic thinking. This new approach emphasizes that the drama of salvation is played out in human history, including international politics, which means that international politics must ultimately be interpreted in a Christological light. There is also a greater emphasis on the way that cultural practices shape not only the identities, interests, and norms of individuals, but also of states themselves, and therefore a moral analysis of war must look at not only the decisions that are made before and during war, but also at the cultural practices that make war a possibility. Within the Catholic world, however, even as these insights were developed and incorporated into official thinking at the Second Vatican Council, their implications for understanding international politics and war have not been realized.

CONCLUSION

In regard to a Catholic perspective on the origins of war, constructivism can help link the past with the present. The ancient Christian tradition developed penetrating insights into the origins of war that unfortunately have been neglected in more recent centuries, and constructivism can help Catholics recover those insights. An increasing awareness of historicity and a renewal of the traditional understanding of the relationship between nature and grace profoundly shaped Catholic theology in the twentieth century, and constructivism is largely compatible with those two developments. Recent Catholic theology and constructivism together suggest a Catholic perspective on war and its origins that recognizes that culture is a human creation that nonetheless plays an important role in creating, or constituting, human persons and their identities, interests, and norms of behavior. Culture also plays an essential role in shaping the social institutions, including states, that persons create to fulfill their needs and desires. Because human history is the stage on which the drama of salvation is played out and on which persons accept or reject God's offer of grace, culturally constituted institutions such as states will inevitably be affected by both sin and grace. When speaking of states, then, this means that war is ultimately caused by clashing cultural practices that foster sin, particularly violence. In the following chapters I will show how Catholic theologians and official Catholic teaching on war and peace have failed to explain the origins of war in a way fully consistent with the Catholic worldview, and in fact have been influenced by tenets of modern political thought that they otherwise reject.

NOTES

1. MacIntyre, *After Virtue*, 204–25. MacIntyre describes the modern turn away from teleological morality on pages 51–61.

2. O'Malley, "Reform," 592.

3. Ibid.

4. Lonergan, "The Future of Thomism," 48–49.

5. Rousselot, *The Eyes of Faith*.

6. Maréchal, *A Maréchal Reader*.

7. Rahner, *Spirit in the World*; Rahner, *Hearer of the Word*.

8. Rahner, *Foundations of Christian Faith*, 41–42.

9. Ibid., 19–20.

10. Ibid., 160.

11. Martinez, *Mystery of God*, 24.

12. Hauerwas, *Truthfulness and Tragedy*; Hauerwas, *A Community of Character*; Hauerwas, *The Peaceable Kingdom*.

13. Von Balthasar, *Theo-Drama*.

14. Schreiter, *Constructing Local Theologies*; Schreiter, *The New Catholicity*; Bevans, *Contextual Theology*.

15. Fuchs, "Historicity and Moral Norm," 106.

16. Porter, *Natural and Divine Law*; Schockenhoff, *Natural Law*.

17. Dussel, *Ethics and Theology*; Dussel, *Ethics and Community*.

18. De Lubac, *Mystery of the Supernatural*, 19–36.

19. De Lubac, *Surnaturel*, 452–58.

20. Ibid., 105–7. My own translation.

21. Some believe that Pope Pius XII meant to censure de Lubac in his encyclical *Humani generis*, which condemns those who "destroy the gratuity of the supernatural order, since God, they say, cannot create intellectual beings without ordering and calling them

to the beatific vision." Pius XII, *Humani generis*, 26. All papal and conciliar documents are from www.vatican.va/.

22. Rahner, "Concerning the Relationship between Nature and Grace," 297–317; Rahner, "Nature and Grace," 165–88; Rahner, "Order of Redemption," 40–41; Coffey, "Whole Rahner," 96; Vandervelde, "Grammar of Grace," 447.

23. Rahner, "Order of Redemption," 49–50.

24. De Lubac, *Mystery of the Supernatural*, 53–74. Emphasis in original.

25. Ibid., 31–36, 75–82, 95.

26. Rahner, "History of the World," 98–99. Elsewhere Rahner argues that this is true because the human person is a unity of the spiritual and the material, and therefore his or her spiritual fulfillment must be expressed through the material, concrete, and historical. Rahner, "Order of Redemption," 47.

27. Rahner, "History of the World," 100 102.

28. Ibid., 97–98; Rahner, "Order of Redemption," 56–57.

29. Rahner, "History of the World," 106–10.

30. Ibid., 114.

31. Rahner, "Order of Redemption," 50–51.

32. Ibid., 66–67.

33. De Lubac himself understood that his ideas had political implications. Joseph A. Komonchak describes the connections between de Lubac's theology and his resistance to the Nazis and the Vichy regime in France, in contrast to many neoscholastic theologians who supported the Vichy government. "Theology and Culture," 579–602.

34. John Paul II, *Centesimus annus*, 11.

35. For example, the policy of North Korea is governed by the philosophy of *juche*, which is a combination of communism and Confucian ideas.

36. Again, United States policy in the Nicaraguan civil war in the 1980s demonstrates the way that competing ideological positions were channeled through political institutions such as the United States Congress and the cabinet of President Ronald Reagan. R. Kagan, *Twilight Struggle*.

37. For example, the international spread of democracy as an ideal, even if it has unfortunately not led to the worldwide spread of democracy, has led nondemocratic states, such as the Democratic People's Republic of Korea, to at least claim the mantle of democracy.

38. An obvious example is that the overwhelming military and economic power of the United States today plays an essential role in forming American identities and interests, but by itself does not tell us exactly what those identities and interests would be.

39. Second Vatican Council, *Gaudium et spes*, 22.

40. For example, today we recognize slavery as incompatible with the Gospel. Objectively speaking, the slavery of the Roman Empire was an unjust institution, but we do not find the Christians of the time entirely culpable for not resisting that institution.

41. This idea is further developed both by Daniel M. Bell Jr. and by Tobias Winright: see Bell, *Just War as Christian Discipleship*; and Winright, "Gather Us In," 281–306.

42. Capizzi, "War and International Order," 294–95.

CHAPTER SIX
· · · · · · · · · · · · · · · · · ·
TWENTIETH-CENTURY CATHOLIC THINKERS

J. BRYAN HEHIR has written, "If one takes the nuclear age from its inception, it is still true to say that papal writing on war and peace has been the driving force of the [Catholic] tradition."[1] Nevertheless, the popes' writings depended on the thought of theologians and other Catholic thinkers, and because theologians are typically able to give more detailed accounts of their reasoning than popes and councils, it is important to consider the work of some of the more prominent Catholics who have examined the issues of war and international order. In the mid-twentieth century, there was a convergence of Catholic neoscholasticism and liberalism in the writing of both Jacques Maritain and John Courtney Murray, the dominant Catholic thinkers writing on these topics. Partly through their influence, this convergence between neoscholasticism and liberalism would become the leading Catholic perspective on issues of war and peace in the twentieth century, reflected in the official teachings of the popes and the Second Vatican Council. Another and more radical strand represented by Dorothy Day showed affinities with the Marxist approach to international relations theory. These three thinkers had important insights into the origins of war, but each of their perspectives had significant drawbacks because of the influence of certain liberal or Marxist ideas.

JACQUES MARITAIN

The French philosopher Jacques Maritain (1882–1973) was perhaps the most influential Catholic social thinker of the twentieth century. Not only did he influence the thought of at least four popes—especially his personal friend Paul VI, but also Pius XII, John XXIII, and John Paul II—but he also helped to bring about the Catholic Church's endorsement of democracy and human rights as expressions of human dignity.[2] Maritain held many academic posts in France, Canada, and the United States, and served as France's ambassador to the Holy See. Maritain did not write extensively on the question of war, but he indirectly influenced Catholic thought on war through his writings on the nature of the state and international order, which in turn rested on his treatment of the natural law and natural rights, as well as the relationship between nature and grace.

Maritain on International Order

According to Maritain, the primary problem of international order is the modern notion of the state as sovereign. For Maritain, the state is properly understood as only part of the body politic, or political society; it is responsible for the promotion of public order.[3] Maritain contrasts this view of the state with the more modern view of the state as sovereign, separate from the body politic and ruling it from above.[4] Within his domain, the modern sovereign is not limited by morality or any countervailing power, a situation that is mirrored in foreign relations: "As concerns the *external or foreign* activity of the State, that is, its relations with the other States, there is nothing to check the trend of modern States . . . toward supreme domination and supreme amorality, nothing except the opposite force of the other States."[5] This notion of sovereignty is responsible for both the violation of human rights domestically and for disorder internationally. At one level, then, Maritain shared with the constructivists a concern with the development of the notion of sovereignty in international politics.

Maritain claims that the modern understanding of the state makes peace unlikely, and therefore a revised conception of the state is necessary. After the destruction of World War II and the development of nuclear weapons, the establishment of peace is the primary problem of humankind, and for Maritain, world government is the only possible solution.[6] States must learn to limit their autonomy, but according to the modern notion of sovereignty, state power is unlimited and inalienable.[7] Political societies must recognize that their autonomy exists only insofar as they are "perfect," or self-sufficient; but because modern political societies are no longer self-sufficient, they must limit their autonomy by establishing some form of world government.[8] Like the state, the world government should not be considered sovereign; it must be considered only a part of the whole world society, thus ensuring the rights of both individuals and lower political societies.[9] Maritain's reasons for a world government are quite similar to those of the neoscholastic theologian Francisco Suarez, although unlike Suarez, Maritain clearly believes that world government is possible.

Although Maritain suggests that the establishment of a world government depends on the universal will of humankind, this universal will does not depend on ideological consensus. Here he makes an important distinction between practical conclusions and their rational justifications that will play a central role in the writings of Popes John XXIII and Paul VI, described in the following chapter. Maritain writes that humankind is increasingly aware of certain "practical truths" that all share in common, despite the different theoretical warrants given for those truths. Maritain gives as an example the almost universal acceptance of the Universal Declaration of Human Rights as a set of practical conclusions despite the differing and often opposed justifications for those rights.[10] He affirms that Christianity provides the best rational justification for democracy and human rights, but Christianity cannot be imposed politically; the shared practical conclusions must remain a "secular faith."[11] These shared practical conclusions can form the basis for a world government as well as national political societies.

Maritain expresses a relative optimism about the possibilities for international order. If political societies all assent to certain practical conclusions about their conduct, then the resolution of conflicts ought to be simply a matter of establishing the appropriate institutional means for negotiation, as many liberal international relations theorists have argued. Maritain's distinction between people's theological and philosophical beliefs, on the one hand, and the practical truths of politics that can form the basis for international cooperation and peace, on the other, is very similar to the core tenets of liberalism, although there are some key differences. But what justifies Maritain's distinction between practical conclusions and theoretical justifications, and his optimism that all people share the former despite their disagreements on the latter?

Maritain on Natural Law and Natural Rights

Some idiosyncratic elements of Maritain's account of the natural law form the basis for his separation of the practical and the theoretical. Maritain departs from the older natural law tradition in his description of how we know the natural law. He writes that we do not come to know the natural law through "rational knowledge," but rather "through inclination": "The intellect, in order to bear judgment, consults and listens to the inner melody that the vibrating strings of abiding tendencies make present in the subject."[12] Yet for Aquinas, the natural law is known through practical reason, which is a form of rational knowledge; the natural law does reflect the inclinations of human nature, but that does not mean that the natural law is "known through inclination."[13] Maritain's novel claim that knowledge of the natural law arises from natural inclination makes this knowledge at least potentially universal despite differences in theoretical beliefs, which are a form of "rational knowledge." The knowledge of the natural law is thus also immune from the ways in which theoretical beliefs are shaped historically by particular cultures.

Maritain does not totally lack a sense of historical consciousness, though, since he recognizes that humanity's knowledge of the natural law and its implications has developed over time. The natural law is written on the human heart, but this does not mean that all people have immediate access to what it entails, or that humanity's knowledge of the natural law cannot develop.[14] In fact, the primary flaw of rationalist, non-Thomist, accounts of the natural law (such as those of Grotius and Pufendorf) has been their attempt to "regard positive law as a mere transcript traced off from natural law," therefore forgetting "the immense field of human things which depend on the variable conditions of social life and on the free initiative of human reason, and which natural law leaves undetermined."[15] When the natural law is applied in these particular conditions, it becomes the law of nations. Drawing on his peculiar way of understanding how the natural law is known, Maritain adds in a note that if the natural law is known through inclination and not reason, then the law of nations is known through the application of reason to the principles of natural law.[16]

Maritain argues not only that the application of the natural law changes in particular circumstances, but also that as a whole this change has a progressive direction. Historical progress is the progress of liberty.[17] This progress will include "liberation from the bondage of material nature," "liberation from the diverse forms of political bondage," and "liberation from the diverse forms of economic and social bondage."[18] The development of a proper understanding of human rights is therefore an integral part of this historical progress.

In his political works, Maritain argues that natural rights should be understood as an outgrowth of the natural law. According to Maritain, the natural law imposes certain duties on us, and therefore, logically, we must have the right to fulfill those duties.[19] Yet the basis for our rights goes beyond the need to fulfill duties: "A person possesses absolute dignity because he is in direct relationship with the absolute, in which alone he can find his complete fulfillment."[20] This absolute dignity of the human person is the reason why society must respect the freedom and conscience of every person. Even so, just as humanity's knowledge of the natural law develops through time, so too does society's ability to uphold the rights of persons. He gives as one example the right to an education, which could hardly be fully exercised in earlier historical periods but today is achievable.[21] Therefore both our understanding of and ability to implement the natural law and natural rights are historically conditioned.

Individual and Person, Nature and Grace

Maritain's distinction between the individual and the person sheds further light on his account of natural rights. We tend to think of "individual" and "person" as synonymous, but, according to Maritain, individuality corresponds to the material pole of the human being, personality to the spiritual pole. He associates the individual with the material because of the traditional Thomist notion that matter is what differentiates things that share the same nature. Yet human persons are distinguished by more than material individuation. Each human person possesses a unique, interior, spiritual dimension. It is at the level of the person that we relate to one another and love one another.[22] Although Maritain draws a distinction between the human being's individuality and personality, they are not separate entities; the two are united within the single human being.[23]

Maritain then applies this distinction to the political realm. Both dimensions of the human being, the individual and the person, are involved in the temporal sphere governed by the state, but only the individual "belongs" to the temporal. The person, because it is spiritual, transcends the temporal.[24] This claim leads to Maritain's important conclusion that even though we (as individuals) must subordinate ourselves to the common good by serving it and obeying what is required for its achievement, persons cannot be sacrificed for the sake of the common good because the common good consists in the good of the persons who make up society.[25] He also concludes that the state has the authority to enforce the natural law, which pertains to the temporal, but has no authority over personal conscience, which is spiritual.[26] The existence of the spiritual dimension of the human person places limits, in the form of human rights, on what the state can legitimately do to bring about temporal well-being, but does not really change the way we think about temporal well-being as such. Maritain's distinction between the temporal and spiritual dimensions would be influential for Pope Paul VI's similar distinction in his encyclical *Populorum progressio*, among other writings.

Maritain adds to his distinctions between the individual and the person and the temporal and the spiritual the distinction between the natural and the supernatural. He argues that the temporal order of society has its own intermediate, or "infravalent," end that is subordinate to but distinct from humanity's ultimate end, the kingdom of God.[27] He considers these two ends of humanity natural and supernatural, respectively.[28] Because he connects the temporal with the natural and the spiritual with the supernatural, for Maritain supernatural revelation sheds little light on our understanding of temporal well-being, which is based on the natural law. Nevertheless, he concludes that because Christianity alone makes the proper distinctions between the natural and supernatural, the temporal and spiritual, while holding them together in unity, Christianity alone is truly capable of defending the freedom of the person and therefore the proper ordering of the temporal sphere.[29] Yet the Christian is a "Christian as such" only in the spiritual plane; in the temporal plane, the Christian acts simply according to the natural law, although "vivified" by Christian principles.[30] Maritain proposes a New Christendom, not the Old Christendom in which Christianity was imposed on society, but one in which the autonomy of the temporal is respected.[31] Non-Christians can participate in the temporal order as the equals of Christians because the temporal order is governed by a "common practical task" rather than a "common theoretic minimum."[32]

Theologian William T. Cavanaugh argues that Maritain's association of the supernatural with the spiritual and the personal, and the natural with the temporal and the individual, has the effect of erasing the physical, social presence of the church. The church does not have significant "bodily performances" or social practices of its own that form identities and norms.[33] Cavanaugh notes that this is a significant departure from Thomas Aquinas's account of the virtues, in which even the supernatural virtues such as charity are only expressed through concrete bodily practices.[34] Because, according to Cavanaugh, Maritain associates the "social" with what is natural and corporeal, he has little way of explaining why even humanity's most spiritual and transcendent pursuits are communal rather than individual.[35] Cavanaugh is primarily concerned with how this erasure of the social presence of the church hinders the church from resisting an oppressive state, but it also suggests a weakness in Maritain's way of understanding the origins of war and its possible prevention.

Maritain's dualism of spirit and matter keeps him from fully developing a sense of how practices constitute identities and norms, both at the individual and the political levels. This means that he misses the important role that practices play both in the origins of war and in its possible prevention. If, as Christians such as the church fathers and Thomas Aquinas suggest, Christian practices are necessary for forming the virtues that will make peace a possibility, then Maritain's downplaying of the social and bodily dimensions of the church's life is a weakness in understanding the possibilities for peace. Likewise, if the practices that lead to war are in a way "idolatrous," then they find their roots in the spiritual depths of the human person. Maritain, on the other hand, limits the political to the temporal sphere, in which people should be able to agree on basic principles, despite significant differences at the level of the spiritual and theoretical. Maritain's understanding of practical reasoning in politics is also quite ahistorical, not only because of his peculiar view that it is a faculty of inclination rather than reason, but also because he ignores the role that particular communities play in forming people's beliefs through their practices.

Maritain's account of international order, which has had such an influence on the thought of the popes from Pius XII to John Paul II, is based on an account of the natural law that brings together the neoscholastic natural law approach with liberalism. Positively, Maritain did play a significant role in leading the Catholic Church to accept democracy and human rights as moral ideals, and he made major contributions to a Catholic understanding of international institutions. Nevertheless, there are problems with Maritain's thought as well. Maritain's sharp division between the temporal and the spiritual mirrors the modern separation of the political from the transcendent that has been resisted in Catholic thought. He argued that even if societies diverge fundamentally at the spiritual and theoretical level, they ought to be able to agree on certain practical conclusions concerning the temporal order. Therefore conflict among states is typically the result of the failure to establish institutions that reflect those practical conclusions. For Maritain, the deep spiritual differences among peoples are not reflected in the bodily, cultural practices that shape political motivations and behavior. These conclusions led Maritain to positions very similar to those of liberalism, which are not completely adequate from a Catholic perspective.

The American John Courtney Murray also moved in the direction of liberalism, although by a different path.

JOHN COURTNEY MURRAY

Like Jacques Maritain, John Courtney Murray (1904–67) was among the most significant Catholic social thinkers of the mid-twentieth century. According to Robert W. McElroy, after World War II the two mutually influenced each other.[36] Murray is most well known for his development of a Catholic understanding of religious freedom and his coauthorship of the Second Vatican Council's *Dignitatis humanae*, which made respect for religious freedom part of official Catholic teaching. He is also known, however, for his attempt to develop a public philosophy that he believed was necessary for the health of society, as well as for a few short essays on the morality of war and the foundations of international order.

Murray on War and International Order

Murray provides a strong critique of realism and its influence on American foreign policy. He first argues that the United States' approach to war is trapped between the poles of pacifism and realism, asserting that it would be much better served by the natural law and the just war tradition.[37] He then turns more specifically to realism. The realist view of international politics is shaped by certain philosophical assumptions: "So far as one can see by an independent look 'out there,' the dilemmas and ironies and paradoxes are, like the beauty of the beloved, in the eye of the ambiguist [i.e., realist] beholder. They represent a doctrinaire construction of the facts in terms of an antecedent moral theory."[38] The realists are fundamentally misguided in their attitude toward power, according to Murray, with regard to both its exercise within a society and its pursuit in international politics. In the natural law tradition, power or authority is morally neutral, or even good. Therefore there is nothing morally ambiguous about a state pursuing its national interest if that interest is rightly conceived; the state has a moral obligation to promote the welfare of its people. The pursuit of the national interest can even involve the use of force; Murray distinguishes between force, or the exercise of power by the state necessary for achieving its purposes, and violence, the excessive use of force.[39] He believes that this distinction between force and violence is the basis for the just war doctrine.

In the modern world, Murray sees the pursuit of international order as necessary to the pursuit of the national interest. His detailed writings on international order are from an early period in his career, when he reflected on Pope Pius XII's call for postwar international cooperation and organization, yet these ideas are consistent with his later thought. Some form of international organization is necessary for states to resolve their conflicts without the use of violence, and Murray is heartened to see more and more people recognize this. Like Maritain, he believes that this international organization should be governed by the principle of subsidiarity, not seeking to replace already-existing states with a world state, but only performing those functions that states are unable to perform. Such an international organization would represent not the creation of international society, but the institutionalization of the present natural society of humanity.[40] Murray continued to hold this vision of international organization as an ideal throughout his career, although he grew pessimistic about the possibility for its realization because of the influence of the Soviet Union in world politics.

Murray on the Natural Law

Murray turns to the natural law as the basis for the public philosophy that should guide just war reasoning and international cooperation. Yet, as Jean Porter claims, "While much of what Murray says presupposes a doctrine of the natural law, and much of his energy is devoted to correcting false understandings of the natural law, Murray devotes relatively little space to setting forth his own positive understanding of the doctrine of natural law."[41] What he does say is that the natural law is in theory accessible to everyone: "The doctrine of natural law has no Roman Catholic presuppositions. Its only presupposition is threefold: that man is intelligent; that reality is intelligible; and that reality, as grasped by intelligence, imposes on the will the obligation that it be obeyed in its demands for action or abstention."[42] As to how we come to know these principles, Porter argues convincingly that somewhat like Maritain, Murray believes we know them through moral intuition.[43] His account of natural law, in its basics, pays little heed to the way tradition and historical location shape our reasoning.

In his account of the natural law, Murray also demonstrates the neoscholastic separation of the natural from the supernatural. He writes that the natural law "does not promise to transform society into the City of God on earth, but only to prescribe, for the purposes of law and social custom, that minimum of morality which must be observed by the members of a society, if the social environment is to be human and habitable."[44] Here he seems to be drawing on Thomas Aquinas's claim that the human law should not prohibit all vices, only the most grievous.[45] As individuals, we are given the higher calling of the Gospel. Yet, as Murray writes, it would be a mistake "to imagine that the invitation, 'Come, follow me,' is a summons somehow to forsake the universe of human nature, somehow to vault above it, somehow to leave law and obligation behind." The Gospel builds on and perfects the natural law, and the latter is included within the former.[46] In an earlier essay Murray had made a similar argument about the implementation of the natural law in the social order: "The natural law exists within the Gospel; and a social order which would conform to the demands of the natural law would already be fundamentally Christian."[47] Nevertheless, Murray insists that society should be governed by the natural law, whereas individuals in their private lives can choose to follow the fullness of the Gospel; supernatural revelation sheds little light on how society ought to be governed.

Murray has been criticized for failing to recognize the theological presuppositions of his theory of the natural law. For example, John A. Coleman, SJ, points out Murray's "failure to admit that his own theory of natural law rests on particularistic Catholic theological principles and theories which do not command widespread allegiance."[48] Likewise, David L. Schindler points out that even though Murray claims that his natural law framework can provide a "neutral" way of thinking about politics, in fact it reflects a definite worldview. Schindler is particularly concerned that Murray's neoscholastic natural law framework describes society as if it were indifferent to any relation to God rather than intrinsically oriented to God.[49] Not only does Murray fail to fully recognize that our knowledge of the natural law comes through tradition, he also does not fully acknowledge that the natural law is inextricably linked with philosophical and theological beliefs about humanity, the world, and God. Surprisingly, then, Murray does provide important insights into the role of culture and ideology in international politics.

Murray on the Public Consensus

Despite Murray's ahistorical view of our knowledge of the natural law, he also makes room for historicity in his claims about the more particular conclusions of natural law. As William J. Gould Jr. writes, "Despite his strong commitment to a natural law methodology with its insistence upon the permanent features of human nature, Murray was also keenly sensitive to the historical dimension of human experience."[50] According to Murray, there is a fundamental structure to human nature, and yet the human reality changes in history, and the natural law must be worked out in particular historical situations. Therefore, to a certain extent, what the natural law requires changes over time. The more particular or remote applications of the natural law depend on detailed knowledge of the historical situation and are typically only discernable by "the wise." The wise have a responsibility to shape the public consensus of society so that it reflects those applications of the natural law that are appropriate to historical circumstances.[51]

Murray argues that the application of the natural law in particular historical circumstances underlies the public consensus that is the foundation of any civilized society. By "consensus," Murray does not mean simply the shared opinions of the majority of a society, but rather a set of substantive truths that are acknowledged by a critical mass of the populace and that form the basis for deliberations about public affairs. Without this consensus, society is reduced to "barbarism."[52] According to Murray, the truths of the public consensus really are truths, knowable by reason.[53] This is why he considers them "remote precepts of natural law"; they are the results of applying the natural law to changing historical circumstances.[54] Because the public consensus emerges through the application of the natural law to particular historical circumstances, the consensus also reflects the unique character of a society and develops through that society's traditions. The public consensus of a society, such as Western society, has a "growing end," and "there is always the possibility and need of progress in the consensus that sustains [the West's] life, as there is likewise the possibility and the danger of decadence."[55] This danger of decadence is particularly acute, Murray recognizes, because maintaining the public consensus depends on maintaining virtue and self-discipline in the people.[56]

Murray senses the danger of decadence in American culture and thus is concerned with the fate of the public consensus in the United States. As David Hollenbach, SJ, writes: "The entire Murray project—and the precise form the project took—is based upon the hope that there is enough life in the American public philosophy effectively to establish justice, promote the general welfare, and secure the blessings of liberty for all. But throughout his writings runs the counterpoint theme of a fear that this may not be so."[57] Murray's concern for the public consensus in America is twofold. The first part is the practical concern that America's religious pluralism might prevent the establishment of a true consensus. He argues that the differing theological presuppositions of America's religious groups, but more importantly their histories of hostility, make true conversation difficult, although not impossible.[58] The second part is the more philosophical concern that American political life has been too much shaped by the convictions of modern political thought. Murray particularly focuses on the modern rejection of authorities independent of the state, particularly the church. Modern political thought has tended to be "monist," placing all authority in the hands of the state, whether it is a monarchy, dictatorship, or democracy.[59]

Murray on the Soviet Union

In the intriguing essay "Doctrine and Policy in Communist Imperialism," Murray discusses the ideology of Soviet foreign policy and the American response to it. He argues that because of the American tendency to see states as rational actors motivated by utilitarian reason, American foreign policy thinkers have failed to understand Soviet foreign policy correctly. They must look at the ideological sources of state behavior to truly understand world politics. To a certain extent, then, Murray anticipated the constructivists in his critique of political science based on a limited view of reason and in his emphasis on the importance of norms and values.

The pragmatic belief that politics is governed by utility-maximizing reason and not moral truths or ideology leads the United States to an inept approach to the Soviet Union, according to Murray. "The American mind is consciously pragmatist. When questions can no longer be postponed, they are approached with an empirical, experimentalist attitude that focuses on contingencies of fact. The search is for a compromise, for the 'deal' that will be acceptable to both parties in the dispute. The notion of action being controlled by theory is alien to this mentality. The further notion of a great state submitting its purposes and actions to the control of a dogmatic philosophy seems absurd. The pragmatist mind instinctively refuses to take in this notion or to study its implications." The practical American ignores Stalin's dogmatic statements and "rapidly overlooks the essential fact that the purposes and actions of the Soviet Empire are unintelligible without reference to the ideas on which its leaders act."[60] Much like the constructivists thirty years later, Murray is critical of the tendency to see states as benefit-maximizers uniformly guided by utilitarian reason.

Murray suggests that for the United States to craft an adequate policy toward the Soviet Union, it must understand the values that guide Soviet foreign policy. The Soviet Union must be understood not only in material terms, such as geographic size and military and economic power, but also in terms of its ideology and its cultural past.[61] Murray claims that American foreign policy thinkers tend to focus only on size and power, as if the mere fact that two world powers exist necessarily leads to conflict between them or suggests ways of resolving that conflict. Americans must learn to take into account the Soviet Union's whole identity, which in a way makes the task easier: "The major value of a full view of the unique character of the Soviet Union is that it creates a limited but useful set of expectations on which to base American policy."[62] Here Murray's thinking anticipates that of constructivists such as Alexander Wendt on the different facets of the national interest. Murray denies that the incompatibility between the Soviet and American views of reality must necessarily lead to the use of force, although it must be used if moral judgment demands it. This incompatibility does suggest, however, that we should not be optimistic about the possibility for a worldwide public authority. In fact, Murray is critical of Pope John XXIII's *Pacem in terris* (described in the next chapter) for this reason, writing that "there may be some warrant for the thought that the spirit of confident hope which the Pontiff courageously embraces fails to take realistic account of the fundamental schism in the world today." The public consensus that would be necessary for such a public authority to function properly does not exist in the international community.[63] In other words, international institutions themselves cannot establish peace; a culture of peace must also develop among states.

Some of Murray's ideas, therefore, anticipated a constructivist approach to war and its origins, although these existed in tension with his neoscholastic moral framework. Murray seemed to recognize that the origins of international conflict lie in clashes of identities, interests, and norms. Just international institutions depend on at least a minimum of shared values, and in the absence of such shared values, international institutions do not function properly and may in fact make problems worse. Therefore Murray clearly differed from Maritain, who was relatively optimistic that states already possess those shared values.

Whether discussing domestic politics or international politics, however, according to Murray, those shared values must be based on the natural law. We know the natural law through a form of moral intuition independent of our cultural formation. Therefore, although his notion of the public consensus functions much like the notion of culture in constructivist thought, it is also true that Murray sees religious and cultural particularities as a threat to the public consensus. There is a real tension in Murray's thought between the idea that the public consensus is worked out by a particular society in concrete circumstances and the idea that the consensus is a conversation based on reason and natural law. Murray therefore has much in common with liberals such as John Stuart Mill who admit that the spirit of liberty and reasonable institutions develop in particular societies, but who see this development as a move away from the tyranny of particular customs, rather than the embodiment of a particular set of customs. This similarity with liberals is also seen in Murray's own inability to recognize the philosophical and theological presuppositions of his theory of the natural law. Murray failed to take into consideration how even knowledge of the natural law is passed on through cultural tradition. Therefore, like Maritain, Murray demonstrated a certain accommodation with liberalism, although in a different way. Unlike Maritain and Murray, Dorothy Day offered a radical critique of liberalism, but she, too, reflected the influence of certain trends in modern political thought on Catholic thinking about the origins of war, although in her case that influence came from Marxism.

DOROTHY DAY

Dorothy Day (1897–1980) was the cofounder of the Catholic Worker movement and one of the most influential Catholic pacifists of the twentieth century. A convert to Catholicism, Day established the Catholic Worker movement with Peter Maurin in 1933. Through its actions and its newspaper the *Catholic Worker*, the group promoted the corporal and spiritual works of mercy for those in need, the rights of workers, farming communes, and pacifism. Day and other Catholic Workers opposed the United States' involvement in the Second World War, the Korean War, and the Vietnam War, as well as the accoutrements of a militarized society such as the draft, the armaments industry, and civil defense drills. Day defended her positions with a unique blend of Catholicism and radicalism. She was neither a professional theologian nor a political theorist, yet her way of understanding war proved very influential in the second half of the twentieth century, so much so that Anne Klejment calls Day "the spiritual leader of American Catholic pacifism."[64]

Day on Nature and Grace

At one level, Day bases her opposition to war on her reading of the Gospels. For example, in her essay "Our Country Passes from Undeclared War to Declared War," published in the *Catholic Worker* in 1942, Day says of the Catholic Worker movement, "We are still pacifists. Our manifesto is the Sermon on the Mount, which means that we will try to be peacemakers." According to Day, Jesus's command to love our enemies is incompatible with the practice of war.[65] Elsewhere Day writes that followers of Christ must live according to the laws of the kingdom of heaven, which is spiritual rather than temporal. Therefore, they must use spiritual means such as prayer and the sacraments to oppose violence, rather than temporal means such as force.[66]

Michael J. Baxter, CSC, argues that Day's turn to the Sermon on the Mount and a "supernaturalized" way of understanding society departs significantly from the perspective of her Catholic contemporaries. The social theories of American Catholic social ethicists such as John A. Ryan, Moorehouse F. X. Millar, and John Courtney Murray depended on the neoscholastic separation of nature and grace. In this view, the supernatural virtues might apply in the life of the individual, but society is governed by the natural law, which is knowable by reason alone. The natural law includes the just war criteria, which govern the use of force by the state. Baxter argues that by denying the separation between personal and public morality, and by claiming that all are called to a life of holiness, not just to the minimum of morality, Dorothy Day and Peter Maurin rejected the neoscholastic division between nature and grace. According to Baxter, Day and Maurin put forward a "supernaturalized" social theory of which pacifism was a central feature.[67]

Baxter therefore claims that Day and Maurin's ideas demonstrate an affinity with the thought of Henri de Lubac, SJ, on the relationship between nature and grace. He writes that Day and Maurin express in social terms Henri de Lubac's assertion that human nature has a natural orientation to the supernatural and cannot be understood apart from that orientation. Day herself was at least familiar with de Lubac, whom she mentions when discussing the controversy over the relationship between nature and grace.[68]

To a certain extent, Baxter is correct when he notes that Day's thought reflects some of de Lubac's theological insights and shows some similarities to the theological perspective I described in the previous chapter. For example, Day's conviction that holiness is not reserved for a special class within the church (priests and religious), but rather is a calling for all, because every human person is oriented to a supernatural destiny, is clearly similar to the theology of de Lubac. Likewise, Day's claim that our understanding of society must be supernaturalized, or understood in explicitly theological language, parallels Rahner's insights into the presence of sin and grace in human history and culture. Finally, Day's contention that our moral reasoning about war should be theological, and not simply "natural," is consistent with the perspective I described in chapter 5. On the other hand, Baxter misses some of the ways that Day's understanding of nature and grace differs from de Lubac's, especially because of the influence of the Lacouture retreat movement on her thought.

Day's involvement in the controversy over nature and grace came largely through the influence of the Lacouture retreat movement. Onesimus Lacouture, SJ, was a Canadian priest who gained recognition for a distinctive style of spiritual retreat, beginning in the early 1930s. The Lacouture retreat movement, particularly through the retreats given by the priests Pacifique Roy and John Hugo, had a profound influence on the Catholic Worker movement in the 1930s and 1940s.[69] Day continued to take part in Lacouture retreats off and on until her final retreat in 1976.[70] Mark and Louise Zwick rank Onesimus Lacouture second only to Peter Maurin as having the greatest influence on Day spiritually and intellectually.[71] The Lacouture retreat movement deeply affected Day's understanding of the relationship between nature and grace.

Keeping in mind that Day was not a systematic theologian, there are nonetheless significant differences between her own thought and that of Henri de Lubac that, at first only implicitly, show the influence of the Lacouture retreat movement. In her earliest writing where she mentions the topic, *House of Hospitality*, Day suggests that there is a fundamental conflict between nature and grace: "As long as we live there will be a war, a conflict between nature and grace, nature again and again getting the upper hand for the moment, only to be put down rigidly. If we have faith and hope, it is impossible to be discouraged." Here she associates "nature" with "an evil, complacent nagging," "complacency, [and] self-satisfaction."[72] Later she claims that the cause of dissensions within the Catholic Worker movement, and within the church as a whole, is that "there is always a war between nature and grace."[73] Considering their similarity to Day's later writings on the retreat movement, these statements seem to show its early influence on her thought.[74]

Day develops her thought on the question of nature and grace in *On Pilgrimage*, now relating it explicitly to the retreats led by Pacifique Roy and John Hugo. She describes how the theology behind the retreats has created controversy, and she writes, "The teaching has been that love which is of the Lover for the Beloved can only be between equals, and so to achieve this we must die to the natural and live supernatural lives, doing everything for the love of God."[75] Later she writes, concerning what is taught on the retreats, "Good actions may be human or divine. There is confusion in regard to these. The only actions which lead to God are divine actions. Supernatural action has God for its end. The natural has ourselves. Action has value according to whom the action is directed." Only supernatural actions have a true reward. Natural actions, on the other hand, even though good in themselves, "are imperfect actions and lead to venial sin, which leads to mortal sin."[76] Day provides similar reflections on nature and grace and the Lacouture retreats in her autobiography, *The Long Loneliness.*[77]

Day's statements are clearly drawing on both the Augustinian notion that the things of this world should only be used in relation to God and Augustine's statement in the *City of God* that "the earthly city was created by self-love reaching the point of contempt for God, the Heavenly City by the love of God carried as far as contempt of self."[78] But Augustine never considers the misuse of worldly things or self-love "natural" in contrast to the "supernatural." In Day's comments outlined above, she seems to fail to distinguish between natural and unnatural desires for a good. It is as if God were a supernatural thing that must compete for our attention with the natural things of the world. In Augustine and de Lubac's true human fulfillment, however, natural goods and our supernatural end are not in conflict, but rather integrated. The pursuit of the supernatural end sometimes involves the sacrifice of natural goods, but not because they are natural, but rather because something in us is unnatural. This integral understanding of natural and supernatural goods seems to be the view of the bishops at the Second Vatican Council, who in *Gaudium et spes* claim that natural goods are not only means to our supernatural end, but will in fact be united with our supernatural end: "For after we have obeyed the Lord, and in His Spirit nurtured on earth the values of human dignity, brotherhood and freedom, and indeed all the good fruits of our nature and enterprise, we will find them again, but freed of stain, burnished and transfigured, when Christ hands over to the Father: 'a kingdom eternal and universal, a kingdom of truth and life, of holiness and grace, of justice, love and peace.'"[79]

Other influences on Day's spirituality emphasized the presence of grace in the everyday world, balancing this negative view of the natural. For example, in *The Long Loneliness*, Day notes how Peter Maurin's emphasis on the presence of God in the world balanced the otherworldliness of Pacifique Roy, and she quotes St. Catherine of Siena as saying, "All the way to heaven is heaven."[80] Day also often reflects on the presence of grace in our everyday lives, an idea that eventually led her to promote the "little way" of St. Thérèse of Lisieux, on whom Day wrote a book.[81] Lacouture himself emphasized finding Christ present in the poor.[82] Yet the Lacouture movement, with its particular understanding of nature and grace, was central to Day's thinking about war, and she consciously drew on the retreats when formulating her pacifism during World War II, even turning to John Hugo for help in crafting a theological understanding of pacifism and what it entailed for the Christian believer.[83]

The influence of the Lacouture retreat movement is clearly evident in Day's editorial "CW Stand on the Use of Force." Day writes, "From the human natural standpoint men are doing good to defend their faith, their country. But from the standpoint of the Supernatural—there is the 'better way'—the way of the Saints—the way of love." Those who say, as John Courtney Murray would later on, that this supernatural ethic is for individuals, while the political must be governed by a natural ethic, are mistaken. Because we are called to a supernatural destiny, relying only on the natural will have disastrous consequences, including an escalation in brutality.[84] Day, as a Christian anarchist, seems to hold that the state is a natural institution that even if it is good in its own way, should be rejected by the Christian in light of our higher divine calling. The just war ethic is a natural ethic characteristic of the modern state, and must also be rejected.

There seems to be a close connection between Day's statements on war in 1938 and her writings on nature and grace ten years later in *On Pilgrimage*. Just as she wrote in 1948 that even if the natural is good in itself, from the perspective of the divine it is imperfect, so in 1938 she had written that the just war ethic is good in itself, but is imperfect compared with the supernatural way of love. Just as she wrote in 1948 that the natural leads to sin because of its imperfection, so in 1938 she had written that the just war ethic inevitably leads to savagery. As I attempted to show in the previous chapter, however, it is not necessary to think of the state as a natural community in competition with our supernatural end, God, and the just war ethic as a natural ethic inferior to the supernatural ethic of Jesus. The theological perspective on war's origins that I outlined in chapter 5 provides an interpretation of war that is very different from Day's, but theology was not the only source for her understanding of war.

Day on the Origins of War

Day's understanding of the origins of war was shaped by both her theological beliefs and her radicalism. Day had been involved in radical politics before her conversion to Catholicism, and this experience shaped her views on war's origins even after her conversion. She drew on a theory of imperialism centered on the exploitation of workers through the wage system, and therefore her perspective on war's origins shares much in common with Marxist theories. There was a tension in Day's thought between this Marxist influence and the broader theological framework of her thinking about war.

Day's pacifism was at least in part rooted in the account of the origins of modern war that she learned during her time as a radical anarchist, prior to her conversion to Catholicism. As Anne Klejment writes, "Day's openness to peacemaking dates back to World War I and the war resistance she encountered in the lyrical left. From the peacemakers of this earlier time, Day absorbed an analysis of the causes of war."[85] In 1917, Day worked for the socialist newspaper the *New York Call* and was assigned to write on socialists' efforts to prevent the United States from entering the First World War. Through this exposure to the socialist peace movement, she began to develop her own views on war.[86] Day also began to work at the Collegiate Anti-Militarism League, also known as the Anti-Conscription League, which advocated peace through legislation and education, although as Klejment notes, at this point Day herself believed that only a violent revolution would bring about justice and peace.[87] Over time, however, Day's views became more and more similar to those of the International Workers of the World, who favored a nonviolent revolution. From all of these groups, though, Day picked up the idea that modern war stemmed from the structures of capitalism, and she continued to hold this position even after her conversion to Catholicism.

Day never systematically lays out her beliefs on war's origins, but from what can be gleaned from her writings, she espouses many principles that could be classed within a broadly Marxist school of international relations. One of the most fundamental of these is the labor theory of value, according to which the worker contributes all of the value to a product, and therefore a system in which capitalists pay workers wages and keep profits for themselves is necessarily exploitative. Like Marx and Lenin, both Day and Peter Maurin subscribe to this theory; Day continued to hold these beliefs from her early radical days until late in her life.[88] Like Lenin, Day holds that this situation of exploitation leads to underconsumption, because the great majority of workers are no longer able to purchase the goods that are produced.

Day also develops positions significantly different from those of Marx or Lenin that could nevertheless be considered to be inspired by Marxism because of their emphasis on the role of capitalist structures in leading to war. Unlike Lenin, Day concludes that the capitalist class attempts to resolve the contradictions caused by the wage system not through imperialism, but rather through the production of armaments for war: "Our whole modern economy is based on preparation for war."[89] The capitalist class therefore pushes for war in order to maintain both its profits and the capitalist system itself.[90] Day also writes that the increasing mechanization of production under capitalism leads to unemployment; this weakness of capitalism is overcome by employing workers in the production of armaments for war.[91] In this regard Day also differs from Marx and Lenin, who believed that industrialization was a necessary condition for the development of communism, but her use of structural features of the economy to describe the origins of modern war nevertheless shows an affinity with Marxist thought.

Despite these similarities to Marxist thought, it would be wrong to conclude that Day entirely shares Marxism's economic reductionism. First of all, although she agrees with many of Marx's criticisms of capitalism, Day does not believe that capitalism emerged solely as a result of impersonal historical forces. Rather, capitalism developed because of the love of the world and the love of self, which Day contrasts with the love of God, as described earlier. Second, even though Day emphasizes the role of economic structures in contributing to war, she does not do so in a rigidly deterministic way; she also includes the role of human agency, particularly when it is dominated by the vices. This balance between the structural and the personal is found, for example, in a 1967 statement on the Vietnam War: "The war goes on in Vietnam. If it ceased tomorrow, it would be going on in some other quarter of the globe and we, as the richest nation, making so much money out of our armaments, would be very much involved still. The causes of war are still with us: fear, hatred, greed, and 'each man seeking his own.'"[92] Finally, unlike most Marxists, Day does not believe that capitalist exploitation should be or will be overturned by a violent revolution, but rather by voluntary poverty and self-reliance, and further, this change can only come about through the transformation of hearts by grace.[93] Thus Day's understanding of war's origins is fundamentally theological, even if founded on a theology of nature and grace somewhat different from that described in chapter 5.

There is a tension in Day's understanding of war's origins between her theological orientation and her use of Marxist-inspired theories. Perhaps the most important area of tension is in the ambiguous relationship between human agency and economic structures. For example, Day claims that capitalism has its roots in human selfishness and turning away from God, but her interpretation of capitalism through the lens of the labor theory of value seems to stand as the basis for this claim. More concretely, is Day's claim that the Vietnam War, like other modern wars, was caused by "fear, hatred, greed, and 'each man seeking his own'" founded on the prior belief that war is caused by capitalists seeking to deal with underconsumption and unemployment? Secondly, Day's way of understanding war's origins is rather uniform, and fails to take into consideration the varying motivations involved in, for example, World War I, World War II, and the Vietnam War. Therefore, although Mark and Louise Zwick's claim that for Day, "the causes of war were very frequently, at bottom, economic," may not be quite right, there are ambiguities in her thought, and her perspective on war's origins lacks a suitably complex conception of the interrelationship of cultural beliefs and practices with economic institutions.[94]

There is much of value in Day's approach to the origins of war, although it also has significant limitations. Her claim that society must be "supernaturalized" because both sin and grace are active in all areas of human life is an improvement over the neoscholasticism of Maritain, Murray, and, as will be described in the next chapter, many of the twentieth-century popes. It acknowledges that humanity's end is fundamentally supernatural and not disconnected from our earthly pursuits, and also that theology has important things to say about political life. Still, her view that the natural and supernatural are in conflict not only poses problems for ethical reasoning but also provides an inadequate understanding of "natural" communities such as the state. Her Marxist-influenced views on the origins of war also provide useful criticisms of liberal societies ignored by thinkers such as Maritain and Murray, and they also begin to tackle the ways that material and cultural factors influence state behavior. Yet in Day's thought economic structures play a more determinative role than is warranted in comparison to human agency and cultural factors.

CONCLUSION

In different ways, Jacques Maritain, John Courtney Murray, and Dorothy Day each struggled to integrate an understanding of the politics behind war within a theological framework. Maritain separated the spiritual sphere of the church from the temporal sphere of the state and therefore had no way of describing how religious (or idolatrous) beliefs can be embodied in social practices that have a profound impact on the political. Both Maritain and Murray concluded that the temporal sphere is governed by the natural law, which in turn is made up of practical conclusions that are knowable to all regardless of their philosophical and theological beliefs. This conclusion led Maritain to the optimistic belief that international institutions can establish world peace regardless of the deep spiritual divisions of the world, whereas Murray seemed to recognize that these divisions make peace unlikely. This was because Murray partially recognized the importance of culture for understanding state behavior, although he did not fully realize how even reasonable behavior and institutions must be sustained by cultural tradition. Finally, Day's understanding of war's origins had a theological framework, but one in which the natural and the supernatural are opposed to one another. Day also incorporated Marxist ideas, broadly construed, into this framework, creating tensions that were not fully resolved in her own writings. All three of these thinkers were shaped to some degree by modern presuppositions in their views on war's origins; through their influence, they ensured that the same would be true of subsequent Catholic thought.

NOTES

1. Hehir, "Catholic Teaching on War and Peace," 369.
2. Torre, "Maritain's 'Integral Humanism,'" 202–8. Torre mentions only John XXIII, Paul VI, and John Paul II, but it seems clear that Maritain also had an influence on Pius XII.
3. Maritain, *Man and the State*, 9–12.
4. Ibid., 34.
5. Ibid., 193–94. Emphasis in original.
6. Ibid., 189–90.
7. Ibid., 50–51.
8. Ibid., 197–99, 206–7.
9. Ibid., 203, 210–11.
10. Ibid., 76–77.
11. Ibid., 61, 109–11.
12. Ibid., 91–92.
13. Doolin, "Maritain, St. Thomas Aquinas," 127–39; Aquinas, *Summa Theologica*, I, q. 79, a. 11; I-II, q. 91, a. 3; q. 94, a. 1–2.
14. Maritain, *Rights of Man*, 62–64; Maritain, *Integral Humanism*, 137–39.

15. Maritain, *Man and the State*, 97.

16. Ibid., 98 n. 13.

17. Maritain, *Rights of Man*, 29–34.

18. Ibid., 44–45.

19. Ibid., 64–68.

20. Ibid., 4; see also Fay, "Maritain on Rights," 442–43.

21. Maritain, *Man and the State*, 102.

22. Maritain, *Person and the Common Good*, 21–32; Maritain, *Rights of Man*, 2–3; Maritain, *Integral Humanism*, 9.

23. Maritain, *Person and the Common Good*, 33.

24. Maritain, *Rights of Man*, 11–17; Maritain, *Person and the Common Good*, 60–66.

25. Maritain, *Person and the Common Good*, 39–41.

26. Maritain, *Rights of Man*, 77–78.

27. Maritain, *Integral Humanism*, 133–36.

28. Ibid., 97–98.

29. Ibid., 160.

30. Ibid., 291–301.

31. Ibid., 162–84.

32. Ibid., 205–7.

33. Cavanaugh, *Torture and Eucharist*, 181.

34. Ibid., 183.

35. Ibid., 172.

36. McElroy, *Search for an American Public Theology*, 80.

37. Murray, "Doctrine Is Dead," 275–83.

38. Ibid., 283.

39. Ibid., 285–89; see also Hooper, "Cups Half Full," 162–65; McElroy, *Search for an American Public Theology*, 122.

40. Murray, "Juridical Organization," 28–41.

41. Porter, "In the Wake," 27.

42. Murray, "Origins and Authority," 109.

43. Porter, "In the Wake," 33–36.

44. Murray, "Doctrine Lives," 297.

45. Aquinas, *Summa Theologica*, I-II, q. 96, a. 2.

46. Murray, "Doctrine Lives," 297–98.

47. Murray, "Pattern for Peace," 15.

48. Hollenbach, Lovin, Coleman, and Hehir, "Current Theology," 705–6.

49. Schindler, *Heart of the World*, 60–71.

50. Gould, "Liberal Political Culture," 122.

51. Murray, "Origins and Authority," 110–13.

52. Murray, "Civilization of the Pluralist Society," 6–15.

53. Murray, "Two Cases for the Public Consensus," 80.

54. Murray, "Origins and Authority," 117–18.

55. Ibid., 99.

56. Murray, "E Pluribus Unum," 36–37; see also Murray, "Freedom in the Age of Renewal," 182.

57. Hollenbach, "Public Theology in America," 297.

58. Murray, "Civilization of the Pluralist Society," 15–22.

59. Murray, "Two or One," 201–11.

60. Murray, "Doctrine and Policy," 228–29.

61. Ibid., 222–27.

62. Ibid., 227–33.

63. Murray, "Things Old and New," 251–54.

64. Klejment, "Radical Origins," 23–24; see also Chatfield, "Catholic Worker," 1.

65. Day, "Our Country Passes," 52–53.

66. Day, "CW Stand on the Use of Force," 36–37.

67. Baxter, "'Blowing the Dynamite,'" 79–87.

68. Day, *Long Loneliness*, 77–79.

69. Ibid., 243–65.

70. Merriman, *Searching for Christ*, 158–63.

71. Zwick and Zwick, *Catholic Worker Movement*, 235.

72. Day, *House of Hospitality*, 112.

73. Ibid., 125.

74. According to Merriman, Day had not taken part in a Lacouture retreat by this point, but had possibly read notes from such a retreat that were given to her by Maisie Ward, the publisher of *House of Hospitality*. Merriman, *Searching for Christ*, 139–41.

75. Day, *On Pilgrimage*, 136.

76. Ibid., 191–93.

77. Day, *Long Loneliness*, 246–47.

78. Augustine, *On Christian Doctrine*, 1.4–5, 22; Augustine, *City of God*, 4.28.

79. Second Vatican Council, *Gaudium et spes*, 39.

80. Day, *Long Loneliness*, 247.

81. Day, *Therese*; see also Hooper, "Dorothy Day's Transposition," 68–86.

82. Merriman, *Searching for Christ*, 145.

83. McNeal, "Catholic Peace Organizations," 40; Yocum Mize, "'We Are Still Pacifists,'" 466–73.

84. Day, "CW Stand on the Use of Force," 36–37.

85. Klejment, "Radical Origins," 26. "Lyrical left" is Klejment's term for the assorted intellectual socialists and anarchists of the time.

86. Ibid., 15–16.

87. Ibid., 18–19.

88. Day, "Catholic Worker Positions."

89. Day, *Loaves and Fishes*, 86.

90. Although Day differed from Marx and Lenin in this regard, she was hardly alone in her views. See, for example, Beard, *Devil Theory of War*.

91. For example, Day writes, "Employment in this machine age is tied up with preparedness, armaments, war, and recovery from war." *On Pilgrimage*, 93–94. See also ibid., 100, 152–53.

92. Day, "On Pilgrimage—Sept. 1967."

93. Day, *Long Loneliness*, 178; Day, *On Pilgrimage*, 151.

94. Zwick and Zwick, *Catholic Worker Movement*, 262.

CHAPTER SEVEN

· ·

THE TWENTIETH-CENTURY POPES
AND THE SECOND VATICAN COUNCIL

BEGINNING WITH POPE Leo XIII, the neoscholasticism exemplified by the works of Francisco de Vitoria and Francisco Suarez has been central to papal thinking on war and peace. On the other hand, papal thinking in this period also gradually shifted toward the modern view of politics as a practical realm divorced from transcendent ends, culminating in the thought of Pope John XXIII. This conception of politics sat uneasily with the natural law tradition that provided the basic framework for papal thought, but it nevertheless led John XXIII to adopt three principles typical of liberal international relations theory: the assumption that states are rational actors; the assertion that fear, partiality, and ignorance are the root causes of war; and the belief that these weaknesses can be overcome by the establishment of international institutions. The neoscholastic-liberal framework that John XXIII developed in his encyclicals has continued to shape official Catholic teaching on the origins of war ever since. The Second Vatican Council, which met from 1962 to 1965, accepted and ratified the mid-century shifts in Catholic theology described in chapter 5, but its treatment of war continued to be based on the mix of neoscholasticism and liberalism found in Pope John's writings. This theoretical framework continued to influence John's successor, Paul VI, as well.

THE PRECONCILIAR POPES

In several of his encyclicals, Pope Leo XIII (1810–1903, pope 1878–1903) laid out the neoscholastic view of politics, which can be summarized by three main points. The first is that both human society and government are natural, rather than human inventions.[1] The second is that the government's authority over society originates with God, with the implications that leaders must govern according to the natural law established by God and that the people have a moral obligation to obey the government unless it commands something contrary to the natural law.[2] The third point is that "the social question," that is, the proper ordering of society, cannot be divorced from religion; according to Leo, "it is, above all, a moral and religious matter, and for that reason must be settled by the principles of morality and according to the dictates of religion."[3] Although he believes that the natural law, and therefore the right ordering of political society, is knowable by reason apart from revelation, Leo maintains the essential role of religion for two reasons: Sin weakens humanity's faculty of reason, and therefore we need the aid of revelation in discerning the requirements of the natural law; and God's relationship with humanity (as Creator and source of morality) is itself a part of the natural order, discernible to a limited extent by reason. Therefore Leo clearly rejects the modern presuppositions that human life is without a transcendent end and that political life can be separated from religion. The framework Leo outlined would have a significant impact on later popes' writings on issues of war and peace.

One important feature of the preconciliar popes' neoscholastic framework is the claim that conflict is caused by the abandonment of Christianity. Pope Benedict XV (1854–1922, pope 1914–22) writes that World War I was caused by the lack of Christian principles.[4] In his first encyclical *Ubi arcano Dei consilio*, Pius XI (1857–1939, pope 1922–39) claims that although after World War I the nations of Europe had made peace on paper, "the law of violence held sway so long that it has weakened and almost obliterated all traces of those natural feelings of love and mercy which the law of Christian charity has done so much to encourage."[5] Society's evils are caused by "inordinate love of the things of the world," and this inordinate love is "the source of all international misunderstandings and rivalries."[6] In another encyclical, Pius admonishes, "Tear the very idea of God from the hearts of men, and they are necessarily urged by their passions to the most atrocious barbarity."[7] Pius XII (1876–1958, pope 1939–58) writes, "Who can express astonishment if peace and war thus prove to be closely connected with religious truth? Everything that is, is of God: the root of all evil consists precisely in separating things from their beginning and their end."[8] In these statements the preconciliar popes very clearly reject the presuppositions of modern political thought.

These popes also agree that charity is the remedy for conflict. According to Benedict XV, "there can be no stable peace or lasting treaties, though made after long and difficult negotiations and duly signed, unless there be a return of mutual charity to appease hate and banish enmity."[9] Pius XI writes that charity, which is not opposed to justice but goes beyond it, is necessary for curing society's ills.[10] Pius XII also asserts that peace and justice require the grace of God expressed through acts of charity.[11] Other statements by Pius XII reveal the neoscholastic framework behind these popes' statements on charity: Charity is something supernatural added on to what is required for justice and peace, which are natural virtues, rather than something that forms the content of justice and peace; charity does not establish peace, but rather "consolidates" peace; and Christian faith among political leaders is "particularly valuable" for the establishment of moral order in international society, but only belief in God is strictly necessary.[12] Despite its separation of charity from justice, and therefore the supernatural realm from the natural realm of politics, this neoscholastic position is a far cry from the total separation of the religious from the political realm in most liberal thought.

The preconciliar popes also distance themselves from liberalism in their attitudes toward international institutions. Despite initially giving it his support, after seeing the League of Nations in action Benedict decided that it was not a worthy institution. Like the realists, Benedict recognizes that the supposed ideals of the League of Nations and the Treaty of Versailles masked the ambitions of the victorious powers. Unlike the realists, Benedict argues that peace can flourish only in the presence of charity, not the "atheistic and utilitarian" principles that inspired the League.[13] Pius XI claims that the failure to see the spiritual roots of conflict would lead to the failure of the League. Because of the spiritual root of conflict, the church has an essential role in world politics, just as it did in the Middle Ages when it was the "true League of Nations": "There exists an institution able to safeguard the sanctity of the law of nations. This institution is a part of every nation; at the same time it is above all nations. She enjoys, too, the highest authority, the fullness of the teaching power of the Apostles. Such an institution is the Church of Christ."[14] Like Benedict XV, Pius XII in principle supported an international political authority as part of the proper ordering of international society and was initially enthusiastic about the United Nations, which was established in 1945 at the end of World War II. But he became disenchanted with the institution because of its ineffectiveness, brought about by the presence of the Soviet Union on the Security Council; for Pius this ineffectiveness amounted to a failure to respect the moral order.[15] The popes from Leo XIII to Pius XII, therefore, drew on a neoscholastic framework that, although accommodating modern political thought to some extent, continued to resist its basic presuppositions.

POPE JOHN XXIII

John XXIII (1881–1963, pope 1958–63) clearly followed in the tradition of his predecessors in his perspective on international politics, but also departed from them in important ways. Like his predecessors, John emphasized the divine moral order that governs politics, both nationally and internationally, but to an unprecedented degree he also emphasized the importance of human rights and democracy. John also maintained the neoscholastic separation of justice and charity, which was associated with the theological distinction between the natural and supernatural, but at least in some of John's writings this separation also represents a separation of the practical realm of politics from the spiritual or theoretical realm, moving John closer to modern political thought, particularly to certain strands of liberalism. Because of this division between the temporal or practical and the spiritual or theoretical, John taught that people with quite different and even opposing ideologies could significantly cooperate in the practical realm, an attitude that was particularly reflected in his approach to communism.

John XXIII on Peace and Human Rights

In his writings, John considers the sources of war, contending that the causes of war include the violation of human rights, the belief in false ideas about the state, the lack of respect for other nations, cultural oppression, economic exploitation, and the persecution of religion.[16] He particularly emphasizes economic exploitation between nations as a source of conflict in his 1961 encyclical *Mater et magistra*.[17] John writes not only on war's causes but also on its prevention. He rejects the view that peace can be ensured by the balance of armaments. The arms race does not create peace but rather elevates the risk of war, because it creates fear; it is particularly foolish because of the destructive power of nuclear weapons.[18] John claims that "men nowadays are becoming more and more convinced that any disputes which may arise between nations must be resolved by negotiation and agreement, and not by recourse to arms." He concludes: "Thus, in this age which boasts of its atomic power, it no longer makes sense to maintain that war is a fit instrument with which to repair the violation of justice."[19] Brian M. Kane argues that although this last passage seems to suggest that John forbids all war, the prohibition pertains only to offensive wars, since elsewhere John defends a state's right to self-defense.[20] Still, it was the strongest statement against war ever issued by a pope.

John's comments on the morality of war are only part of a broader perspective on international order based on the natural law. John begins his encyclical *Pacem in terris* with the following words: "Peace on Earth—which man throughout the ages has so longed for and sought after—can never be established, never guaranteed, except by the diligent observance of the divinely established order."[21] The moral order is stamped on each person's soul, but many people fall into error, which leads to conflict.[22] Observance of the moral order, on the other hand, leads to harmony. The rights of states are an important component of the moral order. Like individuals, "nations are the subjects of reciprocal rights and duties," and states should be considered equals, differences in development and power not giving one nation the right to dominate another.[23]

John also notes the growing interdependence of nations and believes that it must be managed by international institutions. In *Mater et magistra*, John points to growing international interdependence as one of the "signs of the times."[24] Technology has fostered increasingly intricate relations among states, and states face problems that they cannot manage alone. People feel the need for international cooperation, but are hindered from working toward it by mistrust, which can only be overcome through recognition of the moral order established by God.[25] John also notes this growing interdependence in *Pacem in terris* and argues that the need for international cooperation demands the establishment of a worldwide public authority. Such a public authority cannot be established by force, but rather by free consent, and must operate with fairness and impartiality. It must be guided by the principle of subsidiarity, taking to itself only those responsibilities that states are not able to fulfill on their own. John believes that the United Nations could become this worldwide public authority, especially because the United Nations' 1948 Universal Declaration of Human Rights provides a moral framework for international order.[26]

International institutions are essential for peace, according to John, but peace also requires that states themselves be well ordered. Again, this requirement is expressed primarily in terms of rights and duties. According to John, "individual human beings are the foundation, the cause and the end of every social institution."[27] Every individual "has rights and duties, which together flow as a direct consequence from his nature. These rights and duties are universal and inviolable, and therefore altogether inalienable."[28] Each individual also has the duty to protect the rights of others and to promote a social order in which the rights of all are respected.[29] Political authority is established by God, so political leaders should govern according to God's moral law. Rulers should govern by free consent rather than coercion. Therefore democracy is a particularly suitable form of government, with due concern for "the stage of development reached by the political community."[30] Although John's emphasis on rights clearly reflects a certain rapprochement with liberalism, his description of a moral order established by God is certainly drawn from the neoscholastic natural law tradition.[31]

Along with a conception of international and domestic order governed by the natural law, John XXIII also inherits from his predecessors an emphasis on the importance of charity. In his 1960 Christmas message, John insists that peace demands more than proper external conditions; it must also include interior transformation. Truth is the basis of international peace and must enlighten justice, and "justice in its turn ought to be integrated and sustained by Christian charity."[32] Human unity must be "based on the precepts of justice and nurtured by charity."[33] International peace is beyond human powers and ultimately depends on God's grace.[34] John's insistence on the importance of charity and grace, like his foundation in the natural law, clearly places him in the neoscholastic tradition.

A Conflicting Convergence

Although John stands in the neoscholastic tradition of his predecessors, he also shows signs of convergence with liberalism in his views on conflict and cooperation. In both *Mater et magistra* and *Pacem in terris*, John describes the possibility of Catholics cooperating with those of other religions and ideologies by finding points of agreement in political, economic, and social matters. One practical result of this approach was his more accommodating stance toward communism and the Soviet Union. In Italy, this led to his endorsement of a political coalition of Christian Democrats and Socialists.[35] John's idea of "cooperation" went beyond a temporary coalition of political parties to achieve limited goals, however. He and his foreign minister Agostino Casaroli softened the Vatican's attitude toward the Soviet Union, recognizing that communism was a long-term reality and seeking "sufficient living space" for the church in Eastern Europe.[36] Such a policy depended on long-term cooperation between groups with fundamentally opposed philosophies. What accounts for John's apparently contradictory beliefs that, on the one hand, well-ordered societies that respect human rights and recognize the moral order established by God are necessary for peace, and on the other hand, that peaceful coexistence at the international level was possible with the totalitarian Soviet Union?

The reason for John's optimism is a subtle shift in his understanding of the natural order, including the political order, and the natural law that governs it. When discussing the possibility of cooperation with non-Catholics, John writes in *Pacem in terris* that there is "a clear distinction between a false philosophy of the nature, origin and purpose of men and the world, and economic, social, cultural, and political undertakings, even when such undertakings draw their origin and inspiration from that philosophy."[37] By itself, this phrase could have two interpretations. The first and more conservative interpretation is that in some cases individuals or groups with widely different philosophies can nevertheless cooperate on those projects that they agree are worthwhile. The second, more radical, interpretation is that these temporal projects have their own rationales that could be understood and agreed to by individuals and groups completely independently of the diverse philosophies that divide them. Although John's statements that errors about the moral order are ultimately the cause of conflict point toward the first interpretation, John consistently takes stands like those toward the Soviet Union and other Eastern bloc governments that equally, if not more so, point toward the second interpretation. John's phrasing is a clear reference to the thought of Jacques Maritain, described in the previous chapter, lending further support to the second interpretation. The reference to Maritain also suggests that John accepts some form of the modern notion that political life can be understood in terms of a reason independent of our broader philosophical beliefs, and in particular the liberal variant that emphasizes the possibilities for cooperation based on that reason. In his writings on the temporal sphere, John also seems to share some characteristically liberal views: that states are rational actors; that conflicts arise because of ignorance, fear, and partiality; and that international institutions can resolve conflicts by overcoming those conditions.

John combines the liberal assumption that individuals and states are rational actors with the natural law framework he inherited from his predecessors, leading him to an extreme form of "natural law optimism." In a remarkable sentence from *Pacem in terris*, he writes, "When society is formed on a basis of rights and duties, men have an immediate grasp of spiritual and intellectual values, and have no difficulty in understanding what is meant by truth, justice, charity and freedom."[38] John's statement is unlike anything written by previous popes, but is quite similar to the liberal belief, characteristic of Locke, Kant, and Bentham, that individuals will act in a rational and moral manner once they have established political institutions that overcome their shortcomings as individuals. Unlike the utilitarians, who argued that such institutions allow people to harmonize their rational self-interests for the good of the whole, or Kant, who claimed that political institutions lead people to obey the dictates of practical reason, for John the purpose of such institutions is to lead people to know what the natural law requires and to act on it. The power of political institutions to foster morality overshadows the lingering effects of sin emphasized by John's predecessors. Because John considers the United Nations Universal Declaration of Human Rights an adequate moral basis for international order, it is not a great leap for him to believe that, given the right conditions, under the jurisdiction of the UN states will behave according to the dictates of natural law, regardless of their motivating ideologies.

As further evidence of his optimism about states' capability to act in accord with the natural law, John presents a picture of the possibilities for peace that is practically indistinguishable from that of liberals. In *Pacem in terris*, he writes, "There is general agreement—or at least there should be—that relations between States, as between individuals, must be regulated . . . in accordance with the principles of right reason."[39] John's near equivocation between "is" and "should be" is telling, since elsewhere he seems to assume that most if not all conflicts are the result of misunderstandings between people of otherwise good will. He suggests that every conflict can be reconciled and provides little guidance on what to do when one cannot be. According to John, conflicts between states can be resolved "by establishing contact with one another and by a policy of negotiation."[40] In such a negotiation, "there must be a mutual assessment of the arguments and feelings on both sides, a mature and objective investigation of the situation, and an equitable reconciliation of opposing views."[41] John apparently assumes that this will be sufficient, since he provides no alternative course of action if negotiations fail or if there is no equitable reconciliation.

John's description of international negotiations thus shares two assumptions with liberalism. The first is that states only come into conflict over interests that can be "equitably reconciled" rather than over fundamental values that are difficult, if not impossible, to compromise. The second is that conflicts arise only because of ignorance, bias, and fear: Ignorance of the other's intentions is overcome through "mutual assessment"; the danger of bias is overcome through a "mature and objective investigation of the situation"; and "equitable reconciliation" is necessary so that the parties involved need not fear that the others are gaining an unfair advantage over them. In earlier papal thought, ignorance, bias, and fear would certainly be factors contributing to conflict, but ultimately sin and the lack of charity lay at conflict's roots. John also at times expresses that view, but then it is unclear why negotiations would always be sufficient to overcome conflict.

Finally, John is quite optimistic about the ability of international political institutions to establish peace. As already mentioned, in John's view an international political authority such as the United Nations makes it possible for states to act in accord with the natural law, to which they can all agree despite their diverse ideologies. In terms of war and peace, international institutions do this by facilitating the negotiations that are necessary for resolving conflicts. It is no wonder, then, that John had such hope that the United Nations would be able to maintain peace between the opposing blocs of the cold war, especially when contrasted with Pius XII's pessimism.

The traditional interpretation of John's social thought, exemplified by Charles E. Curran, attributes John's "natural law optimism" solely to his neoscholastic framework.[42] Yet John's predecessors shared that framework, and none of these earlier popes shared his optimism about international cooperation. In particular, his immediate predecessor, Pius XII, held views diametrically opposed to John's on peaceful coexistence with the Soviet Union and on the United Nations' prospects for establishing peace. What distinguished John from earlier popes cannot be explained in terms of the natural law framework that he shared with them. Something changed in John's thought that led to this optimism, and that is the adoption of modern presuppositions into his understanding of the origins of war, despite the fact that when these presuppositions are explicitly stated, he claims to reject them.

John's understanding of the temporal or political sphere became more similar to that of liberalism than that found in traditional neoscholasticism. Neoscholasticism certainly already exhibited some influence from those modern political presuppositions (which, as has already been noted, developed specifically as attacks on the Christian tradition), but at least in its political form, as manifested in the writings of Pope John's papal predecessors, it strongly rejected those presuppositions. Instead of critiquing neoscholasticism at precisely those points where it was open to the negative influences of modern political thought, as theologians such as Rahner and de Lubac did, John modifies neoscholasticism such that what feeble resistance it did mount against modern political thought is, perhaps inevitably, overcome. Although John speaks about recognition of the divine moral order and inner transformation through charity as necessary for peace, these statements have little if any bearing on his more practical statements about the requirements for peace and cooperation. I contend that this is because for John, principally through the influence of Maritain, the truths of the moral order—although connected to metaphysical truths about God, the human person, and the nature of reality—are knowable in a different way than those metaphysical truths; therefore the moral order can be known even by those who reject the truth about these other matters. Regardless of its source, this element of John's thought represents a significant departure from the thought of his predecessors in the papacy. The parallels with political liberalism in John's thought are simply too striking to attribute his optimism to anything other than a shift in his understanding of the political sphere.[43] Official Catholic teaching has continued along these lines, despite the fact that since the middle of the twentieth century, official Catholic teaching has been influenced by theological trends that should have only reinforced the differences between Catholic thought and modern political thought, as described in chapter 5.

THE SECOND VATICAN COUNCIL

The Second Vatican Council, a gathering of all of the bishops of the Catholic Church that met in four sessions between 1962 and 1965, was a time of reform and renewal for the church. The council brought about such needed reforms as a revision of the liturgy and the recognition of religious freedom as a fundamental right. More generally, the council represented an updating of the church's thought, drawing on both the Christian tradition and twentieth-century theology, particularly concerning the nature of the church itself and of the church's relationship to the world as a whole. This renewal included recognizing the insights of theologians into both the historical conditioning of human existence and the relationship between nature and grace. The council served, then, as a ratification of these developments that, as I argued in chapter 5, should have a deep influence on Catholic thinking about war's origins. At the same time, the council sought to address the issues that troubled humanity in the middle of the twentieth century, including questions of war. Despite the Second Vatican Council's many important theological developments, however, its treatment of war remained stuck in the neoscholastic-liberal framework established by John XXIII.

Historical Consciousness at Vatican II

From its very beginning, it was clear that the Second Vatican Council could not be understood apart from the growing sense of historical consciousness in the modern world and within the Catholic Church itself. In his opening speech to the council, Pope John XXIII was clear that the council's purpose was to present the perennial teachings of the church in a way that could be understood by modern persons. He writes that the church "must ever look to the present, to the new conditions and new forms of life introduced into the modern world, which have opened new avenues to the Catholic apostolate." Although the council must preserve the deposit of faith, "the substance of the ancient doctrine of the deposit of faith is one thing, and the way in which it is presented is another."[44] Pope John XXIII therefore set the tone of dialogue with the modern world that would characterize the council.

The documents of Vatican II reflect this openness to dialogue with the world. A central text demonstrating this openness is from the Pastoral Constitution on the Church in the Modern World, *Gaudium et spes*, no. 44: "Since the Church has a visible and social structure as a sign of her unity in Christ, she can and ought to be enriched by the development of human social life, not that there is any lack in the constitution given her by Christ, but that she can understand it more penetratingly, express it better, and adjust it more successfully to our times."[45] The bishops recognize that people's ways of thinking are affected by their historical situation, and the church must therefore learn from the world in order to present the Gospel message in a way that is understandable to the people of the present. The church seeks to discern "the signs of the times" in order to "recognize and understand the world in which we live, its explanations, its longings, and its often dramatic characteristics" and, "in language intelligible to each generation, . . . respond to the perennial questions which men ask about this present life and the life to come, and about the relationship of the one to the other."[46]

The documents of the Second Vatican Council give concrete form to this awareness of the historical conditioning of human existence. The Decree on Ecumenism, *Unitatis redintegratio*; the Declaration on the Relation of the Church to Non-Christian Religions, *Nostra aetate*; and *Gaudium et spes* show a profound sensitivity to the existential situation of non-Catholic Christians, non-Christians, and atheists in their relation to the transcendent.[47] *Gaudium et spes* also for the first time recognizes that there may be diverse ways of solving social problems in different cultures. In chapter III of part II of *Gaudium et spes*, the council recognizes that the developed and developing countries, and even various regions within single countries, face very different social conditions, and therefore require different sorts of policies.[48] The bishops make similar points in chapter IV, on political life. They begin by making the traditional point that "the choice of a political regime and the appointment of rulers are left to the free will of citizens," but then add that this variety stems from "the character of different peoples and their historic development."[49]

Gaudium et spes expresses the church's recognition of historical consciousness above all in the chapter on culture. Chapter II of part II begins, "Man comes to a true and full humanity only through culture, that is, through the cultivation of the goods and values of nature." Culture is the use and development of natural goods by free human beings. Likewise, the document states, "From day to day, in every group or nation, there is an increase in the number of men and women who are conscious that they themselves are the authors and the artisans of the culture of their community." The council recognizes that there is a diversity of cultures, and it is through their being passed on "that there is formed the definite, historical milieu which enfolds the man of every nation and age and from which he draws the values which permit him to promote civilization."[50]

Chapter II of part II of *Gaudium et spes* also explores the relationship between the Christian faith and the diverse cultures of the world. Christians are called to take part in the various cultures in which they find themselves, and in fact their lives ought to reveal the full meaning of culture found in Jesus Christ. The cultures of the world remain open to Christ, "for God, revealing Himself to His people to the extent of a full manifestation of Himself in His Incarnate Son, has spoken according to the culture proper to each epoch," and the church is not bound to any one culture, but rather adapts to the different cultures of the world. At the same time, "the Gospel of Christ constantly renews the life and culture of fallen man, it combats and removes the errors and evils resulting from the permanent allurement of sin."[51] Human culture is fulfilled by grace, and grace only transforms humanity by means of culture.[52] Clearly, besides reflecting the historicity of the human person, this chapter's emphasis on the presence of sin and grace in culture reflects the influence of twentieth-century theology concerning nature and grace.

Nature and Grace at Vatican II

As a whole, the documents of the Second Vatican Council reflect the changes in Catholic theology concerning the relationship between nature and grace. In fact, a study of the history of the writing of the council documents reveals that the bishops rejected the positions of the Roman Curia's neoscholastic theologians in favor of the new trends in theology. Many of the documents demonstrate this shift, but above all this is true of *Gaudium et spes*, which emphasizes that Jesus Christ is the key to understanding all of human existence and that human history must be understood as the stage on which salvation history plays out.

Several of the documents' themes reflect the council's understanding of nature and grace. The Dogmatic Constitution on the Church, *Lumen gentium*, recovers traditional ways of thinking about the church that were critical for renewing the Catholic understanding of the church's relationship with the world.[53] *Lumen gentium* also insists that all Christian believers, including laypeople, are called to holiness, thereby rejecting the view that the layperson's life in the world is a life concerned only with natural goods, not with the supernatural.[54] The Decree on the Apostolate of Lay People, *Apostolicam actuositatem*, makes the same point.[55] As Charles E. Curran notes, even the Constitution on the Sacred Liturgy, *Sacrosanctum concilium*, "insists on a close relationship between liturgy and life. The liturgy, especially the Eucharist, constitutes the summit toward which all of the activity of the church is directed and the font from which all of its power and life flows," including the life of the faithful in the world.[56] It is in *Gaudium et spes*, however, that the renewed understanding of nature and grace becomes most clear.

The council best expresses the renewed sense of nature's fulfillment by grace in the Christological focus of part I of *Gaudium et spes*. In paragraph 10, the bishops affirm, "The Church firmly believes that Christ, who died and was raised up for all, can through His Spirit offer man the light and the strength to measure up to his supreme destiny," and further, that the church "likewise holds that in her most benign Lord and Master can be found the key, the focal point and the goal of man, as well as of all human history."[57] Perhaps the most important passage comes from paragraph 22: "The truth is that only in the mystery of the incarnate Word does the mystery of man take on light. For Adam, the first man, was a figure of Him Who was to come, namely Christ the Lord. Christ, the final Adam, by the revelation of the mystery of the Father and His love, fully reveals man to man himself and makes his supreme calling clear."[58] This passage presents a bold Christological interpretation of human life. Later the bishops write that the unity of humanity is fulfilled in communion with Christ and is a likeness of the communion of the three Persons of the Trinity.[59] These passages represent a clear shift from the natural law approach of earlier social encyclicals to a more theological and scriptural approach, demonstrating a fresh emphasis on the significance of theology for interpreting human existence in all its aspects.[60] The church seeks dialogue with others not by beginning with certain natural truths knowable to all through reason, but by presenting humanism as a shared ideal, then showing how the light of Christ transforms this ideal.[61]

Gaudium et spes presents not only a more theological understanding of the human person than do previous documents, but also of human history as a whole. For example, the bishops claim that sin is not simply a personal reality, but rather that "all of human life, whether individual or collective, shows itself to be a dramatic struggle between good and evil, between light and darkness."[62] Later they expand on this point in stark terms: "For a monumental struggle against the powers of darkness pervades the whole history of man. The battle was joined from the very origins of the world and will continue until the last day, as the Lord has attested. Caught in this conflict, man is obliged to wrestle constantly if he is to cling to what is good, nor can he achieve his own integrity without great efforts and the help of God's grace."[63] Human activity in the world is corrupted by sin but can also be transformed by God's grace. What we do in this world is integrally related to our ultimate supernatural destiny, in which our work will be transformed and fulfilled.[64] The Holy Spirit is at work in human efforts to bring about societies in which the human person flourishes.[65] In fact, the "communitarian character [of society] is developed and consummated in the work of Jesus Christ."[66]

Because we primarily find Christ through the church, the church has a critical role to play in history. *Gaudium et spes* states, "Since it has been entrusted to the Church to reveal the mystery of God, Who is the ultimate goal of man, she opens up to man at the same time the meaning of his own existence, that is, the innermost truth about himself."[67] Even though the church's mission is religious, not political or economic, the church sheds light on the ultimate significance of the political and economic spheres.[68]

Even if its true meaning lies in the church, the world retains a "legitimate autonomy," because "by the very circumstance of their having been created, all things are endowed with their own stability, truth, goodness, proper laws and order. Man must respect these as he isolates them by the appropriate methods of the individual sciences or arts." But if the concept of legitimate autonomy "is taken to mean that created things do not depend on God, and that man can use them without any reference to their Creator, anyone who acknowledges God will see how false such a meaning is."[69] This passage seems to be primarily concerned with the legitimate autonomy of the natural sciences, which is a fairly uncontested claim, but it also refers to the human sciences and therefore to our understanding of human society. How can the idea that human society has its "own stability, truth, goodness, proper laws and order" be reconciled with the idea that human society finds its ultimate significance in Christ through the church and can only fully be understood in a theological light?

In a way, the "stability, truth, goodness, proper laws and order" of human society correspond to the "natural order" within the human person described by Henri de Lubac. That natural order has its own integrity and yet has no final end of its own; rather, it is fulfilled by a supernatural end and therefore is only fully understood in light of the supernatural. Likewise, human society is an essential part of human nature and is necessary for the pursuit of certain human goods. To some extent, the institutions that humans develop for these purposes have their own order and can be studied by the social sciences. At the same time, human society only finds its fulfillment in communion with Christ and must be understood in that light.[70] Clearly, then, *Gaudium et spes* reflects the two significant changes in twentieth-century Catholic theology—the awareness of historicity and the renewed understanding of nature and grace—but unfortunately these changes are not reflected in the bishops' treatment of war in part II.

Gaudium et spes on War

Despite the new theological approach of part I of *Gaudium et spes*, the treatment of war and peace in chapter V of part II continues to reflect the juxtaposition of neoscholasticism and liberalism found in John XXIII's *Pacem in terris*. Because of the way that *Gaudium et spes* was written, the theological insights evident in part I very rarely found their way into part II, which deals with concrete issues. Chapter V, "Fostering of Peace and Establishment of a Community of Nations," which deals primarily with issues of war and peace, reflects the mix of natural law thinking and liberalism found in *Pacem in terris* and therefore contains many of the same drawbacks concerning war and its origins. Despite its call to examine war "with an entirely new attitude," chapter V presents little that is new in interpreting war as a human phenomenon, although it does take new stands on questions about the morality of war, such as condemning terrorism and arguing for making legal provisions for conscientious objectors.[71]

The chapters of part II of *Gaudium et spes* remain distinct in style and theological emphasis from the chapters of part I. As Charles E. Curran explains, "The lack of integration between the two parts of *Gaudium et spes* derives somewhat from the historical fact that they were developed on separate tracks and really were not integrated to form a coherent whole."[72] From the very beginning of the drafting of the document that became *Gaudium et spes*, parts I and II were crafted separately, and as the theological style of part I changed radically through the revision process, part II remained relatively the same.[73] Chapter II of part II, on culture, is a notable exception.[74] As a result of this process, chapter V, on war and peace, retains the neoscholastic, natural law style of earlier church documents.

This is not immediately evident when one begins to read the chapter, because the preface is written with a theological focus reminiscent of part I. In the later stages of composition of *Gaudium et spes*, many of the bishops and theological advisers began to complain that there was little connection between the two parts; in an attempt to solve this problem, the authors inserted prefaces meant to reflect the more theological themes of part I.[75] Although it does not express the bishops' main points on war and peace, the preface to chapter V is nevertheless significant for understanding the council's views on the origins of war because it deals with the notion of peace. The preface begins by noting the growing horror of war in the modern world; therefore, "the Gospel message, which is in harmony with the loftier strivings and aspirations of the human race, takes on a new luster in our day as it declares that the artisans of peace are blessed 'because they will be called the sons of God' (Matt. 5:9)."[76] The bishops go on to define peace: "Peace is not merely the absence of war; nor can it be reduced solely to the maintenance of a balance of power between enemies; nor is it brought about by dictatorship." Rather, peace involves the establishment of justice, or the pursuit of the common good of humanity, which reflects the eternal law established by God. Yet, the bishops continue, "this is not enough. . . . Peace is likewise the fruit of love, which goes beyond what justice can provide." They elaborate in theological terms: "That earthly peace which arises from love of neighbor symbolizes and results from the peace of Christ which radiates from God the Father." Therefore Christ is the key to overcoming violence: "Insofar as men are sinful, the threat of war hangs over them, and hang over them it will until the return of Christ. But insofar as men vanquish sin by a union of love, they will vanquish violence as well."[77] It is clear in the preface that although peace requires economic and political changes, ultimately it depends on spiritual transformation. In the rest of the chapter, however, the Christological focus of the preface is less evident.

Chapter V of part II of *Gaudium et spes* sounds remarkably similar to John XXIII's *Pacem in terris* when it describes the causes of war and the strategies for preventing war. The bishops write: "Not a few of these causes [of war] come from excessive economic inequalities and from putting off the steps needed to remedy them. . . . Other causes of discord, however, have their source in the desire to dominate and in a contempt for persons." These are all causes that John recognized. Finally, however, "if we look for deeper causes, we find them in human envy, distrust, pride, and other egotistical passions."[78] Here it does sound as if sin plays an important role in the origins of war.

When they offer solutions to these deeper causes, the bishops seem to back-track. To solve the problems that cause war, they propose that "it is absolutely necessary for countries to cooperate more advantageously and more closely together and to organize together international bodies and to work tirelessly for the creation of organizations which will foster peace."[79] The document goes on to assert that humanity must strive to establish more adequate international organizations, building on those already in place.[80] The council fathers also point out that peace is not only a matter of institutions but also of personal attitudes; therefore "there is above all a pressing need for a renewed education of attitudes and for new inspiration in public opinion," although they are not clear about what this education should look like.[81]

The bishops are correct to note that international institutions must play an important role in establishing peace, but other crucial pieces of the puzzle are lacking in their description of what is necessary for peace, such as any descrip-tion of culture as the basis for properly functioning institutions, let alone a culture transformed by the Gospel. For example, they say very little about the cultural preconditions for the establishment of just international institutions: Does there have to be a generally just culture among states for just international institutions to be established? Nor do they discuss how just international institu-tions must be maintained through the practices of the states that compose them, or how states can subvert these institutions through their actions. The bishops almost seem to assume that properly ordered institutions would have a practi-cally automatic effect on state behavior. Their practical proposals in the body of the chapter do not fully correspond to their reflections on peace in the preface.

Of course, institutions do shape the behavior of the actors who are part of them, but this does not take place in an automatic way. As the constructivists argue, the international system, and its embodiment in international institutions, shapes the identities, interests, and norms of the states that constitute it precisely through the same process in which those states shape the international system. By ignoring the role that states play in shaping and maintaining international institutions through their choices, the bishops writing in *Gaudium et spes* also downplay the role of sin in this process. Sin is a persistent part of human life, as the bishops themselves recognize; by downplaying its role in the behavior of states and in the international system itself, the bishops exaggerate the potential for international institutions to establish peace, just as John XXIII had. This pattern would also be found in the thought of John's successor Paul VI, who even more clearly demonstrates the weaknesses in the neoscholastic-liberal view of war's origins.

POPE PAUL VI

In his reflections on war and peace, Pope Paul VI took up the neoscholastic-liberal framework of John XXIII. In his diplomacy, Paul continued to promote peaceful coexistence between East and West. He also reflected more on the origins of war than any previous pope. Like John, Paul believed that international institutions, especially the United Nations, must play a vital role in establishing peace. The highly exalted role he gives to the United Nations, in fact, shows a failure to adequately incorporate contemporary theology's reflections on historicity and nature and grace into his views on war and peace.

The Diplomacy of Pope Paul VI

In many ways, the diplomacy of Pope Paul VI (1897–1978, pope 1963–78) was a continuation of that of Pope John XIII. As substitute for Pius XII's secretary of state and as archbishop of Milan, Giovanni Montini had developed ties with Angelo Roncalli, later John XXIII, and was thought of as "John's chosen and logical successor."[82] In his Vatican career prior to becoming pope, Montini was a leading advocate for Christian Democracy in Italy. As pope, Paul VI continued to seek dialogue with the Communists in Eastern Europe and work for peace between the Eastern and Western blocs. Finally, more than previous popes, Paul became engaged with the third world.

Beginning in the 1930s, Giovanni Montini was a significant figure in the Christian Democracy movement in Italy and became a leader among the anti-Fascist intellectuals in Italy, many of whom, including Montini, were influenced by the French Catholic philosopher Jacques Maritain, discussed in chapter 6.[83] During the Second World War, Montini acted as Pius XII's representative in efforts to plan the democratic future of Italy after the war.[84] He played an important role in establishing the Christian Democracy Party's dominance in post-war Italy.[85] Even after his election as pope, Paul VI supported the ideals of the Christian Democrats and was called "the Christian Democratic Pope."[86] As pope, however, Paul's attention moved beyond Italy to the rest of the world.

As pope, Paul VI continued John's policies toward the Communist East; his concerted diplomatic efforts in this area were known as his *Ostpolitik*.[87] He continued to believe that communication with the Communists was necessary, although he recognized that, because dialogue requires some common ground between the interlocutors, dialogue with the Communists would be "difficult, but not impossible," a case of "hope against hope."[88] In 1967 Paul VI appointed Agostino Casaroli as his secretary for public affairs, in charge of the foreign relations of the Vatican and therefore of its *Ostpolitik*.[89] Based on an interview with Casaroli, George Weigel describes Paul VI and Casaroli's *Ostpolitik* as concerned with maintaining "breathing space" for the Catholic Church in Eastern Europe.[90] Paul VI's *Ostpolitik* understood diplomacy as the pursuit of economic and political interests, and Paul worked to minimize the ideological differences between West and East, while Casaroli saw himself as the representative of the Catholic Church's institutional interests.[91] Paul had some success in protecting the rights of the Church in Eastern bloc countries, but at the price of a constraint on Vatican criticism of communism.[92]

Paul VI's engagement with the third world was perhaps more positive than his *Ostpolitik*. Although John XXIII's 1961 encyclical *Mater et magistra* and Vatican II's *Gaudium et spes* in 1965 expressed concern for the social problems of the third world, Vatican attention to the third world came into its own with Paul VI's 1967 encyclical *Populorum progressio*, which promoted development in all its forms. Paul also demonstrated his concern for the developing world by his unprecedented travels to countries such as India, Uganda, and Colombia.[93] Paul traveled to Colombia for the opening of the second meeting of the Episcopal Conference of Latin America (CELAM) in Medellín. According to Peter Hebblethwaite, the Medellín documents applied the pope's teaching in *Populorum progressio* to the situation of the church in Latin America and were also a milestone in the development of Latin American liberation theology.[94] Paul also sought an end to conflicts in the third world, such as the wars in Biafra and Nigeria, and the Vietnam War.[95]

Pope Paul VI on War and Peace

Paul VI was a tireless promoter of peace, but he was also a defender of the just war ethic defined by his predecessors Pius XII and John XXIII. Perhaps Paul's most well-known statement on war comes from his speech to the United Nations General Assembly in 1965: "Never again one against the other, never, never again! . . . Never again war, never again war! It is peace, peace, that has to guide the destiny of the nations of all mankind!"[96] He also argues that the view that war is inevitable must be rejected.[97] Significantly, he condemns "the realism of facts and interests" that claims "that what matters is force; [that] man will at best reduce the combination of forces to a balance of opposition, but organized society cannot do without force."[98] Paul seems to be referring to the realist notion of the security dilemma, in which all other nations necessarily are threats and the best that can be hoped for is a balance of power. Nevertheless, Paul is clear that countries have the right to defend themselves and that peace should not be confused with cowardice in the face of one's duty to defend country, justice, and liberty.[99] Paul also condemns violent revolution, terrorism, and other acts of political violence.[100]

Paul spends relatively little time describing the causes of war. In *Populorum progressio*, he specifically mentions as sources of violence the injustices caused by colonialism as well as racism among both the former colonizers and the newly independent nations.[101] In his message for the 1975 World Day of Peace, Paul mentions "new forms of jealous nationalism," "touchy rivalries based on race, language and traditions," "sad situations of poverty and hunger," "exclusive and arrogant ideologies," "territorial conflicts," and the nuclear arms race as sources of conflict.[102] On the same occasion in 1976, Paul writes that the world is "radically divided by irreconcilable ideologies" that cause conflict among states and within states.[103] Paul seems to see ideology as having a larger role in the causes of international conflict than John XXIII did, although he does not go into much detail describing that role.

Besides making these brief claims about the origins of war, Paul VI offers important reflections about what is necessary for peace. Like his predecessors Pius XII and John XXIII, he claims that peace can only exist when justice prevails. Justice is above all found in respect for the dignity and equality of human persons. Significantly, Paul asserts that the modern demand for equality and participation, which are necessary for peace, can only be achieved through democracy.[104] He also declares that the justice required for peace among states includes faithfully following international agreements. According to Paul, this is one reason why international institutions are necessary: to help establish and enforce these agreements.[105]

Like John XXIII, Paul VI assigns international organizations, especially the United Nations, an important role in preserving peace. Early in his career, Montini had already been critical of the Vatican's hostility to the League of Nations in the 1930s.[106] In *Populorum progressio*, Paul writes that international collaboration is necessary to overcome poverty, one of the sources of conflict, and praises international organizations like the United Nations that are engaged in fostering development.[107] International organizations that have been established to promote peace must be respected and supported, and this is above all true of the United Nations.[108] Paul's attitude toward international organizations such as the United Nations, however, continued to be shaped by the neoscholastic-liberal framework developed by John. His writings on this subject show very little influence from contemporary theological trends concerning historicity and the relationship between nature and grace, despite their impact on other areas of his thought.

Pope Paul VI on Historicity and Nature and Grace

Paul VI is the first pope to seriously grapple with the issue of historicity in his writings. John XXIII had already begun to think of the church's social teaching as a set of principles that needed to be applied in diverse situations and of the Catholic faith itself as something that must be presented in ways appropriate to each time and place, but Paul takes these ideas even further. In *Ecclesiam suam*, he states that the church must adapt itself to the situations where it finds itself.[109] In a famous passage from *Octogesima adveniens*, Paul states that because of the widely varying situations of the modern world, the church has no unified message when it comes to social teaching: "It is up to the Christian communities to analyze with objectivity the situation which is proper to their own country, to shed on it the light of the Gospel's unalterable words and to draw principles of reflection, norms of judgment and directives for action from the social teaching of the Church."[110] This passage "was heralded as a central expression of a historically conscious methodology in magisterial teaching."[111] In *Evangelii nuntiandi*, Paul echoes *Gaudium et spes* by claiming that the Gospel must be adapted to the diverse cultures of the world.[112] His acknowledgment of the important role of culture and ideology in creating conflict among states is probably due to his recognition of historicity.

When looking at the international system as a whole, however, rather than individual states, Paul does not seem to apply these insights, instead implying that the states share a basic agreement on moral principles. For example, writing in 1970 he claims that "the world's conscience no longer tolerates such crimes [as terrorism, torture, repression, concentration camps, killing hostages, etc.], the fierce inhumanity of which turns back in dishonor on those who perform them."[113] Nevertheless, the world continued to tolerate these things in places such as Latin America, the Middle East, and Southeast Asia. Four years later, Paul writes: "The idea of Peace is already victorious in the thought of all men in posts of responsibility. We have confidence in their up to date wisdom, their energy and ability. No head of a nation can today wish for war; every one yearns for the general Peace of the world."[114] It is not clear on what basis Paul could make such a statement. Whereas elsewhere he describes ideology as a primary cause of war, when he looks at the international system as a whole, and its institutional embodiment in the United Nations, he sees "peaceful coexistence in diversity of ideologies and forms of government" as a realistic possibility.[115] Paul's insistence that the nations of the world share a commitment to peace and can peacefully coexist despite their differences in ideology, besides being naïve, shows that he does not fully consider the ways in which the cultures and ideologies of those nations shape their behavior. As I will demonstrate shortly, Paul shares John's notion that individuals and political entities have immediate access to moral truths independently of their theoretical beliefs and ideologies.

Although Paul shows some awareness of historicity (albeit applying it unevenly), his writings scarcely ever reflect the developments in the Catholic understanding of the relationship between nature and grace. In many of his statements, Paul gives an important place to supernatural charity in establishing peace. For example, in his "1971 World Day of Peace Message," he writes, "A true brotherhood, among men, to be authentic and binding, presupposes and demands a transcendental Fatherhood overflowing with metaphysical love, with supernatural charity."[116] To the question of how peace can be realized, Paul responds, "We answer in terms that may be inaccessible to those who have closed the horizon of reality to natural vision alone. Recourse must be had to that religious world which we call 'supernatural.'"[117] Paul particularly emphasizes the importance of forgiveness and reconciliation for peace, which seems absurd to the modern ear.[118] This emphasis on the supernatural might seem to show the influence of the mid-century theologians who had such impact on the Second Vatican Council, but other statements by Paul show that this is not the case.

Neoscholasticism's influence on Paul is evident in his World Day of Peace messages. Paul writes that although the substance of what temporal peace entails can be understood without reference to Christ, "for us Christians, . . . peace is above all the result of the implementation of that design of wisdom and love, through which God willed to enter into supernatural relations with mankind."[119] This statement suggests that God's "supernatural relations with mankind" pertain primarily to humanity's spiritual dimension as experienced by "us Christians" and have little concrete significance for the temporal dimension considered in itself. In his 1976 message, Paul writes: "This message too must have its appendix for those properly called followers and servants of the Gospel—an appendix which recalls how explicit and demanding Christ our Lord is in regard to this theme of peace stripped of every weapon and armed only with goodness and love."[120] It is significant that Paul sees the Gospel as important for international peace, but it is telling that he sees it as an "appendix" to temporal peace understood on its own terms, just as in neoscholastic theology grace is an extrinsic addition to a human nature already complete in itself.

Although retaining a neoscholastic framework in his understanding of nature and grace, Paul also adopts the liberal understanding of the temporal order developed by John. This is above all demonstrated in Paul's encyclical *Populorum progressio*, on economic development, which clearly shows the influence of Paul's friend, the philosopher Jacques Maritain.[121] Paul writes that true development includes not only economic development but also spiritual development.[122] Spiritual development involves the human person directing his or her life toward God, and at an even higher level, uniting with Christ.[123] In *Populorum progressio*, the temporal and the spiritual are two distinct spheres; although the proper development of the temporal sphere requires recognition of the spiritual sphere, the temporal sphere remains relatively complete within itself. On the one hand, this distinction has the effect of limiting the direct influence of sin and grace to the spiritual sphere, having only indirect effects on the temporal sphere. On the other hand, Paul makes more explicit the changed understanding of the temporal sphere already implicitly found in John's encyclicals. This sharp distinction between the temporal and the spiritual is essential for Paul's claim that Christians can legitimately take part in socialist political movements at the temporal level, despite the false ideologies of many of their members; here Paul explicitly draws on John's distinction between historical movements and false philosophies.[124] This distinction of course plays an important role both in Paul's optimism about the possibility for peaceful coexistence on the international stage (just as it had in John's) and in his acceptance of many liberal assumptions about international institutions and peace.

In his speeches and writings, Paul presents a highly exalted view of the United Nations that is influenced by the combination of neoscholastic theology and liberal political assumptions. In a 1963 address to United Nations Secretary General U Thant, Paul describes the United Nations as "the steadily developing and improving form of the balanced and unified life of all humanity in its historical and earthly order."[125] In his 1965 address to the UN General Assembly, Paul calls the UN "the obligatory way of modern civilization and world peace." In a remarkable passage reminiscent of Dante's vision of the universal monarch, Paul says that he is "tempted to say" that the United Nations "reflects in the temporal order what our Catholic Church intends to be in the spiritual order: one and universal. Nothing loftier can be imagined on the natural level, as far as the ideological structure of mankind is concerned."[126] Paul describes the United Nations in very idealistic terms, not fully recognizing that the institution is affected by the same material, cultural, and ideological factors that shape the behavior of the very states that compose it. Paul believes that in some way the United Nations fulfills the temporal order, perhaps even functioning, in theological terms, as humanity's "natural end." If the struggle between sin and grace is limited to a supernatural order separate from the natural and temporal order, then one can ignore or at least downplay the permanent effects of sin on the behavior of states and their role in contributing to war. When this is combined with the liberal assumption that states will behave rationally given the right institutional conditions, it contributes to an extremely optimistic perception of international institutions' potential for creating peace.

Paul maintains his optimism about peace despite dread of nuclear destruction, but this optimism about the temporal sphere is in tension with *Gaudium et spes*'s eschatological focus. In a telling passage from his message for the 1973 World Day of Peace, Paul reveals that behind his hope for peace lies dread: "If these modern organizations which are to promote and protect peace were not fit for their specific function, what would be the fate of the world? If their inefficiency were to cause fatal disillusionment in the minds of men, peace would thereby be defeated, and with it the progress of civilization. Our hope and our conviction that peace is possible would be stifled, first by doubt, then by mockery and skepticism, and in the end by denial. And what an end this would be!"[127]

Because he lived at the height of the cold war nuclear standoff, Paul's fear is understandable, yet, for Christians, isn't our hope in the life to come rather than in this world? This does not mean ignoring this world, "for here grows the body of a new human family, a body which even now is able to give some kind of foreshadowing of the new age." But it is only the life to come "whose blessedness will answer and surpass all the longings for peace which spring up in the human heart."[128] Despite his dread, Paul expresses optimism about humanity's progress toward peace: "For, notwithstanding everything, peace marches on. There are breaks in continuity, there are inconsistencies and difficulties. But all the same peace marches on and is establishing itself in the world with a certain invincibility."[129] Paul's optimism about the inevitable progress of temporal life is in striking contrast with the recognition by *Gaudium et spes* (which itself was criticized for being too optimistic) that our earthly existence will always be marked by sin as well as grace. His neoscholastic understanding of nature and grace, however, leads Paul to think of the natural order as potentially complete within itself, the supernatural order alone awaiting fulfillment in the life to come. Because the whole of humanity is the ultimate natural community, then the institutional organization of that community is its perfection. Just as he does not fully apply his insights into historical consciousness to the international system, not recognizing how the culture and ideologies of individual states affect the culture of the international system and its institutional embodiments, Paul VI also does not fully consider the way in which the international system is penetrated by the mysteries of sin and grace.

CONCLUSION

Beginning with Leo XIII, the popes challenged modern political thought by affirming that human life is governed by a divinely established moral order and that political life cannot be separated from humanity's relationship with God. But beginning with John XXIII, a school of thought that in its origins was an explicit rejection of these ideas has shaped official Catholic thinking on the origins of war. John XXIII represents a shift in Catholic thinking on war and peace, involving a convergence of Catholic neoscholasticism and liberal international relations theory. On the one hand, the popes increasingly emphasized human rights and democracy as noble goals. On the other, the growing separation between the temporal and the spiritual in Catholic social thought allowed several principles of liberal international relations theory that were foreign to the older Catholic tradition of thought on war and peace to become influential in official Catholic teaching. These principles include the assumption that states, at least under the right institutional conditions, are rational actors; the locating of the origins of war in fear, partiality, and ignorance; and the belief that these weaknesses can be overcome by the establishment of international institutions.

The Second Vatican Council ratified many of the important developments in twentieth-century Catholic theology, but in its treatment of war the council failed to take advantage of those insights. Partly because of its history of authorship, Vatican II's *Gaudium et spes* presented an understanding of war and its origins similar to that found in Pope John XXIII's *Pacem in terris*. Both of these documents are rooted in a blend of neoscholastic natural law and liberalism that leads to optimism about the behavior of states and the possibilities of international institutions for resolving conflicts between states. Neither document fully recognized the role of culture in determining state behavior, as described by the constructivists and developed in earlier chapters, and neither fully situated international politics and the struggle for peace within the broad sweep of salvation history.

Pope Paul VI inherited the understanding of the international system developed by John XXIII and the Second Vatican Council, and he too failed to fully integrate the insights of twentieth-century Catholic theology into his understanding of international politics. Paul VI did begin to present a more adequate understanding of the behavior of states as shaped by culture and other historically contingent factors. When it came to understanding the international system as a social structure, Paul followed John XXIII by downplaying the constitutive role that the beliefs and behaviors of states play in forming the international system and therefore underemphasizing the importance of culture for international politics. This led to a liberal optimism about the potential of international institutions for resolving conflicts. As I will argue in the next chapter, despite an even more thorough acceptance of the important trends in twentieth-century Catholic theology, Pope John Paul II maintained much of the neoscholastic-liberal framework of his predecessors.

NOTES

1. Leo XIII, *Diuturnum*, 11.

2. Ibid., 2, 4–8, 15–16; Leo XIII, *Immortale Dei*, 3–5; Leo XIII, *Libertas*, 9, 33–34.

3. Leo XIII, *Graves de communi re*, 11.

4. Benedict XV, *Ad beatissimi apostolorum*, 5.

5. Pius XI, *Ubi arcano Dei consilio*, 20–21.

6. Ibid., 24–25.

7. Pius XI, *Divini redemptoris*, 21.

8. Pius XII, "1954 Christmas Message," 188.

9. Benedict XV, *Pacem Dei munus pulcherrimum*, 1.

10. Pius XI, *Divini redemptoris*, 46, 49.

11. Pius XII, *Auspicia quaedam*, 11; Pius XII, *Mirabili illud*, 5–7; Pius XII, *Summi maeroris*, 9.

12. Pius XII, *Summi pontificatus*, 51; Pius XII, "1941 Christmas Message," 47.

13. Pollard, *Unknown Pope*, 146–47.

14. Pius XI, *Ubi arcano Dei consilio*, 44–47.

15. Holmes, *Papacy*, 181–82.

16. John XXIII, "1960 Christmas Message."

17. John XXIII, *Mater et magistra*, 157.

18. John XXIII, *Pacem in terris*, 109–13.

19. Ibid., 126–27.

20. Kane, "John XXIII," 65–68.

21. John XXIII, *Pacem in terris*, 1.

22. Ibid., 4–6.

23. Ibid. 80, 86–89.

24. John XXIII, *Mater et magistra*, 49.

25. Ibid., 200–8.

26. John XXIII, *Pacem in terris*, 130–45.

27. John XXIII, *Mater et magistra*, 219.

28. John XXIII, *Pacem in terris*, 9.

29. Ibid., 28–33.

30. Ibid., 46–52, 67–68, 73–74.

31. By itself, John's emphasis on human rights would not demonstrate an accommodation with liberal thought, since, as Brian Tierney has argued, there was a strong emphasis on natural rights among medieval natural law theorists. See Tierney, *Idea of Natural Rights*.

32. John XXIII, "1960 Christmas Message."

33. John XXIII, *Ad Petri cathedram*, 33.

34. John XXIII, *Pacem in terris*, 167–68.

35. Johnson, *Pope John XXIII*, 226–29.

36. Hanson, *Catholic Church*, 216.

37. John XXIII, *Pacem in terris*, 157–60; see also *Mater et magistra*, 238–39.

38. John XXIII, *Pacem in terris*, 45.

39. Ibid., 114.

40. Ibid., 129.

41. Ibid., 93.

42. Curran, *Catholic Social Teaching*, 29–32.

43. Besides those parallels already mentioned, the very structure of John's encyclical *Pacem in terris*, which is divided into chapters on the relations of individuals with each other and with the state, the relations among states, and the relations of individuals and states to the world community, corresponds to the conceptual framework of Kant's *Perpetual Peace*, in which he distinguishes the *ius civitatis*, the *ius gentium*, and the *ius cosmopoliticum*.

44. Pope John XXIII, "Opening Speech to the Second Vatican Council."

45. Second Vatican Council, *Gaudium et spes*, 44.

46. Ibid., 4.

47. Second Vatican Council, *Unitatis redintegratio*, 3–4; *Nostra aetate*, 2; *Gaudium et spes*, 19.

48. Second Vatican Council, *Gaudium et spes*, 63.

49. Ibid., 74–75.

50. Ibid., 53–55.

51. Ibid., 57–58.

52. Tucci, "Proper Development of Culture," 264.

53. Kasper, "Theological Anthropology," 132.

54. Second Vatican Council, *Lumen gentium*, 30–42.

55. Second Vatican Council, *Apostolicam actuositatem*.

56. Curran, *Catholic Social Teaching*, 32–33.

57. Second Vatican Council, *Gaudium et spes*, 10.

58. Ibid., 22. Significantly, this is a paraphrase of a passage from Henri de Lubac's *Catholicism*: "By revealing the Father and by being revealed by him, Christ completes the revelation of man to himself." De Lubac, *Catholicism*, 339.

59. Second Vatican Council, *Gaudium et spes*, 23–24.

60. Pope, "Natural Law," 54–55; Curran, *Catholic Social Teaching*, 33–34.

61. Kasper, "Theological Anthropology," 136–37; see also Ratzinger, "Church and Man's Calling," 117–20.

62. Second Vatican Council, *Gaudium et spes*, 13.

63. Ibid., 37.

64. Ibid., 39.

65. Ibid., 26.

66. Ibid., 32. By "the communitarian character" of society, *Gaudium et spes* means the idea that individual persons are fulfilled in community, and that the good of the human community consists in the good of the individuals who make it up.

67. Ibid., 41.

68. Ibid., 42. As Yves Congar writes, the world "is capable of becoming Church and is called by the Church, if the Church is understood to be what reveals to the world its own ultimate meaning." Congar, "Role of the Church," 212.

69. Second Vatican Council, *Gaudium et spes*, 36.

70. For a more detailed description of this idea, see Schindler, *Heart of the World*, 11–29; Schindler, "Christology," 159–75.

71. Second Vatican Council, *Gaudium et spes*, 78–80.

72. Curran, *Catholic Social Teaching*, 48.

73. Moeller, "Pastoral Constitution," 2–4, 6–7.

74. Ibid., 57.

75. Ibid., 62.

76. Second Vatican Council, *Gaudium et spes*, 77.

77. Ibid., 78.

78. Ibid., 83.

79. Ibid.

80. Ibid., 84.

81. Ibid., 82.

82. Coppa, *Modern Papacy*, 214.

83. Hebblethwaite, *Paul VI*, 93, 121–22.

84. Ibid., 178–79.

85. Ibid., 205–6, 242–43.

86. Hanson, *Catholic Church*, 135–36.

87. Weigel, *Final Revolution*, 69–70.

88. Hebblethwaite, *Paul VI*, 381.

89. Ibid., 492–95.

90. Weigel, *Witness to Hope*, 227–30.

91. Ibid., 295.

92. Holmes, *Papacy*, 248–49; Weigel, *Witness to Hope*, 280–81.

93. Holmes, *Papacy*, 244–48; Hebblethwaite, *Paul VI*, 483–85.

94. Hebblethwaite, *Paul VI*, 521–24.

95. Coppa, *Modern Papacy*, 231–32; Hebblethwaite, *Paul VI*, 459–60, 477–78, 505–6.

96. Paul VI, "Address to the United Nations," 4.

97. Paul VI, "1969 World Day of Peace Message"; Paul VI, "1970 World Day of Peace Message"; "1973 World Day of Peace Message"; "1974 World Day of Peace Message."

98. Paul VI, "1974 World Day of Peace Message."

99. Paul VI, "1968 World Day of Peace Message"; Paul VI, "1974 World Day of Peace Message."

100. Paul VI, *Populorum progressio*, 31; Paul VI, *Evangelii nuntiandi*, 37; *Mense maio*, 8; "1978 World Day of Peace Message."

101. Paul VI, *Populorum progressio*, 5, 62–63.

102. Paul VI, "1975 World Day of Peace Message."

103. Paul VI, "1976 World Day of Peace Message."

104. Paul VI, "1969 World Day of Peace Message"; Paul VI, "1971 World Day of Peace Message"; *Octogesima adveniens*, 24; "1972 World Day of Peace Message."

105. Paul VI, "1976 World Day of Peace Message."

106. Hebblethwaite, *Paul VI*, 124.

107. Paul VI, *Populorum progressio*, 64, 78.

108. Paul VI, "1968 World Day of Peace Message."

109. Paul VI, *Ecclesiam suam*, 42.

110. Paul VI, *Octogesima adveniens*, 4.

111. Elsbernd, "What Ever Happened," 39–40; see also Curran, *Catholic Social Teaching*, 92.

112. Paul VI, *Evangelii nuntiandi*, 19–20.

113. Paul VI, "1970 World Day of Peace Message."

114. Paul VI, "1974 World Day of Peace Message."

115. Paul VI, "1970 World Day of Peace Message."

116. Paul VI, "1971 World Day of Peace Message."

117. Paul VI, "1977 World Day of Peace Message."

118. Paul VI, "1970 World Day of Peace Message"; Paul VI, "1975 World Day of Peace Message."

119. Paul VI, "1969 World Day of Peace Message."

120. Paul VI, "1976 World Day of Peace Message."

121. Curran, *Catholic Social Teaching*, 35; Pope, "Natural Law," 56.

122. Paul VI, *Populorum progressio*, 14.

123. Ibid., 16, 21.

124. Paul VI, *Octogesima adveniens*, 30–34.

125. Paul VI, "Address to the Secretary General."

126. Paul VI, "Address to the United Nations," 3.

127. Paul VI, "1973 World Day of Peace Message."

128. Second Vatican Council, *Gaudium et spes*, 39.

129. Paul VI, "1971 World Day of Peace Message."

CHAPTER EIGHT

· · · · · · · · · · · · · · · · · · · ·

POPE JOHN PAUL II

PAUL'S SUCCESSOR POPE John Paul II (1920–2005, pope 1978–2005) more fully integrated twentieth-century Catholic theological reflections on historicity and the relationship between nature and grace into his reflections on international politics, including in his account of the origins of war; on the other hand, to a significant extent he maintained the view of the international system as a whole that was developed by John XXIII and Paul VI. John Paul II transformed papal thinking about domestic society and the behavior of states, yet his account of the international system remained mostly untouched by the theological concepts he developed elsewhere.

THE THEOLOGY OF JOHN PAUL II

In his theology, Pope John Paul II demonstrates a profound sense of both historicity and the integral connection between human nature and grace. His theology is extremely Christological, interpreting human existence and history in the light of Jesus Christ. This Christological focus contributes a theological emphasis to his social teaching that is unprecedented among earlier popes. John Paul also displays an awareness of the significant role of culture in forming human consciousness. Culture is necessary for human fulfillment, and the beliefs and values of cultures find their fulfillment in Jesus Christ.

Nature and Grace

John Paul II lays out his Christological vision in his first encyclical, *Redemptor hominis*. He begins the encyclical with the stunning phrase, "The redeemer of man, Jesus Christ, is the center of the universe and of history."[1] All of created reality, including the human person and human society, must be understood in the light of Christ. Christ sheds light on human existence and human relationships of all forms: "in the sphere of [man's] own family, in the sphere of society and very diverse contexts, in the sphere of his own nation or people (perhaps still only that of his clan or tribe), and in the sphere of the whole of mankind."[2] Humanity depends on Christ because it is only fulfilled through the love revealed by Christ: "Man cannot live without love. He remains a being that is incomprehensible for himself, his life is senseless, if love is not revealed to him, if he does not encounter love, if he does not experience it and make it his own, if he does not participate intimately in it."[3]

John Paul also expresses similar ideas in one of his last works, the book *Memory and Identity*. He uses biblical terms to express theological concepts similar to those of de Lubac and Rahner: "In God's plan of salvation, it is only by agreeing to be grafted onto Christ's divine Vine that man can become fully himself. Were he to refuse this grafting, he would effectively condemn himself to an incomplete humanity."[4] Christ shapes human history like the yeast in Jesus's parable, for "from all eternity God's plan has been to accomplish in Christ the divinization of man and of the world."[5] Yet in the world, the weeds grow together with the wheat.[6] Although the Kingdom of God grows in human history, "its goal is the life to come."[7] John Paul's claims about Christ and human nature are very different from the neoscholastic understanding of human nature as complete in itself, apart from grace.

John Paul's theology of nature and grace also found its way into his social encyclicals. In *Sollicitudo rei socialis*, John Paul asserts that "sin and the structures produced by sin as it multiplies and spreads" lie behind the cold war division of the world into East and West, as well as the conflict between North and South.[8] Notably, John Paul applies the theological category of "sin" to economic and political realities, not simply individual actions. John Paul claims that the solution to these world divisions is solidarity, a "Christian virtue" that is modeled on the communion of the three Persons of the Trinity.[9] This theological analysis in *Sollicitudo rei socialis* is balanced by passages that limit Christian faith to an interior inspiration in a quest for justice shared and agreed to by all.[10] In his later encyclical *Centesimus annus*, John Paul is clear that even though the social sciences are necessary to understand social problems and develop solutions for them, "man's true identity is only fully revealed to him through faith, and it is precisely from faith that the Church's social teaching begins. . . . The theological dimension is needed both for interpreting and solving present-day problems in human society."[11] John Paul, therefore, assigns theology a much more prominent role in interpreting political life than had the neoscholastics and the popes influenced by them. Having taken this strong position about the role of theology, it is no surprise then that John Paul uses theological categories to describe war and peace in ways unlike his predecessors.

Historicity

John Paul II also draws on theological insights into historicity, particularly in his views on culture. According to John Paul, culture is a distinctive feature of humanity that plays an essential role in establishing the identity of the individual person and the community. Culture consists in the ways that a society uses the things of the world for the development of human persons.[12] He writes: "Culture is a specific way of man's 'existing' and 'being.' Man always lives according to a culture which is specifically his, and which, in its turn, creates among men a tie which is also specifically theirs, determining the inter-human and social character of human existence." Culture is concerned with "having," or the use of material things, but only as they are used to develop the human person, when "man, as man, becomes more man, 'is' more, has more access to 'being.'" Culture cannot be understood as simply the reflection of a mode of production, as Marxists claim; although modes of production play an important role in forming culture, "it is not such and such a system that is at the origins of culture, but man, man who lives in the system, who accepts it or tries to change it."[13] Because culture is above all the product of human persons in their subjectivity, "Culture is the life of the spirit: It is the key that gives access to the deepest and most jealously guarded secrets of the life of peoples; it is the fundamental and unifying expression of their existence."[14] Culture is "a structuring element of one's personality," an essential constitutive element of an individual's identity.[15] Although culture shapes a person's way of being and acting, John Paul clearly affirms that certain speculative and moral truths remain universal.[16] When a culture distorts these truths, it must be purified by the Gospel, which intrinsically fulfills all cultures.[17]

In *Memory and Identity*, John Paul further reflects on the importance of culture for a nation: "The term 'nation' designates a community based in a given territory and distinguished from other nations by its culture." Like the family, the nation is a natural society and not an artificial construction.[18] The nation is not identical to the state; it is frequently the case that a state is closely linked to a single nation, but often multiple nations exist within one state. Recent decades have seen a tendency to move toward international institutions, "yet it still seems that nation and native land, like the family, are permanent realities"; an increasing emphasis on the universal should not overwhelm the particular.[19] Because the nation is an integral part of human nature, it is also penetrated by sin and grace: "The history of all nations is called to take its place in the history of salvation."[20] Pope John Paul II's diplomacy could be interpreted as his attempt to guide the nations of the world into taking their places in the history of salvation.

THE DIPLOMACY OF JOHN PAUL II

John Paul II's diplomacy clearly had a different style from that of his predecessor Paul VI. Paul certainly promoted human rights, democracy, and economic justice, just as John Paul did, but the two popes differed in how they understood the Catholic Church's role in helping to bring about these goals. Paul VI seems to have focused on the church's political engagement, especially through Vatican diplomacy, but in some cases his efforts were stymied by his sometimes conflicting desire to protect the institutional rights and assets of the church, which depended on political stability. John Paul II, on the other hand, saw the church first and foremost as a cultural force, in fact the most important cultural force: By proclaiming the Gospel of Jesus Christ, the church transforms cultures and reveals the dignity of the human person. This difference between the two approaches to papal diplomacy is above all shown in John Paul's role in the events that led to the collapse of communism in Eastern Europe in 1989. John Paul also actively promoted human rights in third world countries.

John Paul II and Communism

John Paul's approach to communism in Eastern Europe as pope was shaped by his experience as a priest and bishop in Communist-governed Poland. Karol Wojtyla had certainly encountered the Communist authorities as a priest in Poland, but his stance toward communism really began to take shape at the Second Vatican Council. Bishop Wojtyla of Krakow and the other Polish bishops thought that the dialogue with Marxists promoted by some Western bishops was a waste of time: "Wojtyla and his friends thought that Western intellectuals were naïve and ignorant, even downright stupid, when it came to the realities of communism."[21] Nevertheless, Wojtyla believed that an explicit condemnation of communism by the council would be counterproductive. In the 1970s, Wojtyla began to develop an approach to communism that was distinct from the harsh anticommunism of Pius XII, the openness to dialogue of John XXIII and Paul VI, and the anticommunism of Cardinal Stefan Wyszynski of Warsaw, the Primate of the Polish Church: "It seemed as if the Archbishop of Krakow was living in a transcendent dimension. His confrontation with communism took place in the context not of a specific religious denomination or ideological issue, but of the rights of man, pure and simple."[22] After a workers' strike was violently repressed in 1976, Wojtyla more and more put his thoughts into action, speaking out against the government's violation of human rights and giving his support to underground resistance movements.[23]

Upon becoming pope, John Paul II developed a new approach to communism in Eastern Europe that represented a shift from the policies of Paul VI. Ugo Colombo Sacco notes that one of John Paul's critical changes was to focus the Holy See's efforts on making contact with individuals and nations, not only with states, which was consistent with John Paul's emphasis on renewal and transformation from below.[24] George Weigel adds that John Paul's approach to communism differed from Paul VI's in that it focused on culture rather than politics or economics. Communism is not only an oppressive political and economic system but also an oppressive vision of humanity that is hostile to the cultures of the people it governs. John Paul II "knew that cultural resistance could be an effective antidote to the seemingly impregnable position of a criminal state," especially if that cultural resistance was founded on the truth about the human person revealed by Jesus Christ.[25]

John Paul's primary way of opposing communism was his support for the Polish people. Above all, John Paul's 1979 trip to Poland had a galvanizing effect on the Polish people, encouraging them to engage in the cultural resistance that he believed was necessary for the collapse of communism. Weigel calls John Paul's trip to Poland a "lesson in dignity" for the Polish people.[26] Bernstein and Politi describe this trip as "a grand turnabout for the Church" in which it demanded not just space for itself but also respect for human rights and Christian values.[27] John Paul understood his own actions as a way of reviving Polish culture, restoring it to its Christian roots, and bringing a new sense of dignity to the Polish people. This new sense of dignity laid the groundwork for the Solidarity labor movement that began at a strike in Gdansk the next year and soon became a broad cultural resistance movement that would be central to the collapse of communism in Poland.[28] John Paul continued to give his support to Solidarity and other resistance movements in Eastern Europe until the collapse of communism in 1989.

John Paul II and Human Rights

Although he shared interests with the United States during the cold war, John Paul did not hesitate to criticize the human rights abuses of third world governments sponsored by the United States, as well as abuses by governments supported by the Soviet Union. Bernstein and Politi describe how the Vatican and the Reagan White House cooperated with one another in the struggle against Soviet communism, but this did not mean their interests neatly coincided.[29] In a trip to Brazil in 1980, John Paul criticized that country's military dictatorship, speaking out in favor of economic justice and human rights, including the rights of indigenous peoples.[30] On a trip to Central America, the pope visited Guatemala, Haiti, and El Salvador, condemning human rights abuses by right-wing governments in those countries.[31] In his 1987 trip to Chile, John Paul promoted democracy and human rights in a private meeting with Augusto Pinochet. He explained to a reporter: "I am not the evangelizer of democracy, I am the evangelizer of the Gospel. To the Gospel message, of course, belongs all the problems of human rights, and if democracy means human rights then it also belongs to the message of the Church." John Paul sought to foster human rights not only by political means but also by helping to revivify Chilean civil society, demonstrating his understanding of the cultural roots of human dignity.[32] Later that year, he criticized the human rights abuses of Alfredo Stroessner's government in Paraguay.[33]

John Paul continued to promote human rights in the third world after the end of the cold war. One controversial example was the Vatican's leading role in establishing a coalition of third world countries that resisted efforts at the 1995 United Nations Conference on Population and Development in Cairo to make abortion on demand a universal right.[34] According to John Paul II, legalized abortion epitomizes the domination of the weak by the strong that lies at the heart of all human rights violations. Likewise in Beijing in 1995, at the United Nations' Fourth World Conference on Women, the Vatican opposed policies that marginalized the traditional family or promoted abortion, and sought to advocate for the real issues and concerns of poor women around the world.[35] In 1998, John Paul traveled to Cuba, hoping to have an effect on that society similar to the one he had had on Polish society in the 1980s; although thousands of Cubans came to see the pope, the trip had little effect on the Cuban regime.[36] When he was elected pope, many in the media concluded that the election of a Polish cardinal meant that the pope would ignore the third world in favor of relations with the Communists of Eastern Europe, yet in the end human rights in the developing world became the most consistent political concern of John Paul's papacy.[37]

JOHN PAUL II ON THE ORIGINS OF WAR AND PEACE

In his writings and speeches, Pope John Paul II develops official Catholic reflection on the morality of war. He strenuously denies that war is a legitimate means of pursuing interests or resolving conflicts, either internationally or within states, yet upholds the right to military self-defense.[38] At the same time, John Paul was the first pope to articulate a duty of humanitarian intervention.[39] He also strongly condemns terrorism as an unjust recourse to violence and affirms the right to defense against terrorism, within moral and legal limits.[40] Besides developing Catholic thinking on the morality of war, John Paul also contributed to Catholic reflection on war's origins.

The Origins of War

John Paul II develops a multifaceted understanding of the origins of war. In *Centesimus annus*, he praises Paul VI's assertion that true development, economic and spiritual, contributes to peace, and economic injustice contributes to conflict.[41] In his 1999 World Day of Peace message, he writes that the violation of human rights is a potential cause of conflict, as is the political domination of one country by another.[42] In this regard, political and economic exploitation typically go together. In *Sollicitudo rei socialis*, John Paul claims that the division of the world into two blocs in which the superpowers politically and economically dominate weaker countries was one of the most important causes of conflict during the cold war.[43]

Like Paul before him, John Paul insists that economic and political domination always take place in the context of ideology, which is a deeper source of conflict. The material motivations of groups and states are shaped by differing ideologies. This view is consistent with John Paul's understanding of culture, as described earlier, and it is also consistent with the theoretical insights of the constructivists. In *Sollicitudo rei socialis*, John Paul writes that competing ideologies lay behind the economic and political domination of the cold war.[44] Elsewhere he explicitly criticizes the realists for looking only at the material factors of power during the cold war, and therefore seeking "not so much to resolve tensions through justice and equity *as to manage differences and conflicts* in order to maintain a kind of balance that will preserve whatever is in the interests of the dominating party."[45] The realist approach, according to John Paul, ignores the deeper sources of conflict, injustice and ideology, and therefore is not helpful for establishing real peace.

John Paul argues that false ideologies lie at the origins of conflict. He particularly makes this case in his 1980 World Day of Peace message: "It is a fact, and no-one doubts it, that truth serves the cause of peace; it is also beyond discussion that non-truth in all its forms and at all levels (lies, partial or slanted information, sectarian propaganda, manipulation of the communications media, and so on) goes hand in hand with the cause of war. . . . Underlying all these forms of non-truth, and fostering and feeding upon them, is a mistaken ideal of man and of the driving forces within him," including the denial of the dignity of the human person. When this dignity is denied, then the belief that progress can be brought about through violent struggle can more easily be justified. Peace therefore demands telling the truth about acts of violence such as murder, massacres, and torture, as well as the truth about the human person.[46]

This connection between peace and the truth about the human person raises the question of the role of religion in matters of war and peace, and John Paul claims that religion has a generally positive role to play in fostering peace. He consistently insists that morally speaking, religious motivations cannot justify violence, and that violence in the name of God is blasphemy.[47] Fundamentalism and fanaticism, especially when they lead to violence and terrorism, are perversions of religion that seek to impose religious views on others.[48] In his 1992 World Day of Peace message, John Paul cautiously writes that despite their differences, the world's religions can work together for peace, and in 1999 he more boldly asserts, "Recourse to violence in the name of religious belief is a perversion of the very teachings of the major religions."[49] Bernstein and Politi, however, claim that in private, John Paul often expressed reservations about Islam; in a private conversation, he is said to have claimed, "What the Qur'an teaches people is aggression. . . . Islam is a religion that attacks."[50] Whether he

believed that violent interpretations of Islam are false interpretations, or that
there is something problematic about Islam as a religion, true religion is a source
of peace, according to John Paul, because peace can only come from the change
of heart that religion brings.[51]

When it comes to understanding the origins of war, then, John Paul II's
thought is fairly consistent with the perspective I have outlined in earlier chapters. He concludes that cultures, which sometimes take the form of ideologies,
shape the behavior of states. False ideologies, particularly those that present a
distorted notion of the human person, are the primary cause of conflict and
war, both among states and within states. The realm of culture and ideology
is not cut off from the material world, because culture itself pertains to the
way humanity makes use of the things of the world. There is also a material
component to ideology, and conflicts therefore involve both ideological and
material dimensions. The causes of conflict and war cannot be reduced to the
material dimension.

John Paul II on the Origins of Peace

John Paul recognizes that peace is ultimately not the product of human labor
but rather a gift from God: God writes the moral law necessary for peace on the
human heart, and through the Holy Spirit, seeks to interiorly transform each
person. John Paul adds: "History bears witness that men left to themselves have
a tendency to follow their irrational and selfish instincts. They thus experience
the truth that *peace is beyond human powers*."[52] In his 1984 Address to the Diplomatic Corps, John Paul affirms, "In truth, the Church is very conscious that this
patient transformation of international relations surpasses human powers, due
to the limited and sinful character of man. That is why . . . *the Church prays*."[53]
John Paul therefore echoes his predecessors in emphasizing the necessity of
grace for establishing international peace, a neoscholastic theme that was only
amplified by John Paul's more integral understanding of nature and grace.

Because peace is ultimately a gift from God, and it is primarily through the
church that we encounter God, the church plays an important role in establishing peace. In the first place, the church participates in the quest for peace
through its diplomatic activity, including its bilateral relations with individual
states.[54] In its diplomacy, however, the church only has at its disposal the "poor
means" of Christ, not the "rich means" of a true state; this suggests that diplomacy is not the church's primary tool for promoting peace.[55] More important than
diplomacy, then, is the church's proclamation of the transcendent dimension of
the human person as the source of the person's dignity and rights, which form
the foundation of peace.[56] The church also helps to bring about the conversion
and reconciliation necessary for peace, not least by offering us the Eucharist,
through which we join ourselves to Christ and establish the communion that
is at the basis of true peace.[57]

In his 1997 and 2002 World Day of Peace messages, John Paul speaks of the importance of forgiveness for international peace: "No process of peace can ever begin unless an attitude of sincere forgiveness takes root in human hearts." Forgiveness may seem difficult or even impossible according to human logic, which is marked by sin, but "forgiveness is inspired by the logic of love, that love which God has for every man and woman, for every people and nation, and for the whole human family."[58] Forgiveness is also closely related to justice, John Paul claims: "*Forgiveness neither eliminates nor lessens the need for the reparation* which justice requires, but seeks to reintegrate individuals and groups into society, and States into the community of Nations."[59] Forgiveness is not opposed to justice, but rather creates the possibility for justice.[60] Finally, and most importantly, John Paul declares that "*reconciliation comes from God,* who is always ready to forgive those who turn to him and turn their back on their sins."[61] Clearly, for John Paul II, forgiveness is not an interior transformation that inspires individuals or states to pursue justice, but rather a transformation of the very notion of justice. And as a gift from God, as grace, forgiveness reveals that there is no sharp divide between the political and the theological, that the aspirations of international politics for justice and peace are only fulfilled by the reconciliation in Christ found within the church. Despite this significant move away from neoscholasticism in his thinking about international politics, John Paul's understanding of the role of international political authorities in establishing peace continues to be influenced by the neoscholastic and liberal framework of his predecessors John and Paul.

International Political Authority and Peace

Although the insights of twentieth-century theology into historicity and the relationship between nature and grace certainly influenced John Paul II in his thinking about international peace, for the most part his thought remained similar to that of his predecessors John XXIII and Paul VI. John Paul did describe peace as ultimately a gift from God requiring personal transformation, and he offered intriguing reflections on the role of forgiveness in international peace. On the other hand, when it comes to concrete descriptions of the institutional means of securing peace, these theological developments are not fully integrated into his thought. This is above all true in John Paul's statements on the United Nations and international dialogue.

Like his predecessors, John Paul claims that the establishment of peace depends on the establishment of justice, especially the protection of human rights: "Justice goes hand in hand with peace and is permanently and actively linked to peace." Peace demands justice in all of its dimensions, from the good of the individual person to the relations among states.[62] Peace and justice above all require the protection of human rights, and political institutions should be reformed so that they allow for the adequate participation of citizens and the exercise of their rights.[63] John Paul's emphasis on the proper ordering of society definitely draws on the neoscholastic tradition of his predecessors, including the growing liberal influence evident in the importance given to human rights and democracy.

John Paul moves from the individual society to the international scene, arguing that peace requires just relations between states. The common good encompasses all of humanity.[64] Just as states must protect the rights of their citizens, states themselves have rights and must respect the rights of other states.[65] The pursuit of the global common good, which includes respect for the rights of states, is essential for peace today above all because of the growing interdependence of the world, or as it is now called, globalization.[66] International law plays an essential role in the pursuit of peace, and states have an obligation to honor it. The greatest challenge to international law, however, is that by itself it is insufficient for establishing the global common good and therefore true peace; just as his predecessors John XXIII and Paul VI had, John Paul claims that attaining the global common good requires some sort of international political authority.[67]

John Paul argues that international institutions are necessary if peace is to be established. By themselves, states are not able to accomplish what is necessary for peace, and therefore they have established international organizations to help them.[68] John Paul writes of the important role of regional organizations and the International Criminal Court, but above all he points to the United Nations as a source of peace.[69] John Paul points out that the United Nations was established in the aftermath of the Second World War for the purpose of preventing another such catastrophe by limiting the legitimate uses of force to self-defense and collective security, a task that he wholeheartedly supports.[70] He notes that the end of the cold war has allowed the United Nations to more adequately fulfill its role as peacemaker.[71]

Despite his praise for the United Nations, John Paul was the first pope to suggest significant reforms for the organization. In *Sollicitudo rei socialis*, John Paul writes that international institutions need reforming to improve their efficiency, and in his World Day of Peace messages he mentions the need for greater participation.[72] In *Centesimus annus*, however, John Paul is concerned that international organizations have failed to prevent many international conflicts: "The United Nations . . . has not yet succeeded in establishing, as alternatives to war, effective means for the resolution of international conflicts. This seems to be the most urgent problem which the international community has yet to resolve."[73] Although there is nothing surprising about John Paul's call for reform of the United Nations, a call that was heard from many voices at the time, it is notable that after he has given a complex account of the causes of war, combining material, ideological, and theological dimensions, John Paul would suggest that the problem of persistent war could be solved by the reform of international institutions. This is because John Paul ignores the presence of sin in the international system and international institutions, as opposed to in individual states.

John Paul II consistently fails to recognize the presence of sin in the international system as a whole and in its institutional embodiments. Derek S. Jeffreys captures this oversight nicely:

> Despite its moral and rhetorical power, . . . there was something disturbing about John Paul II's speech [to the United Nations in 1995]. Coming on the heels of the United Nations' abject failure to prevent genocide in Rwanda, his comments about a family of nations had an air of unreality about them. The Member States of the UN showed little or no concern for members of their "family" on the African continent. . . . He mentions the Rwandan genocide, and clearly, some of his remarks about virulent nationalism apply to it. However, he never discusses why the so-called international community utterly failed to stop it.[74]

Jeffreys's point is not that John Paul did not recognize the moral failure of "passive indifference" to genocide, but rather that he always attributes moral failure to states individually and never to the international community as a whole or to the United Nations. Later Jeffreys gives the example of John Paul's efforts to prevent the definition of abortion as a universal human right at Cairo and Beijing. In his encyclical *Evangelium vitae*, John Paul speaks of a "culture of death" that is embodied in domestic political institutions and is further reinforced by those institutions, but in the case of Cairo and Beijing, he attributes opposition to his cause solely to a minority of activists and officials, not to the moral culture of the United Nations itself. Jeffreys concludes that unlike in his account of domestic society, John Paul seems to believe that distorted values manifest at the international level can be overcome by institutional means alone, with no need for a deeper cultural and spiritual transformation.[75]

Besides downplaying the role of sin in the international system, John Paul also at times adopts his predecessors' optimism about moral agreement among states, ignoring the role of culture in shaping state behavior. This is particularly true in his description of dialogue. International organizations are "the places and instruments par excellence for true dialogue for peace," but dialogue is possible even without them.[76] John Paul asserts that "there is no peace without readiness for sincere and continual dialogue," regardless of where that dialogue takes place.[77] He notes that some "are doubtful about the possibility of dialogue and its effectiveness, not least when the positions are so tense and irreconcilable that they seem to allow no space for any agreement," but he himself concludes that "*dialogue for peace is possible*, always possible. It is not a utopia." Even when dialogue seems to fail, there is always the possibility of resuming it, and John Paul concludes: "People are finally capable of overcoming divisions, conflicts of interests, even if the oppositions would seem radical ones—especially when each party is convinced that it is defending a just cause—if they believe in the virtue of dialogue, if they accept to meet face to face to seek a peaceful and reasonable solution for conflicts."[78]

But is it not likely that there is radical opposition precisely because at least one party to a conflict does not believe in the virtue of dialogue? John Paul seems to assume that states share the view that dialogue is a virtue, suggesting that dialogue fails for reasons other than irreconcilable values, such as impatience or the lack of an adequate venue. It is also significant that the primary examples John Paul gives of international conflicts that were successfully resolved through dialogue and negotiation without recourse to war are the Beagle Channel dispute between Argentina and Chile in 1978–79 and a dispute between Ecuador and Peru in 1998, both of which were merely border disputes rather than ideological conflicts.[79] It seems implausible to expect conflicts with deep ideological and religious roots, such as the Israeli-Palestinian conflict, to be able to follow the same model. Although he admits the role of culture and ideology in shaping state behavior and even in causing war, when it comes to describing the interactions and negotiations that could lead to peace among states, John Paul largely ignores those factors. Considering that he admits that dialogue primarily takes place in international institutions, he seems to suggest that institutional means can resolve the sources of conflict. Thus John Paul II uses theological insights into historicity and the relation between nature and grace primarily in his treatment of individual states and domestic society, not the international system as a whole.

Domestic Society as a Model

It could be objected that John Paul's approach to communism, fundamentally different from that of John XXIII and Paul VI, shows that his view of the international system was different from that of his predecessors. George Weigel makes this claim. What this argument attributes to a change in papal approach to international politics, however, is really a reflection of John Paul's understanding of the relationship between the state and society, not a new understanding of the international system.

John Paul's critique of communism draws on his understanding of the human person and human society. In *Centesimus annus*, John Paul writes that "the fundamental error of socialism [i.e., communism] is anthropological in nature," meaning that "man is . . . reduced to a series of social relationships, and the concept of the person as the autonomous subject of moral decision disappears, the very subject whose decisions build the social order." Underlying this error about the human person is the more fundamental error of atheism, because "it is by responding to the call of God contained in the being of things that man becomes aware of his transcendent dignity." John Paul continues, "In contrast, from the Christian vision of the human person there necessarily follows a correct picture of society." When the transcendent dimension of the human person is recognized, then it follows that the person is fulfilled not through the state alone, but through other institutions, particularly the family, cultural groups, and the church, through which human subjectivity is developed and whose autonomy must be respected. Therefore, in the Christian view of things, the authority of the state is limited.[80]

So far John XXIII and Paul VI could agree with this, but what is new is John Paul's claim that the error of communism is not only embodied in politics and economics, but is also a corruption of culture. Cultures are humanity's diverse ways of responding to the mystery of God, and therefore when the transcendent dimension of the person is suppressed, a corrupted culture results. John Paul writes that with "the culture and praxis of totalitarianism," the state "tends to absorb within itself the nation, society, the family, religious groups and individuals themselves." It is no surprise, then, that the Eastern European resistance movements drew on their national cultures and "rediscover[ed] the person of Christ himself as the existentially adequate response to the desire in every human heart for goodness, truth and life."[81] The church's true contribution to society is through the realm of culture, and only secondarily through politics; the church plays a decisive role in transforming culture by proclaiming the truth about the human person as revealed in Jesus Christ.[82]

In his encyclicals *Centesimus annus* and *Evangelium vitae*, John Paul applies similar insights to democratic societies. He is clear that the Catholic Church supports democracy, primarily because it is the form of government that best protects human rights and ensures people's participation in society. But democracy cannot stand alone; it must be situated in a culture guided by authentic human values. John Paul writes: "Democracy cannot be idolized to the point of making it a substitute for morality or a panacea for immorality. Fundamentally, democracy is a 'system' and as such is a means and not an end. Its 'moral' value is not automatic, but depends on conformity to the moral law to which it, like every other form of human behavior, must be subject: in other words, its morality depends on the morality of the ends which it pursues and of the means which it employs." When democracy as an institution is divorced from authentic human values, an attitude of "ethical" or "skeptical relativism" gains ground. Were such an attitude to become widespread, "the democratic system itself would be shaken in its foundations, and would be reduced to a mere mechanism for regulating different and opposing interests on a purely empirical basis." John Paul adds, "If there is no ultimate truth to guide and direct political activity, then ideas and convictions can easily be manipulated for reasons of power. As history demonstrates, a democracy without values easily turns into open or thinly disguised totalitarianism."[83] Such a view divorces freedom from the truth, as freedom is reduced to merely doing what one wants without regard for objective values, and truth becomes determined by majority opinion. "Everyone else is considered an enemy from whom one has to defend oneself," because truth is reduced to power and the strong are able to dominate the weak. John Paul adds, "When this happens, the process leading to the breakdown of a genuinely human co-existence and the disintegration of the State itself has already begun."[84]

According to John Paul II, when democratic institutions are separated from authentic cultural values, they begin to embody a culture of death that denies the truth about the human person and leads to the domination of the weak by the strong. The culture of death corrupts society's political institutions, and in turn political institutions reinforce the culture through the law. Such a culture of death is founded above all on the denial of God, which leads to the denial of the dignity of the human person.[85] The well-being of society depends on the truth about the human person revealed in Christ, although the church respects the legitimate autonomy of democracy and seeks to avoid fanaticism and fundamentalism; the church can only propose, never impose.[86]

As Derek S. Jeffreys suggests, John Paul could have applied this line of thinking to the international system and the United Nations, but he does not. What would such an application look like? The United Nations and other international organizations cannot be understood apart from their own bureaucratic culture and the culture of the international system as a whole. Like institutions at the domestic level, the United Nations and other international organizations are divided by a struggle between a culture of life that upholds authentic human values and a culture of death in which the strong dominate the weak and the truth about the human person is denied. Of course no nation or group of nations fully represents either culture; nations themselves are likewise divided, as are individuals. This struggle has been visible at conferences such as those in Cairo and Beijing, but the power of the culture of death in the United Nations is also evident in the so-called Human Rights Commission (and now Human Rights Council), on which notorious human rights abusers can sit and pass judgment on other states while the United Nations does nothing about genocide in places like Rwanda or Sudan.

John Paul does not offer such an analysis, however, because his understanding of the international system is taken largely unchanged from his predecessors John XXIII and Paul VI, and is therefore untouched by the theological insights that John Paul applies to his understanding of domestic society. John XXIII and Paul VI understood international institutions (like all political institutions) as governing a temporal sphere of material interests separate from the spiritual sphere of religion and ideology. Temporal authorities must respect the spiritual sphere, but otherwise the spiritual has little to do with the temporal; therefore, the temporal order can be perfected through peace even if humanity's supernatural end is not perfected until the life to come. Likewise, John Paul does not describe the culture of the international system and its institutional embodiments, such as the United Nations, nor does he claim that the international system itself is permeated by sin and grace, except in his theological description of the cold war in *Sollicitudo rei socialis*. By ignoring the cultural dimension in international politics, John Paul almost seems to make the United Nations "a substitute for morality or a panacea for immorality" in international politics, and he presents an overly optimistic view of dialogue among states. Therefore although John Paul II develops a more adequate account of the origins of war at the level of individual states, he exaggerates the possibilities of resolving conflicts internationally and downplays the ways in which the international system itself can contribute to conflict through distorted values.

CONCLUSION

John Paul II began to develop a sophisticated account of the origins of war at the level of individual states, rooting war in the ideological and cultural distortions that lead to violence. His account of the international system, on the other hand, instead suggests the liberal views that the origins of war lie in conflicting material interests, compounded by ignorance, bias, and fear, and that these forces can be overcome through international institutions and dialogue. John Paul developed an account of domestic society as a social structure formed through culture by the individuals who constitute it, and therefore reflecting a mixture of the culture of life and the culture of death; this account could serve as a model for understanding the international system. This new understanding of domestic society lay behind John Paul's new approach to Communist Eastern Europe. John Paul did not view the international system in the same way, however. His understanding of the international system, influenced by the neoscholastic-liberal framework of his papal predecessors, exaggerated the possibilities of international institutions and dialogue to resolve conflicts and downplayed the cultural transformation that is necessary for peace (and which those same predecessors emphasized when speaking of individual societies). It also downplayed the way the international system and its institutional embodiments can themselves contribute to conflict through their influence on the identities, interests, and norms of behavior of states.

NOTES

1. John Paul II, *Redemptor hominis*, 1.
2. Ibid., 14.
3. Ibid., 10.
4. John Paul II, *Memory and Identity*, 98–99.
5. Ibid., 117.
6. Ibid., 4.
7. Ibid., 156.
8. John Paul II, *Sollicitudo rei socialis*, 46.

9. Ibid., 40.

10. Ibid., 35, 38.

11. John Paul II, *Centesimus annus*, 54–55.

12. John Paul II, "1981 Address to the Diplomatic Corps," 23.

13. John Paul II, "Address to UNESCO," 292.

14. John Paul II, "1981 Address to the Diplomatic Corps," 22.

15. John Paul II, "2001 World Day of Peace Message," 6.

16. John Paul II, *Fides et ratio*, 95; John Paul II, *Veritatis splendor*, 53.

17. John Paul II, *Fides et ratio*, 71; see also John Paul II, *Centesimus annus*, 51.

18. John Paul II, *Memory and Identity*, 69–70; see also John Paul II, "Address to UNESCO," 296.

19. Ibid., 66–67.

20. Ibid., 72.

21. Bernstein and Politi, *His Holiness*, 102–3.

22. Ibid., 118–19.

23. Ibid., 126–28.

24. Sacco, *John Paul II*, 18.

25. Weigel, *Witness to Hope*, 295–97.

26. Ibid., 300–325.

27. Bernstein and Politi, *His Holiness*, 7.

28. Ibid., 237–47.

29. Such a close alliance is proposed by Bernstein and Politi, who argue that in his trip to Nicaragua in 1983 and to Chile and Argentina in 1987, John Paul criticized Marxism while saying little about the Contras in Nicaragua, the repression by General Augusto Pinochet in Chile, or the recently fallen military junta in Argentina, supposedly in order to support Reagan's policies of opposition to communism and endorsement of gradual democratic reforms. Ibid., 257–71, 355–69, 461–66.

30. Weigel, *Witness to Hope*, 379–80.

31. Ibid., 451–57.

32. Ibid., 531–36.

33. Ibid., 560–62.

34. Ibid., 715–27; Bernstein and Politi, 524–30.

35. Weigel, *Witness to Hope*, 766–71.

36. Ibid., 805–14.

37. Sacco, *John Paul II*, 16.

38. John Paul II, "1987 Address to the Diplomatic Corps," 78.

39. John Paul II, "1993 Address to the Diplomatic Corps," 126–27.

40. John Paul II, "2002 World Day of Peace Message," 4–5. See also John Paul II, *Sollicitudo rei socialis*, 24; "1989 World Day of Peace Message," 10; "1986 Address to the Diplomatic Corps," 69–70.

41. John Paul II, *Centesimus annus*, 52; see also John Paul II, "1986 Address to the Diplomatic Corps," 69.

42. John Paul II, "1999 World Day of Peace Message," 2.

43. John Paul II, *Sollicitudo rei socialis*, 22; see also John Paul II, "1986 World Day of Peace Message," 2.

44. *Sollicitudo rei socialis*, 20.

45. John Paul II, "1986 World Day of Peace Message," 3. Emphasis in original.

46. John Paul II, "1980 World Day of Peace Message," 1–3.

47. John Paul II, "1998 Address to the Diplomatic Corps," 152–53; John Paul II, "2002 Address to the Diplomatic Corps," 170.

48. John Paul II, "1992 World Day of Peace Message," 7; John Paul II, "2002 World Day of Peace Message," 6.

49. John Paul II, "1992 World Day of Peace Message," 5; John Paul II, "1999 World Day of Peace Message," 5.

50. Bernstein and Politi, *His Holiness*, 439–42.

51. John Paul II, "1984 World Day of Peace Message," 2.

52. John Paul II, "1987 Address to the Diplomatic Corps," 74–75. Emphasis in original.

53. John Paul II, "1984 Address to the Diplomatic Corps," 52. Emphasis in original. See also John Paul II, "1984 World Day of Peace Message," 5; "1992 World Day of Peace Message," 4.

54. John Paul II, "1981 Address to the Diplomatic Corps," 22.

55. John Paul II, "1979 Address to the Diplomatic Corps," 9.

56. John Paul II, "1989 Address to the Diplomatic Corps," 92.

57. John Paul II, "1985 Address to the Diplomatic Corps," 61–62; John Paul II, "2005 World Day of Peace Message," 12.

58. John Paul II, "1997 World Day of Peace Message," 1.

59. Ibid., 5. Emphasis in original.

60. John Paul II, "2002 World Day of Peace Message," 3.

61. John Paul II, "1997 World Day of Peace Message," 6. Emphasis in original.

62. John Paul II, "1998 World Day of Peace Message," 1; John Paul II, "1982 Address to the Diplomatic Corps," 31–32; "1984 World Day of Peace Message," 3; "1986 Address to the Diplomatic Corps," 63; "1988 Address to the Diplomatic Corps," 83; 1995 "World Day of Peace Message," 1.

63. John Paul II, "1981 World Day of Peace Message," 6; John Paul II, "1982 World Day of Peace Message," 9; "1987 World Day of Peace Message," 2; *Sollicitudo rei socialis*, 26; "1988 World Day of Peace Message," 1; "1998 World Day of Peace Message," 2; "1999 World Day of Peace Message," 3, 6.

64. John Paul II, "1979 Address to the Diplomatic Corps," 11; John Paul II, "1981 World Day of Peace Message," 1.

65. John Paul II, "1984 Address to the Diplomatic Corps," 48; John Paul II, "1985 Address to the Diplomatic Corps," 56–57.

66. John Paul II, "1984 Address to the Diplomatic Corps," 1; John Paul II, "2000 World Day of Peace Message," 5–6.

67. John Paul II, "2004 World Day of Peace Message," 5, 9; John Paul II, "1986 World Day of Peace Message," 4.

68. John Paul II, "1982 World Day of Peace Message," 10.

69. John Paul II, "1997 World Day of Peace Message," 4; John Paul II, "2000 World Day of Peace Message," 7.

70. John Paul II, "2004 World Day of Peace Message," 6; John Paul II, "1980 Address to the Diplomatic Corps," 16; "Address to the United Nations General Assembly," 270–71.

71. John Paul II, "1995 Address to the Diplomatic Corps," 140.

72. John Paul II, *Sollicitudo rei socialis*, 43; John Paul II, "2003 World Day of Peace Message," 6; "2004 World Day of Peace Message," 7.

73. John Paul II, *Centesimus annus*, 21.

74. Jeffreys, *Defending Human Dignity*, 148.

75. Ibid., 176–86.

76. John Paul II, "1983 World Day of Peace Message," 11; John Paul II, "2000 World Day of Peace Message," 10.

77. John Paul II, "1980 World Day of Peace Message," 8; see also John Paul II, "1983 World Day of Peace Message," 2.

78. Ibid., 5. Emphasis in original.

79. John Paul II, "Address to the United Nations," 273; John Paul II, "1985 Address to the Diplomatic Corps," 55–56; "1999 Address to the Diplomatic Corps," 157.

80. John Paul II, *Centesimus annus*, 13.

81. Ibid., 24, 45.

82. Ibid., 51.

83. Ibid., 46; John Paul II, *Evangelium vitae*, 70.

84. John Paul II, *Evangelium vitae*, 19–20.

85. Ibid., 21.

86. John Paul II, *Centesimus annus*, 46–47.

CHAPTER NINE

· · · · · · · · · · · · · · · · · ·

CONTEMPORARY CATHOLICS

DESPITE THE POPES' significant statements on war and peace, some of the most important reflection on these themes has continued to come from Catholic intellectuals. Alongside the Catholic radicalism exemplified by Dorothy Day and carried on by later generations of American Catholic activists, J. Bryan Hehir and George Weigel represent the dominant strands in American Catholic intellectual discourse about war. Both Hehir and Weigel openly acknowledge the influence of John Courtney Murray on their own thought, although they have taken his ideas in somewhat different directions. Hehir, a liberal Catholic, has applied Murray's thoughts on the morality of war to contemporary cases such as humanitarian intervention, and has also more closely tied just war reasoning to recent moral theology, as well as to international relations theory, particularly neoliberalism. Weigel, a neoconservative Catholic, has emphasized the role of ideology in shaping state behavior, arguing that the nature of particular regimes is a crucial component of moral reasoning about war. Despite these differences, however, as William J. Gould Jr. notes, "in their common embrace of Murray, today's American Catholic intellectuals reveal themselves to be far less apart in their basic political orientations than their immediate policy differences might suggest."[1] Both Hehir and Weigel inherit from Murray a belief in the value of public reason, expressed in terms of the natural law, which influences their account of war and its origins.

J. BRYAN HEHIR

J. Bryan Hehir, who represents the more liberal wing of thinkers influenced by Murray, has been one of the most influential American Catholic intellectuals of the last quarter of the twentieth century. As Kristin Heyer writes: "As a policy advisor to the United States bishops at the United States Catholic Conference (USCC) for many years, dean and professor at Harvard Divinity School, and recent president of Catholic Charities USA, Hehir has exercised one of the most influential public roles in recent American Catholic history."[2] Hehir has been particularly influential in his writing about international order, war, and peace.

Hehir on International Order

In much of his early work, Hehir attempts to learn from the study of international politics how to better understand the international system in order to provide a more adequate ethical analysis of world politics. He argues that ethics must be interdisciplinary, and therefore ethicists concerned with issues of war and peace must learn from political science. He adds, "In doing interdisciplinary work one inevitably depends upon some analysts more than others; . . . even a choice like this is part of the ethical picture we assume."[3] Hehir himself chooses to draw on the works of his teacher, Stanley Hoffman, who was loosely affiliated with liberal international relations theory, as well as on the neoliberals described in chapter 3.

In a way reminiscent of neoliberals such as Robert O. Keohane and Joseph S. Nye Jr., Hehir attempts to describe the changes in the international system since the end of World War II in order to grasp the situation that ethicists of war and peace must use as their starting point. The fundamental shift was from the "classical" world of power politics to the "contemporary" world of interdependence. The struggle for power is now played out not only on the chessboard of military power, but also on that of economic power, opening the possibilities for not only "the zero-sum logic of win-lose," but also for "win-win" and "lose-lose" situations.[4] Hehir therefore echoes Keohane and Nye's claim that an analysis of contemporary world politics must take into consideration "complex interdependence" as well as the more traditional concerns of realism. He recognizes that interdependence means an erosion of state sovereignty but not the abolition of the state; the state remains the primary actor in international politics. Yet interdependence requires us to rethink how we understand state actors and their behavior, and Hehir maintains that the traditional Catholic view of the state as part of a larger international community shares an affinity with the neoliberal view of interdependent states.[5] Hehir clearly sides with the neoliberals in their debate with the neorealists, arguing that meaningful cooperation among states is possible.[6]

Hehir also argues that the understanding of international politics found in the writings of John Courtney Murray and in the popes from John XXIII to John Paul II remains relevant for the post–cold war world. They had argued that the growing interdependence of the world necessitated the establishment of some form of international political authority. Hehir adds, however, that this understanding of international order could be supplemented by neoliberalism's insight that international institutions or regimes well short of an international political authority can help foster cooperation and peace.[7] He believes that the great changes in world politics at the beginning of the 1990s, however, might make the popes' calls for an international political authority more realistic than in the past.[8] More significant, however, is the fact that Hehir sees the Catholic approach to international politics as fundamentally compatible with the neo-liberal approach.

Hehir on Humanitarian Intervention

One of the most important ethical issues of international politics that Hehir tackles is the question of humanitarian intervention. According to Hehir, humanitarian intervention became a more pressing issue in the 1990s because of the changes in international politics at the beginning of that decade, but this theme was already foreshadowed in Hehir's earlier treatment of human rights in foreign policy. In his 1980 essay "Human Rights from a Theological and Ethical Perspective," he argues that human rights are a legitimate foreign policy concern, but that this concern should be balanced by other issues. For example, security issues such as arms control must take precedence over the promotion of human rights.[9] Like the neoliberals, Hehir disconnects issues of material power, such as nuclear-weapons capability, from issues of ideology, such as human rights; this disconnect is criticized by the constructivists, who argue that *who* possesses nuclear weapons and *why* is just as important as *that* they possess them.

In the changed international situation of the 1990s, according to Hehir, military intervention to prevent massive human rights violations can in some cases be justified. The end of the cold war and the resulting decrease of nuclear tensions created the possibility for human rights to take a more prominent place in foreign policy.[10] Hehir argues that state sovereignty and nonintervention should remain important international norms, but they are not absolute and can be overridden for proportionate reasons.[11] In other words, one begins with the norm against intervention and then applies the just war criteria to determine when humanitarian intervention might be justified. Using this method, Hehir concludes that military intervention might be justified in cases of genocide, ethnic cleansing, or in failed states.[12] For example, he argues that NATO's 1999 intervention in Kosovo was legitimate, although he questions the exclusive use of air power in that war.[13] He distinguishes, however, between these massive violations of human rights and lesser abuses of human rights, which do not justify military intervention. Hehir also concludes that military intervention to prevent the spread of weapons of mass destruction to so-called rogue states, or states with oppressive governments that consistently disregard international law, may be justified, especially if those states also sponsor terrorist groups, but only with the approval of the United Nations Security Council.[14]

According to Hehir, the growing acceptance of humanitarian intervention shows how ethical reflection on war adapts to changes in our understanding of the international system. During the Middle Ages, Christians in Europe believed they were part of a *respublica Christiana*, or a single community governed by a spiritual head, the pope. Because this community was governed by a single, albeit spiritual, authority, thinkers such as Thomas Aquinas more easily justified military intervention in the affairs of other states in terms of universal values. In the modern period, on the other hand, characterized by the collapse of the *respublica Christiana* and the rise of the modern state system, just war theorists such as Emmerich de Vattel developed the principle of nonintervention.[15] This transition also led to just causes for war being understood in terms of the rights of states rather than the maintenance of international order.[16] Today the international system continues to change, which should lead to revisions in the way the just war theory is applied.

Hehir on the Just War Theory

Hehir's understanding of the just war theory reveals certain assumptions about state behavior. In his understanding of the just war theory, Hehir draws on the approach of Protestant moral theologian James F. Childress, who describes state violence as a "prima facie evil," or an action that must be presumed to be wrong unless this wrongness can be overridden by certain positive consequences that the action may bring about.[17] In thinking about the morality of war this way, Hehir links his reflections on war to the Catholic approach to moral theology known as proportionalism.[18] According to Richard McCormick, SJ, a leading proponent of proportionalism, no actions are intrinsically evil, but rather may involve certain disvalues (sometimes called pre-moral or ontic evils); other values (or pre-moral or ontic goods) may provide a proportionate reason for performing the action.[19] In fact, Hehir argues that the just war theory is best understood in proportionalist terms.[20] The destructiveness of war is a pre-moral evil, but the prohibition of this evil can be overridden when there are goods that might be brought about by war, or other evils that could be prevented. Christianity does not provide a *prohibition* against violence, according to Hehir, but rather a *presumption* against violence.[21]

Hehir uses proportionalism and the presumption against violence as primary tools for understanding the morality of war, which suggests a certain way of understanding the behavior of states that correlates with his use of neoliberalism to analyze world politics. Although proportionalism is clearly distinct from utilitarianism, it is similar to utilitarianism in suggesting that the moral decision maker is a rational actor. Proportionalists certainly do not limit the relevant moral values to pleasure and pain, as utilitarians do, instead arguing that values and disvalues are objective realities, rather than mere subjective experiences.[22] Nevertheless, proportionalism does presuppose that the various values and disvalues can be weighed and compared.[23] Therefore a moral actor must, in a sense, rationally maximize the good and minimize evil, just as neoliberalism supposes that states do.

The moral theologian Germain Grisez raises a criticism of proportionalism that demonstrates a further possible convergence between proportionalism and neoliberalism. According to Grisez, if it really were true that we could weigh and compare goods and evils in the way proposed by proportionalists, then we would never have any good reason for choosing anything other than the best choice; any person who has not been overcome by emotion would choose it, unless they were misled about their choices.[24] If Grisez is correct, then there is a clear analogy between the role of proportionalism in Hehir's thought and that of utilitarianism in neoliberal theory: Proportionalism seems to suggest that appropriate international institutions could create the conditions necessary for states to act rationally and cooperatively by providing access to information and eliminating temptations to respond to a situation out of fear or bias. It must be understood that Grisez's argument is a criticism of proportionalism rather than a proportionalist's self-description of his or her own views, but it nonetheless provides insight into Hehir's views.

Proportionalism also influences our understanding of state behavior by shaping our perception of what sorts of goods states might pursue. In his critique of proportionalism, Grisez argues that it downplays the way in which our actions shape our very being as persons.[25] This leads the proportionalists to ignore what he calls "existential goods," or goods for which the choice to pursue that good is itself part of the good, as opposed to "substantial goods," those goods that exist separately from the choice to pursue them. For example, I can choose to eat healthy foods in pursuit of the good of health, but that choice itself is not normally part of what we think of as "health"; health, therefore, is a substantive good. On the other hand, I can choose to keep in touch with my friend when we have moved apart in pursuit of the good of friendship, but in this case my very choice to keep in touch is itself part of what one means by friendship; friendship, therefore, is an existential good. According to Grisez, the existential goods are typically expressive of harmony in some way, whether it is harmony among the various dimensions of the human person, harmony among individuals, or harmony between an individual and God.[26] The proportionalists recognize the existential goods as goods, but only as states of affairs in which individuals are involved, rather than as aspects of persons themselves. They fail to see that choices made in pursuit of the existential goods create new realities that bring with them new moral obligations. For example, marriage is a commitment that changes the identities of those who enter into it and a good that must be preserved for its own sake, not just a mutually beneficial agreement that can be abandoned when it is no longer fulfilling for the parties involved.[27]

This critique of proportionalism is significant for a Catholic perspective on international politics because how one answers the question about existential goods affects how one understands the goods that states pursue. The debate over existential goods almost precisely parallels the debate between constructivists and neoliberals over norms, described in chapter 4. According to many neoliberals, states interact and form institutions so that they can pursue their already existing interests more efficiently through cooperation. For constructivists, on the other hand, states' interests are at least partly formed precisely through their interactions with one another. What Grisez's discussion of existential goods adds to this debate is that not only is it true that social structures partly constitute the interests of the actors who make them up, but morally speaking, the social structures of which an actor is a part and which the actor partly creates or maintains become goods themselves that must be preserved by the actor; they are not simply means of pursuing the actor's interests. For example, just relations between the United States and Canada ought to be preserved as good in themselves, not simply because they are for the moment mutually beneficial. When the proportionalist moral calculus is applied to war, relationships of justice are typically not included as purposes or ends for which war is fought, which could radically change the way war is morally analyzed. Hehir's proportionalist analysis of the morality of war is therefore closely connected with his use of neoliberal analysis in describing international politics.

Hehir on Public Reason

In his writings Hehir also describes the public role of the church in the process of moral reasoning. Because contemporary society is pluralistic, the church must speak in a language accessible to all, and Hehir believes that the natural law provides such a language. This claim clearly demonstrates that, as Heyer argues, "without a doubt, the single most important analytical influence on Hehir, theologically or philosophically, remains Murray."[28] Hehir asserts that it is one thing for the church to use religious language within its own community, but quite another to use religious language within the broader civil society. In civil society, he writes, "the constituency to which [the church] speaks and the community in which it witnesses present more complex challenges to the voice and vision of religious witness."[29] The pluralistic nature of civil society demands that the church speak in philosophical terms in that forum, and particularly using the framework of the natural law, rather than in theological terms.[30] In later essays, Hehir acknowledges that religious and theological arguments may be acceptable in civil society, but "actions that will invoke the coercive power of the state and touch the lives of all citizens . . . should be cast in terms of a public philosophy."[31] He clearly believes that matters of war are public issues that must be dealt with in terms of a public philosophy, and, as outlined earlier, does so in terms of the natural law, albeit a revisionist version of the theory.

The theologian Michael Baxter has criticized the "public theology" developed by Hehir and others. Baxter argues that although the advocates of public theology claim to root their social ethics in the theological insights into nature and grace of such theologians as Henri de Lubac and Karl Rahner, they are really more in continuity with the preconciliar neoscholastic theology that separated the natural sphere of temporal life from the supernatural sphere of grace. As Baxter writes, Catholic public theology "posits two separate spheres—one pertaining to theology, the other pertaining to the affairs of secular society—and then proposes a set of mediating terms that, by means of a process of translation, somehow links the two spheres. . . . In both the pre- and post-conciliar eras, therefore, theology is limited to functioning as a kind of conceptual reservoir providing ideals, principles, and themes to be applied to the policy issues facing the larger public called 'society,'" a society which can nevertheless already be understood on its own terms.[32]

Echoing the criticisms of Murray described in chapter 6, Baxter argues that by suggesting that religious commitments should be excluded from public discourse, the advocates of public theology are themselves expressing a religious commitment. As Baxter writes, according to the advocates of public theology, "the protocols in a pluralistic society require that political discourse be constructed and sustained without appeal to the substantive beliefs and practices of any particular ecclesial body; that is, it must be founded on an extra-theological base, whether that be the neo-scholastic 'nature,' or some surrogate of 'nature,' such as the relatively stable plane of reason-governed procedures."[33] As Baxter goes on to argue, however, the judgment that theological claims should be excluded from public discourse is itself a theological claim—namely, that at least in its political dimension society can be understood independently of theological claims—that not everyone shares and that is contrary to the traditional understanding of the relationship between nature and grace reaffirmed by the Second Vatican Council.

In sum, if official Catholic thinking about war and international order since Pope John XXIII demonstrates a convergence of the liberal understanding of international politics and a natural law approach to morality, then Hehir offers a neoliberal variation of this convergence. Hehir describes the international system in terms similar to those of the neoliberals, and in fact endorses the adoption of neoliberal ideas in Catholic thinking about international politics. In his understanding of the just war theory, Hehir abandons the more traditional natural law framework and adopts a position influenced by proportionalism. Although it is not exactly the same as utilitarianism, proportionalism tends to think of actors as rationally maximizing the good and minimizing evil. This form of moral reasoning is more compatible with the neoliberal view of states as rational actors than traditional natural law theories. Hehir also demonstrates the influence of liberalism in his claim that transcendent, religious commitments should be excluded from public discourse, or at least from actual policy making, although, as Baxter points out, the belief that society (or international politics) can be understood independently of religious commitments is itself the expression of a religious commitment.

There is much to admire in Hehir's perspective on the origins of war, even if there is much to criticize. Above all, Hehir deserves credit for doing more than any contemporary Catholic intellectual to bring Catholic moral reasoning about war into dialogue with international relations theory. Also, he has contributed some valuable insights as a result of that dialogue; for example, his assertion that Catholic thinking on international politics could pay more attention to the role of nongovernmental ties in fostering international cooperation remains true today. Hehir suffers from the limitations of the neoliberal theory he adopts, however, especially when it comes to the motivations for state behavior. His writings on war and peace are shaped by the neoliberal assumption that states are rational actors. This leads him to an unnecessarily narrow view of the reasons why states do, or should, go to war, and to downplay the importance of regime type for issues such as nuclear disarmament. Hehir's insistence that the natural law be a source of public reason also severs it from its theological roots, so that the light that theology can shed on international politics is all but lost.

GEORGE WEIGEL

If J. Bryan Hehir is representative of the liberal Catholic followers of John Courtney Murray, then George Weigel is representative of Murray's neo-conservative Catholic followers. Weigel defines neoconservative Catholicism as an alternative to both the Catholic Right, which unwisely rejected modernity entirely, and the Catholic Left, which threw out too many essential elements of the Catholic faith in its attempts to adapt to modernity.[34] Just as the political neoconservatives were liberals who became disenchanted with the radical turn of many liberals in the 1960s, the neoconservative Catholics were liberal Catholics who came to believe that many other liberal Catholics were too radical in their willingness to drop aspects of the Catholic faith for the sake of passing intellectual trends.[35] Weigel argues that one important feature distinguishing neoconservative Catholics from the Catholic Left and the Catholic Right is that they continue to believe in a fundamental compatibility between the Catholic faith and the American experiment in ordered liberty.[36] Weigel's reflection on this American experiment in ordered liberty is central to his understanding of war, its origins, and what is necessary for peace.

Weigel on *Tranquillitas Ordinis*

Beginning in the early 1980s, Weigel has argued that John Courtney Murray's approach to the just war and international order provides a necessary alternative to the perspectives dominant in American foreign policy debates. In particular, Weigel claims that realism is a flawed approach to foreign policy for three reasons: First, despite its aims, it fails to promote stability because it ignores the role of ideas in international politics; second, it fails to see that the nature of the "national interest" is the result of moral decisions; and third, in America, realism does not square with the character of the people.[37] According to Weigel, to develop an adequate foreign policy we must "rediscover the tradition of moral reasoning as exemplified (but hardly exhausted) by the natural law tradition of Murray and Maritain."[38]

Like Murray, Weigel argues that the natural law provides a way of thinking about the national interest that is not reduced to *raison d'état* and that does not see power as inherently morally problematic.[39] Somewhat like the constructivist scholar Alexander Wendt, Weigel argues that security and other material factors necessary for survival are at the core of every state's national interests, but those interests are only part of and find their meaning within a broader national purpose guided by a society's ideals. Realism ignores ideals for the sake of material factors, according to Weigel, but to go to the other extreme and ignore material security for the sake of moral ideals would be the equally fatal mistake of utopianism.[40] According to Weigel, the prudent balance of security and ideals that the natural law provides should guide the national purpose.

Weigel concludes that what he calls *tranquillitas ordinis*, or the peace that comes from just order, should be at the core of the national purpose. He argues that, at least among Christians, there are three ways of thinking about peace. The first is psychological peace, or the peace that exists within an individual person when they are properly attuned morally and spiritually. It would be futile to try to bring this sort of peace about through social policy. The second type of peace is *shalom*, or the complete fulfillment of justice and the end of all conflict. This type of peace, too, is beyond human efforts, and will only be brought about by God at the end of time. The third type of peace is the public order of laws, particularly of the sort that provide a means of resolving conflict without resort to force.[41] This public order is what Weigel later calls *tranquillitas ordinis*.[42] *Tranquillitas ordinis* at the international level would entail "ordered liberty within a structure of evolving international public life capable of advancing the classic ends of politics—justice, freedom, security, the general welfare, and peace."[43] International institutions will be necessary to meet this goal, but that does not necessarily mean support for currently existing international institutions that may not embody the values of *tranquillitas ordinis*.[44]

Weigel on the Just War

Weigel argues that the pursuit of *tranquillitas ordinis* in international politics has implications for our moral reasoning about war. Because one of the goals of *tranquillitas ordinis* is to resolve conflicts without the use of force, then whenever possible international conflicts should be resolved through peaceful means. Because a true international order has not yet been established, however, the right of states to use limited and discriminate force must be retained. Any use of force must be ordered toward the pursuit of peace, "in all of its component parts: freedom, justice, security, and order."[45] Weigel's argument that the purposes of war must include the complex social order of *tranquillitas ordinis*, at both the international and domestic levels, is a significant counterpoint to

Hehir's view. Weigel seems to see this social order, a set of relationships among individuals and institutions, as good in itself, whereas Hehir, through the influence of proportionalism and neoliberal international relations theory, tends to see international order as merely a means for states to maximize their already-existing interests. Weigel has also challenged Hehir's notion of a "presumption against war," instead arguing that just war reasoning begins with a "presumption for justice."[46]

In his writings Weigel applies his thought on international order and war to particular circumstances, beginning with the nuclear standoff between the United States and the Soviet Union in the 1980s. American Catholic intellectuals, in typically liberal fashion, tended to think of the conflict between the United States and the Soviet Union in psychological terms, as the result of misunderstandings and fear. This psychological reading of the situation was particularly centered on nuclear weapons as the source of fear. Therefore, for many people, the issue of nuclear weapons and their disarmament came to be separated from the issues of human rights and democracy, as it was for Hehir.[47] In the 1980s Weigel argued, like Murray before him, that Americans must take into consideration the totalitarian and Leninist nature of the Soviet Union when making foreign policy, meaning that material factors such as military power, particularly nuclear weapons capability, cannot be separated from the question of ideology. Weigel claims that such an approach would mean meeting Soviet aggression with military power and seeking nonviolent means of transforming the Soviet regime. This combination would be the best approach for defeating Soviet communism.[48]

In later writings Weigel sees the collapse of communism in Eastern Europe in 1989 and in the Soviet Union in 1991—a result of the combination of the exercise of American military power, nonviolent resistance in the Eastern Bloc, and economic stagnation—as vindication of his ideas. Like the constructivists, Weigel points out that most interpreters of international politics failed to predict the fall of communism in Eastern Europe and asserts that most continue to give faulty interpretations of these events. He argues that this is because of the implicit materialism of most Western commentators, who failed to note the spiritual aspect of both communism (in its denial of the spiritual dimension of the human person) and the Eastern European resistance to communism. Weigel claims that the fact that there was no shift in military power behind the collapse of communism in Eastern Europe provides evidence for the claim that military power only has meaning within a cultural and ideological framework, and that the latter has priority over the former.[49] Weigel concludes, "The Revolution of 1989 . . . ought to have driven this message home with irresistible force: the instabilities and aggression that lead to wars are caused not by weapons but by regimes (or by individuals whose regimes are expressions of their personal demons)."[50]

Beginning with the Persian Gulf War in 1991, Weigel has also addressed questions regarding what would later be called "rogue states," that is, states that are massive human rights violators and contemptuous of international law. He considers the problem of the proliferation of nuclear weapons, as well as other weapons of mass destruction. Like Hehir, Weigel believes that the proliferation of such weapons is one of the great dangers in the post–cold war world, and that preemptive military action to prevent nuclear proliferation may be justified. He argues that this is not only because of the unacceptable consequences of proliferation, but also because of regime type; it makes a difference whether nuclear weapons belong to Great Britain or to Iraq.[51] Weigel's point is clearly a development of his critique of mainstream approaches to understanding the nuclear issue during the cold war. He extends his argument about the cultural meaning of material capabilities beyond nuclear weapons, however, suggesting that the same is true of material resources; he at least considers the possibility that war may be justified if a rogue state were to gain a stranglehold on a critical material resource such as oil because of the crippling effects this would have on the world economy.[52] Weigel's argument about the proliferation of weapons of mass destruction was central to his argument in favor of the Iraq War of 2003. He adds that since there is little evidence that current international institutions are committed to the values of *tranquillitas ordinis*, then the United States is justified in acting unilaterally in the name of justice.[53] Elsewhere Weigel claims that the United States, rather than the United Nations, is the best hope for international order, and that were the United States to diminish in power, the likely result would be chaos.[54]

Weigel on the Natural Law

Like Murray, Weigel bases his account of the just war tradition on the natural law and claims that the natural law provides the most appropriate terms for moral arguments in a pluralistic society. According to Weigel, the just war criteria "provide a grammar—a kind of intellectual template—such that people of widely differing views can engage in a purposeful argument over the merits of a proposal." This is so because the just war criteria are based on the natural law, which is known intuitively and can be understood by people of widely differing views.[55] Christians may believe that grace helps us in our knowledge of the natural law, but according to Weigel, "that such a moral logic exists, that it is available to all human beings through rational reflection, and that it can be intelligibly argued in public is . . . a matter of moral common sense."[56]

For Weigel, insisting that arguments about public policy be given in the form of the natural law is consistent with permitting people to draw on their deepest religious convictions. In the United States, the First Amendment does not forbid citizens from making public policy arguments in explicitly religious terms, but according to Weigel, such arguments will be more accessible to people who do not share the Catholic Church's religious beliefs, and therefore more likely to be effective arguments, if they are offered in natural law terms. Yet opting for the natural law does not mean abandoning one's deepest religious convictions. Those convictions are simply translated into natural law terms. It is only when this translation process has taken place that an argument can truly be considered public, rather than being based on "sectarian warrants for its legitimacy."[57] This is true even though, somewhat contradictorily, Weigel claims that the Gospel is a "public Gospel."[58]

Here Weigel, like Murray before him, seems to run into a conundrum: If the natural law is understandable to all and is accessible to all through intuition and rational reflection, then how is it that societies can depart from the natural law on such a massive scale that, for example, the American public consensus guided by natural law can be in jeopardy, or that some states cannot be considered "rational actors" because they are guided by ideologies hostile to the natural law? This conundrum could be avoided by an interpretation that viewed culture, rather than intuition, as the source of understanding of the natural law.

Weigel is ambiguous about the origins of natural law arguments in American public discourse. At times, he suggests that natural law arguments arise from basic moral intuitions that all human beings share. For example, he writes that in the months leading up to the Persian Gulf War in 1991, "cab drivers, talk show hosts, barbers, columnists, and politicians were all working the issue in remarkably similar terms," that is, the terms of the just war theory. He continues: "But this really shouldn't have been a surprise. Americans instinctively argued in these categories because the just war tradition reflects those moral intuitions that natural law theorists have long believed are built into human beings, and because the just war tradition is a rational tradition of moral discourse with the ability to provide a grammar for public moral argument in a pluralistic society."[59] At other times, however, Weigel suggests that the values and purposes that guide political decision making "express the fundamental, constitutive self-understandings and values of a people—understandings and values that are frequently religious in origin and nature."[60] So, for example, Weigel writes that the just war tradition and the natural law on which it is based are part of the American "national cultural memory."[61] Weigel even characterizes American society's instinctive turn to moral categories, and the natural law in particular, as a feature that distinguishes America from other societies, particularly those of Europe.[62]

Weigel thus presents a rather optimistic description of American culture, especially when compared to other cultures. He juxtaposes a belief in instinctive knowledge of the natural law with the claim that natural law categories are part of the American national cultural memory not always found in other societies. This combination suggests the familiar theme of American cultural history that sees America as new, natural, pristine, and even primitive, in contrast to old, artificial, traditional, and even decadent Europe, even if this is not Weigel's intention. His writings imply that a distinguishing feature of American culture is that it trains Americans to reason morally in terms free from the influence of any of their culture's distinguishing features. Weigel admits that some elements of American society are ignorant of or hostile to the natural law, but like many neoconservatives he limits these elements to the so-called new class of secular, intellectual elites, with the majority of Americans remaining true to their cultural principles, although at times Weigel admits that the new class has had an influence on ordinary Americans.[63] Despite the obvious similarities in their views, Weigel's optimistic view of American society distinguishes him from Murray, who held a more mixed view. More recently, though, Weigel has expressed some concern for the health of American society and Western civilization more generally.[64]

Weigel's ambiguous statements about the natural law in American social discourse also recall the traditional liberal contrast between tradition and reason. According to this view, if a society is to be governed rationally, then arguments based on distinctive philosophical or theological beliefs ought to be excluded from public discourse (if not by law, then at least by choice). This line of argument clearly presupposes that political issues can be rationally understood and discussed without reference to the distinctive philosophical or theological beliefs of a cultural tradition or religious community. It must be noted that Weigel, as a Catholic, does not believe that distinctive theological beliefs are necessarily *irrational*, only that they contribute little to our understanding of political life. In his writings on "rogue states," he also seems to suggest that societies that fail to develop a rational social discourse accessible to all and institutions that embody rational principles are more likely to cause war. His claim that regime type is an important factor in assessing the morality of war seems to be in the tradition of John Stuart Mill's liberal imperialism. Likewise, he seems to suggest that a society becomes peaceful and just when it develops such a rational social discourse and rational institutions. A weakness of Weigel's approach, therefore, is that, like the traditional liberals, he fails to recognize that just as the violent behavior of states is fostered by the distinctive beliefs and practices of a society, the same is also true of peaceful behavior. Reason does not come from a source distinct from and contrasting with cultural influences, but emerges out of those cultural influences.

Weigel on Nature and Grace

Because of his understanding of the relationship between nature and grace, Weigel also finds little place for the distinctive beliefs of Christianity in fostering peace. David L. Schindler offers a critique of Weigel's view of American society and culture that is similar to his critique of John Courtney Murray. Schindler claims that twentieth-century theological developments, including the insights of the Second Vatican Council, reaffirm the traditional Christian view that our orientation to a supernatural destiny is fundamental to our being human, and not something added on to an already complete human nature.[65] Schindler argues that the importance of this fundamental orientation is missing in Weigel's thought, leading Weigel to the view that society can be understood apart from our relation with God, or at least apart from our supernatural destiny.[66] This has the effect that, in the neoconservative view represented by Weigel, "the Church adds something definite and gratuitous to the world, but only by way of inspiration (privately), and in anticipation of the life to come."[67] What this means is that the truth of revelation entrusted to the church is not really necessary for understanding political life. According to Weigel, depending on Christian revelation to understand politics would be impractical because Christians themselves do not agree on the content and significance of that revelation, and more importantly, because it seemingly excludes nonbelievers from public discourse.[68]

In his *Soul of the World: Notes on the Future of Public Catholicism*, Weigel attempts to respond to criticisms like that of Schindler. He writes that he has increasingly come to see that human existence is "cruciform": Its meaning is fully revealed in the life, death, and resurrection of Christ.[69] He continues, "As the Swiss theologian Hans Urs von Balthasar put it, the 'historical event of Christ's redemption of mankind' cuts through the entire cosmos 'in longitudinal section,' leaving no person, and indeed no aspect of creation, untouched."[70] The church is of central importance because it is "the 'school' in which we 'saints' learn our true nature and destiny, as revealed by Christ."[71] Likewise, to fulfill its role, the church must be centered on the Eucharist.[72] Weigel's new recognition of the cruciform nature of human existence and his focus on the church and the Eucharist are positive developments, but they lead to little real change in his account of politics.

Weigel interprets the truth claims of Christianity primarily as placing limits on the state from the outside. The church demands the space to proclaim the Gospel, thereby creating an authority independent of the state and limiting the authority of the state. Christianity also provides us with an ultimate hope that lies beyond this world, challenging those who seek ultimate fulfillment in this world through a worldly utopia. Weigel believes this challenge is essential for a pluralist society in which diverse proposals for ordering public life are considered and debated.[73] Thus Schindler seems correct when he argues that for Weigel, the church does add something to society, but only from the outside and only "in anticipation of the life to come." This is reflected in Weigel's earlier sharp distinction between the peace of *tranquillitas ordinis* and the peace of *shalom*; of course the latter cannot be fully established in this world, but that does not necessarily mean that it must be wholly relegated to the life to come, or that its first fruits are not necessary for the peace of *tranquillitas ordinis*.

Despite his insistence that Christ fully reveals the meaning of human existence, Weigel finds that theological concepts contribute little to our understanding of politics that cannot already be known through the natural law. Although he claims that Christian revelation shows the limits of the authority of the state, the state's limited authority is already a truth of the natural law. And even if the church does place limits on society and the state, both are still governed by their own "autonomous" logic, which is expressed in terms of the natural law.

Therefore, in *Soul of the World*, Weigel continues to insist that when making arguments about public policy, Christians should translate their deepest convictions into terms understandable to all.[74] This is because "we cannot debate the oughts of our common life unless we can make moral sense to one another. And we cannot do this without a grammar by which the conversation about those oughts is ordered."[75] In fact, he goes a step further, arguing that "society will descend into . . . Hobbes's dread war of 'all against all,' unless we can talk together in such a way that we make sense to one another—or at least enough sense to conduct the public argument that is the lifeblood of democracy."[76] Here again we see the familiar idea that arguments that draw on particular religious claims imply violence or at least tend toward violence. This suggestion is balanced by some statements in Weigel's later writings, such as his assertion that "how men and women think about God—or don't think about God—has a great deal to do with how they envision the just society, and how they determine the appropriate means by which to build that society"[77] Still, the dominant tendency in his writings is to imply that it is the failure to translate religious or other particular beliefs into public terms that leads to violence.

Weigel's association of violence with particular religious claims not shared by all seems to suggest, at least, that ultimately he finds the origins of war in particularistic truth claims. In his claim that war primarily has its origins in the clash of culturally formed identities, interests, and norms, Weigel seems to be agreeing with much of the understanding of war's origins that I described in chapter 5. Yet he does not conclude that peace can be brought about when identities, interests, and norms are formed according to the particular truths about the human person revealed by Christianity. Rather, Weigel implies that peace can come about when the public order he calls *tranquillitas ordinis* has been established internationally, if *tranquillitas ordinis* is understood to mean a public order in which individuals and states translate their arguments and proposals into terms supposedly understandable to all. American power is essential for the establishment of *tranquillitas ordinis* at the international level not because the United States is a particularly righteous or Christian nation, but because it has most successfully developed domestically the public order that is so desperately needed internationally.

What Weigel fails to see is that this supposedly neutral public order itself has its own hidden theological presuppositions, presuppositions that, as Schindler argues, conflict with those proposed by the Second Vatican Council and recent Catholic theology. If it really is true that we are oriented toward union with God and that this affects all of human existence, including political life, then the denial of this truth would be more likely to lead to violence and conflict than to true peace. One strength of Weigel's work is his emphasis on the importance of culture and regime type in contributing to war, but this emphasis needs to be balanced by a greater focus on the way specific cultural and religious beliefs and practices can contribute to peace.

CONCLUSION

Following John Courtney Murray, J. Bryan Hehir and George Weigel emphasize the importance of public reason for moral discourse, and this emphasis greatly affects their accounts of war and its origins. Hehir claims that arguments about public policy should be given in language that is understandable to all regardless of their religious convictions, and in his moral reflection on war he turns to a moral theory, proportionalism, that helps him explain how political actors can make rational choices. He also embraces neoliberalism as a helpful way of understanding international politics and the origins of war, thereby opening himself to the criticisms made by the constructivists described in chapter 4. Like Murray, Weigel emphasizes the role of ideology in forming state behavior, and therefore in causing war, but for Weigel it is not necessarily the content of these ideologies that is significant as a cause of war, but simply the fact that they are based on particular religious or ideological claims rather than on public reason accessible to all. According to Weigel, peace is most likely to be established when we put aside our distinctive beliefs or at least translate them into something else; he fails to see that peace, just as much as war, depends on the development of a distinctive set of beliefs and practices.

When one considers the thought of Hehir and Weigel alongside that of Dorothy Day, described in chapter 6, it is evident that the dominant strands of recent American Catholic thinking about war and its origins have been profoundly influenced by the characteristic feature of modern political thought, the separation of the political from the transcendent. This influence has led most Catholics who think about war to be blind to the ways in which war originates in the human drama of sin and grace. Of course, each of these thinkers recognizes that ultimately war is rooted in the sinful condition of humanity, but they have lost sight of the Christian tradition's rich and ancient account of this human drama, which ties sin and grace to the cultural practices that form our identities, interests, and norms, both as individuals and as societies, and that ultimately cause war, but also can contribute to its prevention.

NOTES

1. Gould, "Liberal Political Culture," 134.
2. Heyer, *Prophetic and Public*, 60.
3. Hehir, "Ethic of War and Theology of Peace," 24–25.

4. Hehir, "New World Disorders," 224–27; see also Hehir, "Challenge to Theology," 141–50; Hehir, "Use of Force," 86–89.

5. Hehir, "Challenge to Theology," 151–55.

6. Hehir, "Strategy and Ethics," 110–13.

7. Hehir, "Murray on Foreign Policy," 234–37.

8. Hehir, "New World Disorders," 231–33.

9. Hehir, "Human Rights," 1–3, 16–21.

10. Hehir, "United States and Human Rights," 243–49.

11. Hehir, "Strategy and Ethics," 123–24.

12. Hehir, "Military Intervention," 39–46.

13. Hehir, "Kosovo," 399–405.

14. Hehir, "Religion, Realism, and Just Intervention," 29–32; see also Hehir, "Moral Measurement," 50.

15. Hehir, "Intervention and International Affairs," 138–49.

16. Hehir, "Moral Dimension," 14–17.

17. Hehir, "Just-War Ethic and Catholic Theology," 18–19.

18. The proportionalist moral theologian Richard McCormick, SJ, explicitly makes a connection between his own method of proportionate reasoning and the "prima facie evil" approach to moral reasoning about war. *Notes on Moral Theology, 1965–1980*, 584–86.

19. McCormick, *Corrective Vision*, 8–9.

20. Hehir, "Just-War Ethic and Catholic Theology," 30–32. Significantly, he has continued to defend Childress's approach to the just war theory, for example, against the Protestant theologian James Turner Johnson, even after Pope John Paul II's condemnation of proportionalism as an approach to moral theology in his 1993 encyclical *Veritatis splendor*. "In Defense of Justice," 33.

21. Hehir, "Catholic Teaching," 371–72; Hehir, "Just-War Ethic Revisited," 146–47; "Military Intervention," 42.

22. McCormick, *Notes on Moral Theology, 1965–1980*, 645–46.

23. Throughout his notes on moral theology, McCormick uses terms such as "greater good" and "lesser evil," "weighing," and "calculus." *Notes on Moral Theology, 1965–1980*, 356, 358, 366–67, 542. After theologians such as Paul Ramsey, Germain Grisez, and William E. May had made the criticism that the various goods that motivate human choice are incommensurable, McCormick modified his position to state that a good can be harmed if so doing leads to a greater fulfillment of that same good. *Notes on Moral Theology, 1965–1980*, 717–23. Other proportionalists, however, maintained the original position that even disparate goods can be weighed and compared.

24. Germain Grisez, *Christian Moral Principles*, 150–54.

25. For example, McCormick refers to an action carried out by an individual as "the immediate implications of our activity," as if the self through some mysterious process sets in motion a chain of events, rather than being involved in carrying out the choice. The self remains somewhat aloof from the choices it carries out. "Notes on Moral Theology: 1982," 84–85.

26. Grisez, *Christian Moral Principles*, 121–25.

27. Ibid., 154–56.

28. Heyer, *Prophetic and Public*, 65.

29. Hehir, "Social Values," 60–61.

30. Dean, Noll, Bednarowski, and Hehir, "Public Theology," 22.

31. Hehir, "A Catholic Troeltsch?," 203; see also Heyer, *Prophetic and Public*, 62–63.

32. Baxter, "Reintroducing Virgil Michel," 521–22.

33. Baxter, "Non-Catholic Character," 255.

34. Weigel, "Neoconservative Difference," 138–40.

35. Ibid., 144–46.

36. Ibid., 154–57.

37. Weigel, "Poverty of Conventional Realism," 72–87.

38. Weigel, *American Interests, American Purpose*, 17.

39. Weigel, "National Interest," 16–20; Weigel, "World Order," 31–32.

40. Weigel, "National Interest," 20–22; Weigel, *Idealism without Illusions*, 96–97.

41. Weigel, *Peace & Freedom*, 41–47.

42. Weigel, "Churches and the Gulf Crisis," 85–90.

43. Weigel, "National Interest," 21; see also Weigel, "Free and Virtuous Society," 27.

44. Weigel, "John Courtney Murray Project," 294.

45. Weigel, "From Last Resort," 32.

46. Weigel, "Moral Clarity," 22–23; Griffiths and Weigel, "Just War," 34–35; Williams and Weigel, "War & Statecraft," 19.

47. Weigel, *Tranquillitas Ordinis*, 265–67, 359–63.

48. Ibid., 371–77.

49. Weigel, *Idealism without Illusions*, 11–58.

50. Ibid., 77–78.

51. Weigel, *Idealism without Illusions*, 153–56; Weigel, "Low-Intensity Conflict," 258.

52. Weigel, *Idealism without Illusions*, 156–57.

53. Weigel, "Moral Clarity," 20–27.

54. Weigel, "Low-Intensity Conflict," 253–56.

55. Weigel, *Renewal of American Democracy*, 197–200; Weigel, *Tranquillitas Ordinis*, 120.

56. Weigel, "Talking the Talk," 87.

57. Ibid., 88; Weigel, *Renewal of American Democracy*, 115–16.

58. Weigel, *Renewal of American Democracy*, 204.

59. Weigel, "From Last Resort," 39–40; see also Weigel, "Low-Intensity Conflict," 251–52; Weigel, *Soul of the World*, 73–74.

60. Weigel, "Religion and Peace," 242.

61. Weigel, "Moral Clarity," 20–21.

62. Weigel, "Low-Intensity Conflict," 252.

63. Weigel, "Is America Bourgeois?," 82–84; Weigel, "Response to Mark Lowery," 446–47.

64. Weigel, *Cube and Cathedral*.

65. Schindler, "Is America Bourgeois?," 267–71.

66. Ibid., 272–73; Weigel, "Church's 'Worldly' Mission," 382.

67. Schindler, *Heart of the World*, 5.

68. Weigel, *Renewal of American Democracy*, 194–97.

69. Weigel, *Soul of the World*, 3–4.

70. Ibid., 13–14. The citation is from von Balthasar, *Lay Styles*, 100.

71. Weigel, *Soul of the World*, 16.

72. Ibid., 41–43.
73. Ibid., 37–39.
74. Ibid., 68.
75. Ibid., 156.
76. Ibid., 73.
77. Weigel, *Faith, Reason*, 13.

Conclusion

MODERN CATHOLIC THINKING on war, with its emphasis on war's morality, has ignored many of the insights of the long tradition of Christian reflection on the origins of war. Beginning with the Bible and the church fathers and continuing into the Counter-Reformation, Christian thinking about war has coupled the more well-known reflection on the morality of war with a description of the origins of war, in which war is described as being rooted in particular cultural and religious practices that shape the behavior of those responsible for making decisions about war. As modern political thought rejected the basic presuppositions of the traditional Christian view of politics, this perspective on war's origins was lost; modern political thinkers developed ways of understanding the origins of war based on very different presuppositions. Catholics in the modern period challenged some of the basic principles of modern political thought that conflicted with more traditional Christian principles, but at the same time adopted ways of understanding war's origins that are derived from those same modern principles. This appropriation has affected both official Catholic teaching on war and the writings of Catholic theologians. Taken together, the emergence of constructivism in the field of international relations theory and shifts in twentieth-century Catholic theology provide an opportunity for developing a more adequate Catholic perspective on the origins of war. I hope this book has provided the beginnings of just such a perspective.

I began this book by showing how the Iraq War brought to the fore the frustrating diversity of views within the Catholic Church on the ethics of war, and then I undertook to prove that behind that diversity was an unwitting unity: Most Catholics writing or speaking on war have a perspective on the origins of war that is shaped by theories based on certain presuppositions about the political sphere and its relation to the transcendent, presuppositions that those very Catholics would not accept. To conclude the book, it will be useful to look at how major Catholic voices responded to the Iraq War and how their responses reflect the themes laid out in earlier chapters. I will use these observations to point out areas in which Catholic thinking on war and peace needs to continue to develop. I do not claim that the insights of this book will somehow bring Catholics together, and I may end up being just one more voice amidst the diversity. I do believe, however, that these ideas can move the conversation forward.

Pope John Paul II vocally opposed the U.S.-led invasion of Iraq in 2003 because the war did not meet the just war criterion of last resort and because it did not have the authorization of the United Nations Security Council. As he stated in his 2003 Address to the Vatican Diplomatic Corps, "As the Charter of the United Nations Organization and international law itself remind us, war cannot be decided upon, even when it is a matter of ensuring the common good, except as the very last option and in accordance with very strict conditions, without ignoring the consequences for the civilian population both during and after the military operations."[1] In John Paul's view, Saddam Hussein's Iraq was clearly in violation of its obligations toward the United Nations in regards to dismantling its programs for weapons of mass destruction and allowing international inspectors to verify that dismantling, but the international community should have been given more time to force Hussein to comply with those requirements before the United States resorted to violence. The statements of other Vatican officials, such as Jean-Louis Tauran, the Vatican foreign minister, and Pio Laghi, the former Nuncio to the United States, showed that the Vatican was also concerned that military action not take place without the approval of the United Nations.[2]

Although John Paul's point—that the threat from Iraq was not so pressing as to prevent further efforts, short of war, to force compliance with UN mandates—has some merit, he does not consider all of the relevant historical background. The sanctions against Iraq were imposed in 1991, following Iraq's defeat in the Persian Gulf War. By 1995, France and Russia, who had had extensive commercial relationships with Iraq prior to the Persian Gulf War, began advocating for the end of sanctions, despite the ongoing revelations of weapons inspections. Also in 1995, in response to criticisms (including those of John Paul) that the sanctions on Iraq were predominantly harming civilians, the UN Security Council approved the Oil-for-Food Programme, which allowed Iraq to sell oil in order to buy civilian goods. Saddam Hussein soon found that he could exploit the program by providing the rights to Iraqi oil to anyone willing to pay a price to the Iraqi government. Hussein used this scheme to build support for the end of sanctions. After the war, investigators found that the top three countries with individuals or companies benefiting from the scheme were Russia, France, and China. Major beneficiaries of the program included important Russian politicians and political parties, the French and Russian nationally owned oil companies, and the French bank BNP, which was responsible for carrying out the financial transactions. The head of the United Nations agency responsible for overseeing the program also received these oil rights.[3]

French and Russian manipulation of the sanctions continued as war approached in 2003. In mid-2001, the United States and United Kingdom proposed a revision of the sanctions, called "smart sanctions," which would have lifted the embargo completely on civilian goods while keeping in place an embargo on weapons and other military-related goods; the proposal would also have put Iraq oil sales directly under the control of the UN, since the Oil-for-Food Programme would have no longer been necessary. Despite the humanitarian benefits of the proposal, Russia threatened to veto it and instead advocated for the continuation of Oil-for-Food. In return for blocking the revised sanctions, Iraq granted Russia the rights to develop the largest oil field in the Middle East once sanctions were lifted, rights that had belonged to France prior to its signing onto the idea of "smart sanctions."[4] Despite approving of smart sanctions, France had proposed a much smaller list of prohibited military items, likely because since 1998 France had been making illegal arms deals with Iraq.[5] In late 2002, at the urging of the United States, the United Nations Security Council approved Resolution 1441 calling on Iraq to readmit weapons inspectors, who had been pulled out of Iraq in 1998; inspections began later that year. As the inspections continued into 2003, France and Russia made it clear that under no circumstances would they ever support the use of military force, regardless of the results of the inspections.[6] When Iraq showed only limited compliance with the demands of the UN inspections, the United States, the United Kingdom, and several allies declared war on Iraq, but without UN Security Council approval.

Pope John Paul II presented criticisms of the war in Iraq that demonstrated in a concrete way the optimistic view of international institutions attributed to him and to his predecessors John XXIII and Paul VI. John Paul argued that other means should have been attempted to resolve the issue with Iraq before resorting to force, but given the circumstances, it is not clear what those means would have been. France and Russia favored the ending of sanctions entirely, or as a second best option, inspections with no consequences and the continuation of the Oil-for-Food Progamme, from which they were profiting handsomely. Saddam Hussein believed that because France or Russia would veto any resolution in favor of war, he could lead the inspectors along without fully cooperating.[7] Pope John Paul remained optimistic that international cooperation could resolve the crisis without war, but it was in fact international cooperation that had prolonged the humanitarian crisis of sanctions against civilian goods and made meaningful inspections impossible. Under such circumstances, it is also not immediately clear that the Security Council's refusal to authorize war rendered the United States and United Kingdom military action unjust.

As I have argued in the previous chapters, official Catholic teaching on war and peace could benefit from a more explicit understanding of the ways in which sin and grace permeate the international system, including international institutions. In practical terms, this might mean recognizing that there are often limited options besides war for resolving conflict, and that at times international institutions can hinder the pursuit of peace as much as help it. For example, the 1999 NATO humanitarian intervention in Kosovo was technically illegal because it did not have Security Council approval, due to the opposition of China and Russia, but was widely considered legitimate because of its humanitarian purpose. The Catholic Church has a long tradition of thinking about how we ought to respond morally to immoral laws, and it might be useful for official Catholic teaching to apply those insights to international law, rather than giving it the almost absolute authority often found in Vatican pronouncements concerning the Iraq War.

A greater emphasis on the role of culture in the international system suggests the need for official Catholic teaching to define the terms used in a moral analysis of war, such as "aggression" and "defense," with greater precision. In official Catholic documents, definitions of these terms are given with little explanation, are rarely consistent from one document to another, and are not consistently applied to conflict situations. Official Catholic teaching must fully answer the question, raised by George Weigel and others, whether a violent and oppressive ideology combined with means of wreaking massive havoc constitutes "aggression." "Aggression" might include more than just the physical act of military attack; other actions far short of this can take on the status of aggression within the context of a state's culturally formed identities, interests, and norms. In the post–September 11 world, one must also consider that a hostile country could secretly provide weapons of mass destruction to a terrorist organization while maintaining plausible deniability of its own involvement. In 2002, Iraq appeared to be such a nexus of hostility to the United States, disregard for international norms, possession or pursuit of weapons of mass destruction, and support for terrorism.

J. Bryan Hehir's analysis of the Iraq War also illustrates some of the themes of this book. Other than a short article criticizing the Iraq War as a "war of choice" rather than a "war of necessity,"[8] Hehir's major writing on the topic of Iraq is his analysis of the Bush administration's national security strategy, which, as Hehir notes, provided the broader framework for understanding American policy toward Iraq.[9] Hehir outlines some of the main points of the strategy, including U.S. ambition to remain the preeminent world power and its legitimation of preemptive wars to prevent terrorist or rogue states from acquiring weapons of mass destruction. He then surveys reactions to the National Security Strategy, including supporters such as authors John Lewis Gaddis and Joshua Muravchik, and critics such as scholars (and liberal internationalists) G. John Ikenberry and Stanley Hoffmann. Hehir clearly sides with the critics, who believe that the strategy "turns the United States into a global arbitrator of right and wrong and opens the door to force without restraint." Hehir goes on to claim that "the legal restraints [of the UN Charter] are procedural; they seek to contain the dynamic and drive toward war as a means of solving problems." The 2002 national security strategy, in turn, erodes "the restraint and stability" necessary for "managing 'the anarchy' of world politics."[10] The Iraq War, according to Hehir, demonstrated the hubris of this strategy and was needlessly destabilizing.

As I show in chapter 9, Hehir is very much influenced by neoliberal international relations theory, and that influence is demonstrated in his analysis of the national security strategy. According to neoliberalism, states pursue their rational self-interest and in the process form "international regimes," ranging from informal agreements to full-blown international institutions, as a means of mutual benefit. Although these regimes limit the freedom of participating states, in the end they are more beneficial than a pure state of anarchy, not least because they decrease the likelihood of conflict among states. With this perspective, it is clear how the national security strategy could be so dangerous in Hehir's view. It threatens to undermine the international regimes that promote peace and international well-being, including the well-being of the United States itself.

Such an analysis is open to three criticisms, however. First, it assumes that the regimes established by states will necessarily be cooperative and beneficial. In reality, though, regimes will only embody the values and norms of their participants, and these may very well be quite destructive. Second, it assumes that breaking with international regimes will necessarily be destabilizing. But if regimes can embody destructive as well as beneficial values, then some international regimes may themselves be destabilizing, and in those cases where they do promote stability, stability may not necessarily be a virtue. Third, because it assumes as given that states act in their rational self-interest, Hehir's analysis sees any act of breaking with international regimes as an exercise of naked self-interest, but states are governed by norms when acting on their own just as much as when acting within a regime, and those norms may be good or bad.

The preceding is fairly abstract, but it has direct relevance for the 2002 national security strategy and the Iraq War. Although the United States did break from international restraints by invading Iraq in 2003, it would be a hard case to show that those international restraints were fostering international well-being. The status quo of the United Nations Security Council prolonged the humanitarian crisis in Iraq and eroded the sanctions that were keeping Iraq from developing weapons of mass destruction. The U.S. invasion of Iraq did destabilize the Middle East, but as President Bush pointed out on many occasions, it was the stability promoted by decades of American policy that had put in place dictators such as Saddam Hussein and that had led to the resentment fueling terrorist movements. A radical transformation of the Middle East may not lead to positive change, but policies should be judged based on a rational analysis of their possible outcomes, not by the mere fact that they are destabilizing. Finally, by assuming that any break with multilateralism is necessarily an act of naked self-interest, Hehir's analysis of the Iraq War morally evaluates American intentions in Iraq in terms of their relation to international opinion, rather than on their own terms. Hehir himself admits that "given the dangers of weapons of mass destruction . . . a case for intervention is possible," but in such cases, "moral issues of proper authority and last resort, as well as political-legal issues of establishing dangerous precedents for invoking nonproliferation as a basis for intervention remain unresolved."[11] These unresolved issues are at the heart of a situation that neoliberalism has a hard time explaining: when a powerful nation is morally in the right but is constrained by an unjust international regime. There are certainly dangers when one state has the power to act with little restraint, but in any given situation, the values promoted by the powerful state must be compared to the values promoted by the international restraints. To develop a more adequate understanding of war and peace, Catholic thinkers must reconsider the role of power in international politics.

Supporters of the war in Iraq were not without flaws in their perspective on the war, and by arguing that Catholics such as Hehir unjustly distrust American power, I am not endorsing an uncritical "American exceptionalism." As I describe in the previous chapter, George Weigel claims that when considering threats to national security, one must consider states' ideologies. He draws a distinction between societies, such as that of the United States, in which people have largely learned to translate their religious or other deepest values into rational principles of public discourse accessible to all, and "rogue states" that inevitably act in irrational and unjust ways. Weigel applied this argument to Iraq in 2003, arguing that the nexus of Iraq's regime, pursuit of weapons of mass destruction, and support of terrorism justified war, even if the United States had to act without the approval of the United Nations.[12] This analysis is flawed in two major ways: in its characterization of rogue states and in its characterization of American society.

Weigel's description of rogue states is plagued by a limited notion of rationality. In his analysis, rationality is defined in terms of public accessibility; in a sense, it consists in setting aside those particularities, whether cultural or religious, that make one different from others. Rogue states are "irrational" to the extent that they refuse to be governed by this publicly accessible reason and by the political institutions that embody it. As I have tried to show, however, it is precisely the particular communities to which we belong that shape the way we think by giving us our identities, interests, and norms of behavior, and the same is true for societies or states. What this means is that, in effect, rogue states are not irrational, but rather simply governed by a different rationality. I should be clear that I am not advocating relativism, in which we all have our own rationality, and that's that; some rationalities may be more or less rational depending on their correspondence with the deep reality of things. What I am saying is that when looking at state behavior, one must patiently study the identities, interests, and norms that shape the behavior of so-called rogue states, rather than concluding that they are simply irrational and will respond to nothing but force. Such study might lead to ways of resolving international conflicts short of war; if it did reveal that war is in fact called for, this would not be because the state is irrational, but rather because there is a fundamental clash of identities, interest, and norms for which both sides are willing to fight.

Weigel's description of the United States is also flawed because of his limited view of irrationality; this flaw also finds its way into his analysis of war. In

Weigel's view, the American people are mostly good and are open to reasonable arguments. There may be negative influences on American culture from the cultural elites, but the ordinary American people are largely uncorrupted. When the United States faces a decision about war, claims Weigel, the people instinctively turn to just war reasoning. There is certainly much to admire in American culture, but it is also penetrated by a materialism that is sometimes reflected in Americans' attitudes toward foreign policy; the consumerism that Pope John Paul II so often criticized is only one symptom of this materialism. On the one hand, many Americans take the "base and slothful concept of life" described by Pope Paul VI and "seek only a flight from their responsibility, from the risks that are necessarily involved in the accomplishment of great duties and generous exploits," promoting a type of isolationism or pacifism.[13] Even those who have tried to use American power to promote American ideals, however, have succumbed to a form of materialism by, for example, focusing on high-tech weaponry instead of the manpower and human capital necessary for actually accomplishing the military goals the United States sets for itself.[14] This failure was above all demonstrated in the contrast between the ease with which the U.S. military toppled Saddam Hussein's regime in Iraq and the military's total unpreparedness for the reconstruction to follow. Rather than being instinctive just warriors, the American people tend to favor easily winnable wars against threats to America's own national interests, while avoiding humanitarian interventions.[15] Therefore there is much room for improvement when it comes to the values shaping American foreign policy.

These two limitations in Weigel's perspective are reflected in his views on the Iraq War. Weigel, like many American conservatives, was quick to point to Iraq as a necessary target of American military action. This perception of Iraq as an immediate threat was shaped by Weigel's notion of the rogue state as inherently irrational. Although, as I have already shown, there were serious flaws in the argument that the war with Iraq failed the test of last resort, a more nuanced understanding of Iraq's interests might have suggested serious means the United States might have attempted to use to neutralize Iraq without resorting to war. A more realistic assessment of American culture and its influence on American foreign policy also might have led to a more accurate forecasting of the results of the invasion of Iraq, such as the reluctance to rebuild what had been destroyed, and therefore a more nuanced analysis of the costs and benefits of the war.

An examination of the thought of Hehir and Weigel suggests that Catholics need a better account of the natural law, and in particular, a better approach to moral reasoning about war. Hehir and Weigel, like Maritain and Murray before them, share an understanding of the natural law as a set of principles that can be rationally understood by all regardless of their particular religious and cultural background. When seen in the light of the modern sense of historicity, or the way in which human thinking and acting are shaped by a person's cultural, political, and economic location, this way of understanding the rationality of the natural law is untenable. Without giving up the belief that the natural law reflects what is reasonable, it is more appropriate to think of awareness of the natural law as emerging from within one's culture rather than apart from it. Placing moral reasoning about war in a natural law framework, this means that Catholic thinkers need to pay much more attention to the ways in which state behavior related to war is shaped by culture. Both evil behavior that leads to war and behavior in accord with the natural law that leads to peace come about because of the particular shape of the culture that forms state behavior.

Looking at Hehir and Weigel's thought also shows that Catholics who are concerned with promoting peace must not only condemn actions that contribute to war, but also seek to promote a culture that embodies the beliefs and practices that foster peaceful behavior. Hehir downplays the importance of culture for international institutions, and Weigel downplays its importance for just political institutions. In recent decades, some moral theologians have emphasized the virtues, in contrast to moral theories that focus exclusively on moral decision making. These moral theologians argue that if we wait until we have a decision to make to begin to think about morality, it is already too late. We should already be working on becoming the sort of person who makes good decisions, and that means developing the virtues. The same is true for states when it comes to making decisions about war. A society's first priority is not making the right choice when it has to make decisions about war; its first priority should be to develop the sort of culture that is more likely to make the right choices when faced with those decisions. I believe that the perspective on war's origins that I have developed provides a useful framework for beginning to consider how we can go about doing that.

NOTES

1. John Paul II, "2003 Address to the Diplomatic Corps."
2. Catholic World News, "Still Fighting against War."
3. Duelfer, *Comprehensive Report*, 20–45.
4. Boehlert, "Will Russia Protect Iraq?"
5. Duelfer, *Comprehensive Report*, 111–12.
6. Sciolino, "France to Veto Resolution."
7. Woods, Lacey, and Murray, "Saddam's Delusions," 2–3.
8. Hehir, "An Unnecessary War," 7–8. What such an analysis fails to recognize is that even in cases of self-defense, war is always a choice; of course, Hehir is referring to moral necessity, but to use necessity as a criterion for moral judgment about war simply begs the question, since moral judgment is required to know what is morally necessary.
9. Hehir, "New National Security Strategy," 8.
10. Ibid., 9–12.

11. Ibid., 12.
12. Weigel, "Moral Clarity," 24–26.
13. Paul VI, "1968 World Day of Peace Message."
14. Kagan, "U.S. Military's Manpower Crisis," 97–110.
15. Eichenberg, "Victory Has Many Friends," 140–77.

BIBLIOGRAPHY

Adler, Emanuel. "Constructivism and International Relations." In *Handbook of International Relations*, edited by Walter Carlsnaes, Thomas Risse, and Beth Simmons, 95–118. Thousand Oaks, CA: Sage, 2002.

Alighieri, Dante. *Monarchia*. Translated by Prue Shaw. Cambridge & New York: Cambridge University Press, 1995.

Angell, Norman. *The Great Illusion: A Study of the Relation of Military Power in Nations to Their Economic and Social Advantage*. With an introduction by S. J. Stearns. New York: Garland Publications, 1972.

Aquinas, Thomas. *On Kingship, to the King of Cyprus*. Translated by Gerald B. Phelan. Revised by I. T. Eischmann. Toronto: Pontifical Institute of Mediaeval Studies, 1949.

———. *Summa Theologica*. Translated by Fathers of the English Dominican Province. New York: Benziger, 1947–48.

Ashley, Richard K. "Political Realism and Human Interests." *International Studies Quarterly* 25 (1981): 204–36.

———. "The Poverty of Neorealism." In Keohane, *Neorealism and Its Critics*, 255–300.

———. "Three Modes of Economism." *International Studies Quarterly* 27 (1983): 463–96.

Augustine. *City of God*. Translated by Henry Bettenson. London & New York: Penguin Books, 1984.

———. *The Confessions*. Translated by R. S. Pine-Coffin. New York: Penguin Books, 1961.

———. *Free Choice of the Will*. Translated by Robert P. Russell, OSA. Fathers of the Church: A New Translation, vol. 59, 63–241. Washington, DC: Catholic University of America Press, 1968.

———. "Letter 189." Translated by Sister Wilfrid Parsons. Fathers of the Church: A New Translation, vol. 30, 266–271. New York: Fathers of the Church, 1955.

———. *On Christian Doctrine*. Translated by D. W. Robertson. New York: Macmillan, 1987.

———. *Reply to Faustus the Manichaean*. Select Library of Nicene and Post-Nicene Fathers of the Christian Church, edited by Philip Schaff, first series, vol. 4, 155–345. New York: Christian Literature Co., 1887. Reprint, Peabody, MA: Hendrickson, 1995.

Bainton, Roland H. *Christian Attitudes toward War and Peace: A Historical Survey and Critical Re-Evaluation*. Nashville, TN: Abingdon Press, 1960.

Baxter, Michael J., CSC. "'Blowing the Dynamite of the Church': Catholic Radicalism from a Catholic Radicalist Perspective." In Thorn, Runkel, and Mountin, *Dorothy Day and the Catholic Worker Movement: Centenary Essays*, 79–94.

_____. "Reintroducing Virgil Michel: Towards a Counter-Tradition of Catholic Social Ethics in the United States." *Communio* 24 (1997): 499–528.

_____. "Review Essay: The Non-Catholic Character of the Public Church." *Modern Theology* 11 (1995): 243–58.

Beard, Charles A. *The Devil Theory of War: An Inquiry into the Nature of History and the Possibility of Keeping Out of War.* New York: Greenwood Press, 1969.

Bell, Daniel M., Jr. *Just War as Christian Discipleship: Recentering the Tradition in the Church Rather than the State.* Grand Rapids, MI: Brazos Press, 2009.

Pope Benedict XV. *Ad beatissimi apostolorum.* 1914.

_____. *Pacem Dei munus pulcherrimum.* 1920.

Bentham, Jeremy. *A Fragment on Government.* Edited and with an introduction by F. C. Montague. London: Oxford University Press, 1951.

_____. "Anarchical Fallacies." In *The History of Economic Thought: A Reader,* edited by Steven G. Medema and Warren J. Samuels, 188–91. London & New York: Routledge, 2003.

_____. *Plan for an Universal and Perpetual Peace.* With an introduction by C. John Colombos. Peace Classics, 6. London: Peace Book Co., 1939. Reprinted in *Peace Projects of the Eighteenth Century.* With an introduction by M. C. Jacob. Garland Library of War and Peace, edited by Blance Wiesen Cook, Sandi E. Cooper, and Charles Chatfield. New York & London: Garland, 1974.

Bernstein, Carl, and Marco Politi. *His Holiness: John Paul II and the History of Our Time.* New York: Penguin Books, 1997.

Bevans, Stephen B. *Models of Contextual Theology.* Rev. ed. Maryknoll, NY: Orbis Books, 2002.

Boehlert, Eric. "Will Russia Protect Iraq from the U.S.?" *Salon,* November 15, 2001. http://www.salon.com/news/feature/2001/11/15/iraq (accessed May 24, 2010).

Boucher, David. *Political Theories of International Relations: From Thucydides to the Present.* Oxford & New York: Oxford University Press, 1998.

Brewer, Anthony. *Marxist Theories of Imperialism: A Critical Study,* 2nd ed. London & New York: Routledge, 1990.

Brown, Michael E., Sean M. Lynn-Jones, and Steven E. Miller, eds. *Debating the Democratic Peace.* Cambridge, MA: MIT Press, 1996.

Bueno de Mesquita, Bruce, James D. Morrow, Randolph M. Siverson, and Alastair Smith. "An Institutional Explanation of the Democratic Peace." *American Political Science Review* 93 (1999): 791–807.

Burchill, Scott. "Realism and Neo-realism." In *Theories of International Relations,* 2nd ed., edited by Scott Burchill et al., 70–102. Houndmills, UK & New York: Palgrave, 2001.

Cahill, Lisa Sowle. *Love Your Enemies: Discipleship, Pacifism, and Just War Theory.* Minneapolis: Fortress Press, 1994.

Calvin, John. *Institutes of the Christian Religion.* Edited by John T. McNeill. Translated by Ford Lewis Battles. Library of Christian Classics, edited by John Baillie, John T. McNeill, and Henry P. Van Dusen, vols. 20–21. Philadelphia: Westminster Press, 1960.

Capizzi, Joseph E. "War and International Order." *Communio* 31 (2004): 280–301.

Catholic World News, "Still Fighting against War," April 15, 2003. http://www.catholicculture.org/news/features/index.cfm?recnum=21822 (accessed May 24, 2010).

Cavanaugh, William T. *Torture and Eucharist: Theology, Politics, and the Body of Christ.* Challenges in Contemporary Theology, edited by Gareth Jones and Lewis Ayres. Oxford: Blackwell, 1998.

Chatfield, Charles. "The Catholic Worker in the United States Peace Tradition." In Klejment and Roberts, *American Catholic Pacifism: The Influence of Dorothy Day and the Catholic Worker Movement,* 1–13.

Coffey, David. "The Whole Rahner on the Supernatural Existential." *Theological Studies* 65 (2004): 95–118.

Congar, Yves, OP. "Part I, Chapter IV: The Role of the Church in the Modern World." In *Commentary on the Documents of Vatican II,* Vol. 5, *Pastoral Constitution on the Church in the Modern World,* edited by Herbert Vorgrimler, 202–23. Translated by W. J. O'Hara. New York: Herder & Herder, 1969.

Coppa, Frank J. *The Modern Papacy Since 1789.* In Longman History of the Papacy, edited by A. D. Wright. London & New York: Longman, 1998.

Cox, Robert W. "Social Forces, States and World Orders: Beyond International Relations Theory." In Keohane, *Neorealism and Its Critics,* 204–54.

———. "Towards a Post-Hegemonic Conceptualization of World Order: Reflections on the Relevancy of Ibn Khaldun." In *Governance without Government,* edited by James N. Rosenau and Ernst-Otto Czempiel, 132–59. Cambridge Studies in International Relations, edited by Steve Smith, 20. Cambridge & New York: Cambridge University Press, 1992.

Curran, Charles E. *Catholic Social Teaching, 1891–Present: A Historical, Theological, and Ethical Analysis.* Washington, DC: Georgetown University Press, 2002.

Day, Dorothy. "Catholic Worker Positions." *The Catholic Worker,* May, 1972. http://www .catholicworker.org/dorothyday/daytext.cfm?TextID=519

———. "Editorial—CW Stand on the Use of Force." In *A Penny a Copy: Readings from the Catholic Worker,* edited by Thomas C. Cornell and James H. Forest, 35–38. New York: Macmillan, 1968.

———. *House of Hospitality.* New York: Sheed & Ward, 1939.

———. *Loaves and Fishes.* Maryknoll, NY: Orbis Books, 1997.

———. *The Long Loneliness: The Autobiography of Dorothy Day.* New York: Harper & Brothers, 1952.

———. *On Pilgrimage.* Ressourcement: Retrieval & Renewal in Catholic Thought, edited by David L. Schindler. Grand Rapids, MI: W. B. Eerdmans, 1999.

———. "On Pilgrimage—Sept. 1967." *The Catholic Worker,* September 1967. http://www .catholicworker.org/dorothyday/daytext.cfm?TextID=855

———. "Our Country Passes from Undeclared War to Declared War; We Continue Our Christian Pacifist Stand." In *A Penny a Copy: Readings from the Catholic Worker,* edited by Thomas C. Cornell and James H. Forest, 51–54. New York: Macmillan, 1968.

———. *Therese.* Notre Dame, IN: Fides, 1960.

Dean, William, Mark A. Noll, Mary Farrell Bednarowksi, and J. Bryan Hehir. "Public Theology in Contemporary America." *Religion and American Culture* 10 (2000): 1–27.

De Lubac, Henri, SJ. *Catholicism: Christ and the Common Destiny of Man.* Translated by Lancelot Sheppard and Elizabeth Englund. San Francisco: Ignatius Press, 1988.

———. *The Mystery of the Supernatural.* Translated by Rosemary Sheed. New York: Crossroad, 1998.

———. *Surnaturel: Études Historiques*. Nouvelle édition. Paris: Desclée de Brouwer, 1991.

Dessler, David. "What's at Stake in the Agent-Structure Debate?" *International Organization* 43 (1989): 441–74.

Deutsch, Karl W., Sidney A. Burrell, Robert A. Kann, Maurice Lee Jr., Martin Lichterman, Raymond E. Lindgren, Francis L. Loewenheim, and Richard W. Van Wagenen. *Political Community and the North Atlantic Area: International Organization in the Light of Historical Experience*. Princeton, NJ: Princeton University Press, 1957.

Doolin, Gregory. "Maritain, St. Thomas Aquinas, and the First Principles of Natural Law." In *Reassessing the Liberal State: Reading Maritain's Man and the State*, edited by Timothy Fuller and John Hittinger, 127–39. Washington, DC: American Maritain Association, 2001.

Doyle, Michael W. "Kant, Liberal Legacies, and Foreign Affairs: Part I." *Philosophy and Public Affairs* 12 (1983): 205–54.

———. *Ways of War and Peace: Realism, Liberalism, and Socialism*. New York: W. W. Norton, 1997.

Dubois, Pierre. *The Recovery of the Holy Land*. Translated by Walther I. Brandt. New York: Columbia University Press, 1956.

Duelfer, Charles. *Comprehensive Report of the Special Advisor to the DCI on Iraq's WMD: Regime Finance and Procurement*. Washington, DC: Central Intelligence Agency, 2004.

Dunne, Tim. "Liberalism." In *The Globalization of World Politics: An Introduction to International Relations*, edited by John Baylis and Steve Smith. 3rd ed. Oxford & New York: Oxford University Press, 2005.

Dussel, Enrique. *Ethics and Community*. Translated by Robert R. Barr. Maryknoll, NY: Orbis Books, 1988.

———. *Ethics and the Theology of Liberation*. Translated by Bernard F. McWilliams. Maryknoll, NY: Orbis Books, 1978.

Eichenberg, Richard C. "Victory Has Many Friends: U.S. Public Opinion and the Use of Military Force, 1981–2005." *International Security* 30 (2005): 140–77.

Elsbernd, Mary. "What Ever Happened to *Octogesima adveniens*?" *Theological Studies* 56 (1995): 39–60.

Epp, Roger. "The Ironies of Christian Realism: The End of an Augustinian Tradition in International Politics." In Patterson, *The Christian Realists: Reassessing the Contributions of Niebuhr and His Contemporaries*, 199–232.

Erasmus, Desiderius. *The Complaint of Peace*. Amsterdam: Theatrum Orbis Terrarum; New York: Da Capo Press, 1973.

———. *The Education of a Christian Prince*. Cambridge & New York: Cambridge University Press, 1997.

———. *Enchiridion Militis Christiani: An English Version*. Edited by Anne M. O'Donnell. Oxford & New York: Oxford University Press, 1981.

Farber, Henry S., and Joanne Gowa. "Polities and Peace." In Brown, Lynn-Jones, and Miller, *Debating the Democratic Peace*, 239–62.

Fay, Thomas A. "Maritain on Rights and Natural Law." *Thomist* 55 (1991): 439–48.

Finnemore, Martha. *National Interests in International Society*. Cornell Studies in Political Economy, edited by Peter J. Katzenstein. Ithaca, NY: Cornell University Press, 1996.

———. "Norms, Culture, and World Politics: Insights from Sociology's Institutionalism." *International Organization* 50 (1996): 325–47.

_____. *The Purpose of Intervention: Changing Beliefs about the Use of Force.* Cornell Studies in Security Affairs, edited by Robert J. Art, Robert Jervis, and Stephen M. Walt. Ithaca, NY: Cornell University Press, 2003.

Finnemore, Martha, and Kathryn Sikkink, "International Norm Dynamics and Political Change." In *Exploration and Contestation in the Study of World Politics*, edited by Peter J. Katzenstein, Robert O. Keohane, and Stephen D. Krasner, 247–78. Cambridge, MA: MIT Press, 1999.

Freppert, Lucan. *The Basis of Morality according to William of Ockham.* Chicago: Franciscan Herald Press, 1988.

Fuchs, Josef, SJ. "Historicity and Moral Norm." In *Moral Demands and Personal Obligations.* Translated by Brian McNeil, 91–108. Washington, DC: Georgetown University Press, 1993.

Gentili, Alberico. *De Jure Belli Libri Tres,* Vol. 2, *The Translation of the Edition of 1612.* Translated by John C. Rolfe. With an introduction by Coleman Phillipson. Classics of International Law, edited by James Brown Scott, 16. Oxford: Clarendon Press; London: Humphrey Milford, 1933.

George, Jim, and David Campbell. "Patterns of Dissent and the Celebration of Difference: Critical Social Theory and International Relations." *International Studies Quarterly* 34 (1990): 269–94.

Giddens, Anthony. *The Constitution of Society: Outline of the Theory of Structuration.* Berkeley: University of California Press, 1984.

Gilpin, Robert G. *The Political Economy of International Relations.* Princeton, NJ: Princeton University Press, 1987.

_____. "The Richness of the Tradition of Political Realism." In Keohane, *Neorealism and Its Critics*, 301–21.

_____. *War and Change in World Politics.* Cambridge: Cambridge University Press, 1981.

Gould, William J., Jr. "The Challenge of Liberal Political Culture in the Thought of John Courtney Murray." *Communio* 19 (1992): 113–44.

Griffiths, Paul J., and George Weigel. "Just War: An Exchange." *First Things* (Apr 2002): 31–36.

Grisez, Germain. *The Way of the Lord Jesus,* Vol. 1, *Christian Moral Principles.* Chicago: Franciscan Herald Press, 1983.

Grotius, Hugo. *De Jure Belli Ac Pacis, Libri Tres,* Vol. 2, *The Translation.* Translated by Francis W. Kelsey. With an introduction by James Brown Scott. Classics of International Law, edited by James Brown Scott, 3. Washington, DC: Carnegie Institution of Washington, 1925. Reprint, New York: Oceana Publications, 1964.

Haas, Ernst B. *Beyond the Nation-State: Functionalism and International Organization.* Stanford, CA: Stanford University Press, 1964.

_____. *The Uniting of Europe: Political, Social, and Economic Forces, 1950–1957.* Stanford, CA: Stanford University Press, 1958.

Haas, Guenther H. "Calvin's Ethics." In *The Cambridge Companion to John Calvin,* edited by Donald K. McKim, 93–105. Cambridge Companions to Religion. Cambridge & New York: Cambridge University Press, 2004.

Hamilton, Bernice. *Political Thought in Sixteenth-Century Spain: A Study of the Political Ideas of Vitoria, De Soto, Suarez, and Molina.* Oxford: Clarendon Press, 1963.

Hancock, Ralph Cornel. *Calvin and the Foundations of Modern Politics.* Ithaca, NY: Cornell University Press, 1989.

Hanson, Eric O. *The Catholic Church in World Politics*. Princeton, NJ: Princeton University Press, 1987.

Hauerwas, Stanley. *A Community of Character: Toward a Constructive Christian Ethic*. Notre Dame, IN: University of Notre Dame Press, 1981.

_____. *The Peaceable Kingdom: A Primer in Christian Ethics*. Notre Dame, IN: University of Notre Dame Press, 1983.

_____. *Truthfulness and Tragedy: Further Investigations in Christian Ethics*. Notre Dame, IN: University of Notre Dame Press, 1977.

Hebblethwaite, Peter. *Paul VI: The First Modern Pope*. New York: Paulist Press, 1993.

Hehir, J. Bryan. "Catholic Teaching on War and Peace: The Decade 1979–1989." In *Moral Theology: Challenges for the Future: Essays in Honor of Richard McCormick*, edited by Charles E. Curran, 355–84. New York: Paulist Press, 1990.

_____. "A Catholic Troeltsch? Curran on the Social Ministry of the Church." In *A Call to Fidelity: On the Moral Theology of Charles E. Curran*, edited by James J. Walter, Timothy E. O'Connell, and Thomas A. Shannon, 191–207. Washington, DC: Georgetown University Press, 2002.

_____. "A Challenge to Theology: American Wealth and Power in the Global Community." In Catholic Theological Society of America, *Proceedings of the Thirtieth Annual Convention*, edited by Luke Salm, FSC, 141–62. New York and Mahwah, NJ: Catholic Theological Society of America, 1975.

_____. "Christians and New World Disorders." In *Being Christian Today: An American Conversation*, edited by Richard John Neuhaus and George Weigel, 223–45. Washington, DC: Ethics and Public Policy Center, 1992.

_____. "Conflict and Security in the New World Order." In *Globalization and Catholic Social Thought: Present Crisis, Future Hope*, edited by John A. Coleman and William F. Ryan, 72–86. Maryknoll, NY: Orbis Books, 2005.

_____. "Human Rights from a Theological and Ethical Pespective." In *Moral Imperatives of Human Rights: A World Survey*, edited by Kenneth W. Thompson, 1–23. Washington, DC: University Press of America, 1980.

_____. "In Defense of Justice." *Commonweal*, March 10, 2000, 32–33.

_____. "Intervention and International Affairs: A Normative and Empirical Assessment." In *The American Search for Peace: Moral Reasoning, Religious Hope, and National Security*, edited by George Weigel and John P. Langan. Washington, DC: Georgetown University Press, 1991.

_____. "The Just-War Ethic and Catholic Theology: Dynamics of Change and Continuity." In *War or Peace?: The Search for New Answers*, edited by Thomas A. Shannon, 15–39. Maryknoll, NY: Orbis Books, 1980.

_____. "The Just-War Ethic Revisited." In *Ideas & Ideals: Essays on Politics in Honor of Stanley Hoffmann*, edited by Linda B. Miller and Michael Joseph Smith, 144–61. Boulder, CO: Westview Press, 1993.

_____. "Kosovo: A War of Values and the Value of War." In *Kosovo: Contending Voices on Balkan Interventions*, edited by William Joseph Buckley, 399–405. Grand Rapids, MI: W. B. Eerdmans, 2000.

_____. "Military Intervention and National Sovereignty: Recasting the Relationship." In *Hard Choices: Moral Dilemmas in Humanitarian Intervention*, edited by Jonathan Moore, 29–54. Lanham, MD: Rowman & Littlefield, 1998.

_____. "The Moral Dimension in the Use of Force." In *The Use of Force after the Cold War*, edited by H. W. Brands, 11–32. College Station, TX: Texas A & M Press, 2000.

_____. "The Moral Measurement of War: A Tradition of Change and Continuity." In *The Sacred and the Sovereign: Religion and International Politics*, edited by John D. Carlson and Erik Owens, 41–65. Washington, DC: Georgetown University Press, 2003.

_____. "Murray on Foreign Policy and International Relations: A Concentrated Contribution." In *John Courtney Murray and the Growth of Tradition*, edited by J. Leon Hooper and Todd David Whitmore, 218–40. Kansas City, MO: Sheed & Ward, 1996.

_____. "The New National Security Strategy." *America*, April 7, 2003, 8–12.

_____. "The Relationship of an Ethic of War and a Theology of Peace: Preliminary Ideas." *Annual of the Society of Christian Ethics* (1984): 19–41.

_____. "Religion, Realism, and Just Intervention." In *Liberty and Power: A Dialogue on Religion and U.S. Foreign Policy in an Unjust World*, edited by J. Bryan Hehir et al., 11–33. Washington, DC: Brookings Institution Press, 2004.

_____. "Social Values and Public Policy: A Contribution from a Religious Tradition." In *Democracy, Social Values, and Public Policy*, edited by Milton M. Carrow, Robert Paul Churchill, and Joseph J. Cordes, 57–71. Westport, CT: Praeger, 1998.

_____. "Strategy and Ethics in World Politics." In *At the End of the American Century: America's Role in the Post–Cold War World*, edited by Robert L. Hutchings, 110–28. Washington, DC: Woodrow Wilson Center Press, 1998.

_____. "The United States and Human Rights: Policy for the 1990s in Light of the Past." In *Eagle in a New World: American Grand Strategy in the Post–Cold War Era*, edited by Kenneth A. Oye, Robert J. Lieber, and Donald Rothchild, 233–55. New York: HarperCollins, 1992.

_____. "An Unnecessary War: How Will It Be Conducted?" *Commonweal*, March 28, 2003, 2–3.

_____. "The Use of Force and the International System Today." In *The Moral Dimensions of International Conduct: The Jesuit Community Lectures, 1982*, edited by James A. Devereux, 83–110. Washington, DC: Georgetown University Press, 1983.

Helgeland, John, Robert J. Daly, and J. Patout Burns. *Christians and the Military: The Early Experience*. Philadelphia, PA: Fortress Press, 1985.

Heyer, Kristin. *Prophetic and Public: The Social Witness of U.S. Catholicism*. Washington, DC: Georgetown University Press, 2006.

Hobbes, Thomas. *Leviathan*. Edited by Richard Tuck. Cambridge Texts in the History of Political Thought, edited by Raymond Geuss, Quentin Skinner, and Richard Tuck. Cambridge & New York: Cambridge University Press, 1991.

Hobbs, T. R. *A Time for War: A Study of Warfare in the Old Testament*. Old Testament Studies, 3. Wilmington, DE: M. Glazier, 1989.

Hoffman, Mark. "Critical Theory and the Inter-Paradigm Debate." *Millennium: Journal of International Studies* 20 (1987): 169–85.

Hollenbach, David, SJ. "Public Theology in America: Some Questions for Catholicism after John Courtney Murray." *Theological Studies* 37 (1976): 290–303.

Hollenbach, David, SJ, Robin Lovin, John A. Coleman, SJ, and J. Bryan Hehir. "Current Theology: Theology and Philosophy in Public: A Symposium on John Courtney Murray's Unfinished Agenda." *Theological Studies* 40 (1979): 700–715.

Holmes, J. Derek. *The Papacy in the Modern World, 1914–1978.* London: Burns & Oates, 1981.

Holsti, Kalevi J. *Peace and War: Armed Conflicts and International Order, 1648–1989.* Cambridge Studies in International Relations, edited by Steve Smith, 14. Cambridge & New York: Cambridge University Press, 1991.

Hooper, J. Leon, SJ, ed. *Bridging the Sacred and the Secular: Selected Writings of John Courtney Murray.* Washington, DC: Georgetown University Press, 1994.

———. "Cups Half Full: John Courtney Murray's Skirmishes with Christian Realism." In Patterson, *The Christian Realists: Reassessing the Contributions of Niebuhr and His Contemporaries,* 159–76.

———. "Dorothy Day's Transposition of Thérèse's 'Little Way.'" *Theological Studies* 63 (2002): 68–86.

Hopf, Ted. "The Promise of Constructivism in International Relations Theory." *International Security* 23 (1998): 171–200.

Horsley, Richard A. "Ethics and Exegesis: 'Love Your Enemies' and the Doctrine of Nonviolence." In Swartley, *Love of Enemy,* 72–101.

Humphrey, Hugh M. "Matthew 5:9: 'Blessed Are the Peacemakers, For They Shall Be Called Sons of God.'" In Tambasco, *Blessed Are the Peacemakers,* 62–78.

Hunter, David G. "A Decade of Research on Early Christians and Military Service." *Religious Studies Review* 18 (1992): 87–94.

Huntington, Samuel P. *The Third Wave: Democratization in the Late Twentieth Century.* Norman, OK: University of Oklahoma Press, 1991.

Irenaeus of Lyons. *Against Heresies.* Ante-Nicene Fathers: The Writings of the Fathers Down to A.D. 325, edited by Alexander Roberts and James Donaldson, 315–567. New York: C. Scribner's Sons, 1885–1897. Reprint, Peabody, MA: Hendrickson, 1995.

Jackson, Robert, and Georg Sørensen. *Introduction to International Relations: Theories and Approaches.* 2nd ed. Oxford & New York: Oxford University Press, 2003.

Jeffreys, Derek S. *Defending Human Dignity: John Paul II and Political Realism.* Grand Rapids, MI: Brazos Press, 2004.

Jepperson, Ronald L., Alexander Wendt, and Peter J. Katzenstein. "Norms, Identity, and Culture in National Security." In Katzenstein, *The Culture of National Security,* 33–75.

Pope John XXIII. *Ad Petri cathedram.* 1959.

———. "Christmas Message." 1960.

———. *Mater et magistra.* 1961.

———. "Opening Speech to the Second Vatican Council." 1962.

———. *Pacem in terris.* 1963.

John of Salisbury. *Policraticus: Of the Frivolities of Courtiers and the Footprints of Philosophers.* Edited and translated by Cary J. Nederman. Cambridge Texts in the History of Political Thought, edited by Raymond Geuss and Quentin Skinner. Cambridge & New York: Cambridge University Press, 1990.

Pope John Paul II. "Address to the United Nations General Assembly (1979)." In O'Connor, *Papal Diplomacy,* 270–80.

———. "Address to UNESCO (1980)." In O'Connor, *Papal Diplomacy,* 290–301.

———. "Addresses to the Diplomatic Corps Accredited to the Holy See." 1978–2005. In O'Connor, *Papal Diplomacy,* 7–177.

———. *Centesimus annus.* 1991.

———. *Evangelium vitae.* 1995.

———. *Fides et ratio.* 1998.

———. *Memory and Identity: Conversations at the Dawn of a Millennium.* New York: Rizzoli, 2005.

———. *Redemptor hominis.* 1979.

———. *Sollicitudo rei socialis.* 1987.

———. *Veritatis splendor.* 1993.

———. "World Day of Peace Messages." 1979–2005. http://www.vatican.va.

Johnson, Paul. *John XXIII.* Library of World Biography, edited by J. H. Plumb. Boston & Toronto: Little, Brown & Co., 1974.

Johnston, Alastair Iain. "Cultural Realism and Strategy in Maoist China." In Katzenstein, *The Culture of National Security,* 216–68.

Justin Martyr. *Dialogue with Trypho.* Translated by Thomas B. Falls. Fathers of the Church: A New Translation, vol. 6, 147–366. New York: Christian Heritage, 1948.

———. *The First Apology.* Translated by Thomas B. Falls. Fathers of the Church: A New Translation, vol. 6, 33–111. New York: Christian Heritage, 1948.

———. *The Second Apology.* Translated by Thomas B. Falls. Fathers of the Church: A New Translation, vol. 6, 119–135. New York: Christian Heritage, 1948.

Kagan, Frederick W. "The U.S. Military's Manpower Crisis." *Foreign Affairs* 85 (July 2006): 97–110.

Kagan, Robert. *A Twilight Struggle: American Power and Nicaragua, 1977–1990.* New York: Free Press, 1996.

Kane, Brian M. "John XXIII and Just Cause for Modern War." *New Blackfriars* 80 (1999): 56–72.

Kant, Immanuel. *The Idea for a Universal History with a Cosmopolitan Purpose.* Translated by H. B. Nisbet. In *Political Writings,* edited by Hans Reiss, 41–53. 2nd ed. Cambridge Texts in the History of Political Thought, edited by Raymond Geuss, Quentin Skinner, and Richard Tuck. Cambridge: Cambridge University Press, 1991. First published 1970.

———. *The Metaphysics of Morals.* Translated by H. B. Nisbet. In *Political Writings,* edited by Hans Reiss, 131–75. 2nd ed. Cambridge Texts in the History of Political Thought, edited by Raymond Geuss, Quentin Skinner, and Richard Tuck. Cambridge: Cambridge University Press, 1991. First published 1970.

———. *Perpetual Peace: A Philosophical Sketch.* Translated by H. B. Nisbet. In *Political Writings,* edited by Hans Reiss, 93–130. 2nd ed. Cambridge Texts in the History of Political Thought, edited by Raymond Geuss, Quentin Skinner, and Richard Tuck. Cambridge: Cambridge University Press, 1991.

Kasper, Walter. "The Theological Anthropology of *Gaudium et spes.*" Translated by Adrian Walker. *Communio* 23 (1996): 129–40.

Katzenstein, Peter J., ed. *The Culture of National Security: Norms and Identity in World Politics.* New Directions in World Politics, edited by John Gerard Ruggie. New York: Columbia University Press, 1996.

Keohane, Robert O. *After Hegemony: Cooperation and Discord in the World Political Economy.* Princeton, NJ: Princeton University Press, 1984.

———, ed. *Neorealism and Its Critics.* The Political Economy of International Change, edited by John Gerard Ruggie. New York: Columbia University Press, 1986.

_____. "Realism, Neorealism and the Study of World Politics." In Keohane, *Neorealism and Its Critics*, 1–26.

Keohane, Robert O., and Joseph S. Nye Jr. *Power and Interdependence*, 3rd ed. New York: Longman, 2001.

Klassen, William. "'Love Your Enemies': Some Reflections on the Current Status of Research." In Swartley, *Love of Enemy*, 1-31.

Klejment, Anne. "The Radical Origins of Catholic Pacifism: Dorothy Day and the Lyrical Left During World War I." In Klejment and Roberts, *American Catholic Pacifism: The Influence of Dorothy Day and the Catholic Worker Movement*, 15–32.

Klejment, Anne, and Nancy L. Roberts. *American Catholic Pacifism: The Influence of Dorothy Day and the Catholic Worker Movement*. Westport, CT & London: Praeger, 1996.

Klotz, Audie. *Norms in International Relations: The Struggle against Apartheid*. Cornell Studies in Political Economy, edited by Peter J. Katzenstein. Ithaca, NY: Cornell University Press, 1995.

Komonchak, Joseph A. "Theology and Culture at Mid-Century: The Example of Henri de Lubac." *Theological Studies* 51 (1990): 579–602.

Koslowski, Rey, and Friedrich V. Kratochwil. "Understanding Change in International Politics: The Soviet Empire's Demise and the International System." In *International Relations Theory and the End of the Cold War*, edited by Richard Ned Lebow and Thomas Risse-Kappen, 127–65. New York: Columbia University Press, 1995.

Kowert, Paul, and Jeffrey Legro. "Norms, Identity, and Their Limits: A Theoretical Reprise." In Katzenstein, *The Culture of National Security*, 451–97.

Kratochwil, Friedrich V. "The Force of Prescriptions." *International Organization* 38 (1984): 691–703.

_____. *Rules, Norms, and Decisions: On the Conditions of Practical and Legal Reasoning in International Relations and Domestic Affairs*. In Cambridge Studies in International Relations, edited by Steve Smith, 2. Cambridge & New York: Cambridge University Press, 1989.

Kubálková, V., and A. A. Cruickshank. *Marxism and International Relations*. Marxist Introductions, edited by Raymond Williams and Steven Lukes. Oxford: Clarendon Press, 1985.

Lapid, Yosef. "The Third Debate: On the Prospects of International Theory in a Post-Positivist Era." *International Studies Quarterly* 33 (1989): 235–54.

Lenin, Vladimir Ilich. *Imperialism, the Highest Stage of Capitalism: A Popular Outline*. New York: International Publishers, 1972.

Pope Leo XIII. *Diuturnum*. 1881.

_____. *Graves de communi re*. 1905.

_____. *Immortale Dei*. 1885.

_____. *Libertas*. 1888.

Locke, John. *First Treatise*. In *Two Treatises of Government*, student edition, edited and with an introduction by Peter Laslett, 141–263. Cambridge Texts in the History of Political Thought, edited by Raymond Geuss and Quentin Skinner. Cambridge & New York: Cambridge University Press, 1988.

_____. *Second Treatise*. In *Two Treatises of Government*, student edition, edited and with an introduction by Peter Laslett, 265–428. Cambridge Texts in the History of

Political Thought, edited by Raymond Geuss and Quentin Skinner. Cambridge & New York: Cambridge University Press, 1988.

Lonergan, Bernard J. F., SJ. "The Future of Thomism." In *A Second Collection: Papers by Bernard J. F. Lonergan, SJ*, edited by William F. J. Ryan and Bernard J. Tyrrell, 43–53. London: Dartman, Longman, and Todd, 1974.

Machiavelli, Niccolò. *Discourses on Livy*. Translated by Harvey C. Mansfield and Nathan Tarcov. Chicago: University of Chicago Press, 1996.

_____. *The Prince*. Translated by George Bull. London: Penguin Books, 1999.

MacIntyre, Alastair. *After Virtue: A Study in Moral Theory*, 2nd ed. Notre Dame, IN: University of Notre Dame Press, 1984.

Maréchal, Joseph, SJ. *A Maréchal Reader*. Edited and translated by Joseph Donceels. New York: Herder & Herder, 1970.

Maritain, Jacques. *Integral Humanism: Temporal and Spiritual Problems of a New Christendom*. Translated by Joseph W. Evans. Notre Dame, IN: University of Notre Dame Press, 1973.

_____. *Man and the State*. Washington, DC: Catholic University of America Press, 1998.

_____. *The Person and the Common Good*. Translated by John J. Fitzgerald. New York: Charles Scribner's Sons, 1947.

_____. *The Rights of Man and Natural Law*. Translated by Doris C. Anson. New York: Charles Scribner's Sons, 1943.

Marsilius of Padua. *Defensor Pacis*. Translated and with an introduction by Alan Gewirth. New York: Columbia University Press, 1956. Reprint, New York: Columbia University Press, 2001.

Martinez, Gaspar. *Confronting the Mystery of God: Political, Liberation, and Public Theologies*. New York: Continuum, 2001.

McCormick, Richard A., SJ. *Corrective Vision: Explorations in Moral Theology*. Kansas City, MO: Sheed & Ward, 1994.

_____. *Notes on Moral Theology, 1965–1980*. Lanham, MD: University Press of America, 1981.

_____. "Notes on Moral Theology: 1982." *Theological Studies* 44 (1983): 71–122.

McDonald, Patricia. *God and Violence: Biblical Resources for Living in a Small World*. Scottdale, PA: Herald Press, 2004.

McElroy, Robert W. *The Search for an American Public Theology: The Contribution of John Courtney Murray*. New York and Mahwah, NJ: Paulist Press, 1989.

McGrade, Arthur Stephen. *The Political Thought of William of Ockham: Personal and Institutional Principles*. London & New York: Cambridge University Press, 1974.

McKeogh, Colm. *The Political Realism of Reinhold Niebuhr: A Pragmatic Approach to Just War*. New York: St. Martin's Press, 1997.

McNeal, Patricia. "Catholic Peace Organizations and World War II." In Klejment and Roberts, *American Catholic Pacifism: The Influence of Dorothy Day and the Catholic Worker Movement*, 33–45.

Mearsheimer, John J. "Back to the Future: Instability in Europe after the Cold War." *International Security* 15 (1990): 5–56.

_____. "The False Promise of International Institutions." *International Security* 19 (1995): 5–49.

_____. *The Tragedy of Great Power Politics*. New York: W. W. Norton, 2001.

Merriman, Brigid O'Shea. *Searching for Christ: The Spirituality of Dorothy Day*. Notre Dame, IN & London: University of Notre Dame Press, 1994.

Mill, John Stuart. *On Liberty*. Edited by David Bromwich and George Kateb. Rethinking the Modern Tradition. New Haven, CT & London: Yale University Press, 2003.

Miller, Kenneth E. "John Stuart Mill's Theory of International Relations." *Journal of the History of Ideas* 22 (1961): 493–514.

Mitrany, David. *The Functional Theory of Politics*. London: London School of Economics & Political Science, 1975.

———. *A Working Peace System: An Argument for the Functional Development of International Organization*. Chicago: Quadrangle Books, 1966.

Moeller, Charles. "Pastoral Constitution on the Church in the Modern World: History of the Constitution." In *Commentary on the Documents of Vatican II*, Vol. 5, *Pastoral Constitution on the Church in the Modern World*, edited by Herbert Vorgrimler, 1–76. Translated by W. J. O'Hara. New York: Herder & Herder, 1969.

Morgenthau, Hans J. *Politics among Nations: The Struggle for Power and Peace*. 7th ed. Edited by Kenneth W. Thompson and W. David Clinton. Boston: McGraw-Hill Higher Education, 2006.

———. *Scientific Man vs. Power Politics*. Chicago: University of Chicago Press, 1965.

Murray, John Courtney, SJ. "Are There Two or One?: The Question of the Future of Freedom." In Murray, *We Hold These Truths*, 197–217.

———. "The Civilization of the Pluralist Society." In Murray, *We Hold These Truths*, 3–24.

———. "Doctrine and Policy in Communist Imperialism: The Problem of Security and Risk." In Murray, *We Hold These Truths*, 221–47.

———. "The Doctrine Is Dead: The Problem of the Moral Vacuum." In Murray, *We Hold These Truths*, 275–94.

———. "The Doctrine Lives: The Eternal Return of Natural Law." In Murray, *We Hold These Truths*, 295–336.

———. "E Pluribus Unum: The American Consensus." In Murray, *We Hold These Truths*, 27–43.

———. "Freedom in the Age of Renewal." In Hooper, *Bridging the Sacred and the Secular*, 181–86.

———. "The Juridical Organization of the International Community." In Hooper, *Bridging the Sacred and the Secular*, 28–41.

———. "The Origins and Authority of the Public Consensus: A Study of the Growing End." In Murray, *We Hold These Truths*, 97–123.

———. "The Pattern for Peace and the Papal Peace Program." In Hooper, *Bridging the Sacred and the Secular*, 6–27.

———. "Things Old and New in *Pacem in Terris*." In Hooper, *Bridging the Sacred and the Secular*, 248–54.

———. "Two Cases for the Public Consensus: Fact or Need." In Murray, *We Hold These Truths*, 79–96.

———. *We Hold These Truths: Catholic Reflections on the American Proposition*. New York: Sheed and Ward, 1988. First published 1960.

Musto, Ronald G. *The Catholic Peace Tradition*. Maryknoll, NY: Orbis Books, 1986.

Nadelmann, Ethan. "Global Prohibition Regimes: The Evolution of Norms in International Society." *International Organization* 44 (1990): 479–526.

Niditch, Susan. *War in the Hebrew Bible: A Study in the Ethics of Violence.* New York & Oxford: Oxford University Press, 1993.

Niebuhr, Reinhold. "The Christian Church in a Secular Age." In Niebuhr, *Christianity and Power Politics,* 203–26.

———. *Christianity and Power Politics.* New York: C. Scribner's Sons, 1940. Reprint, Hamden, CT: Archon Books, 1969.

———. "Ideology and Pretense." In Niebuhr, *Christianity and Power Politics,* 107–15.

———. "Modern Utopians." In Niebuhr, *Christianity and Power Politics,* 141–58.

———. *Moral Man and Immoral Society: A Study in Ethics and Politics.* New York: Scribner, 1960.

———. *The Structure of Nations and Empires: A Study of the Recurring Patterns and Problems of the Political Order in Relation to the Unique Problems of the Nuclear Age.* New York: Charles Scribner's Sons, 1959.

Nye, Joseph S., Jr. *Soft Power: The Means to Success in World Politics.* New York: Public Affairs, 2004.

———. *Understanding International Conflicts: An Introduction to Theory and History,* 4th ed. Longman Classics in Political Science. New York: Pearson/Longman, 2003.

O'Collins, Gerald, SJ *Fundamental Theology.* New York & Ramsey, NJ: Paulist Press, 1981.

O'Connor, Bernard J. *Papal Diplomacy: John Paul II and the Culture of Peace.* South Bend, IN: St. Augustine's Press, 2005.

O'Malley, John W., SJ. "Reform, Historical Consciousness, and Vatican II's *Aggiornamento.*" *Theological Studies* 32 (1971): 573–601.

Origen. *Against Celsus.* Ante-Nicene Fathers, Vol. 4, Fathers of the Third Century. American ed. Edited by Alexander Roberts and James Donaldson, 395–669. Peabody, MA: Hendrickson, 1995.

———. *Commentary on the Epistle to the Romans, Books 6-10.* Translated by Thomas P. Scheck. Fathers of the Church: A New Translation, vol. 104. Washington, DC: Catholic University of America Press, 2002.

Orosius, Paulus. *The Seven Books of History against the Pagans.* Translated by Roy J. Deferrari. Fathers of the Church: A New Translation, vol. 50. Washington, DC: Catholic University of America Press, 1964.

Owen, John M. "How Liberalism Produces Democratic Peace." In Brown, Lynn-Jones, and Miller, *Debating the Democratic Peace,* 116–54.

Patterson, Eric. "Niebuhr and His Contemporaries: Introduction to Christian Realism." In Patterson, *The Christian Realists: Reassessing the Contributions of Niebuhr and His Contemporaries,* 1–23.

———, ed. *The Christian Realists: Reassessing the Contributions of Niebuhr and His Contemporaries.* Lanham, MD: University Press of America, 2003.

Pope Paul VI. "Address to the Secretary General of the United Nations Organization." 1963.

———. "Address to the United Nations General Assembly (1965)." In *Paths to Peace: A Contribution: Documents of the Holy See to the International Community.* New York: Permanent Observer Mission of the Holy See to the United Nations, 1987.

———. *Ecclesiam suam.* 1964.

———. Apostolic Exhortation *Evangelii nuntiandi.* 1975.

———. *Mense maio.* 1965.

———. Apostolic Letter *Octogesima adveniens*. 1971.

———. *Populorum progressio*. 1967.

———. "World Day of Peace Messages." 1968–1978.

Pope Pius XI. *Divini redemptoris*. 1937.

———. *Ubi arcano Dei consilio*. 1922.

Pope Pius XII. *Auspicia quaedam*. 1948.

———. *Humani generis*. 1950.

———. *The Major Addresses of Pope Pius XII*, Vol. 2, *Christmas Messages*. Edited by Vincent A. Yzermans. St. Paul, MN: North Central, 1961.

———. *Mirabile illud*. 1950.

———. *Summi maeroris*. 1950.

———. *Summi pontificatus*. 1939.

Pollard, John F. *The Unknown Pope: Benedict XV (1914–1922) and the Pursuit of Peace*. London: G. Chapman, 1999.

Pope, Stephen J. "Natural Law in Catholic Social Teachings." In *Modern Catholic Social Teaching: Commentaries & Interpretations*, edited by Kenneth R. Himes, OFM, et al., 41–71. Washington, DC: Georgetown University Press, 2005.

Porter, Jean. "In the Wake of a Doctrine: A Reassessment of the Doctrine of the Natural Law as Developed in *We Hold These Truths*." In *John Courtney Murray and the Growth of Tradition*, edited by J. Leon Hooper and Todd David Whitmore, 24–40. Kansas City, MO: Sheed & Ward, 1996.

———. *Natural and Divine Law: Reclaiming the Tradition for Christian Ethics*. Ottawa: Novalis; Grand Rapids, MI: W. B. Eerdmans, 1999.

Price, Richard, and Nina Tannenwald. "Norms and Deterrence: The Nuclear and Chemical Weapons Taboos." In Katzenstein, *The Culture of National Security*, 114–52.

Pufendorf, Samuel von. *De Jure Naturae et Gentium Libri Octo*, Vol. 2, *The Translation*. Translated by C. H. Oldfather and W. A. Oldfather. Classics of International Law, edited by James Brown Scott, 17. Oxford: Clarendon Press, 1934.

Rahner, Karl, SJ. "Concerning the Relationship between Nature and Grace." In *Theological Investigations*, Vol. 1, *God, Christ, Mary and Grace*. Translated and with an introduction by Cornelius Ernst, OP, 297–317. Baltimore: Helicon Press, 1961.

———. *Foundations of Christian Faith: An Introduction to the Idea of Christianity*. Translated by William V. Dych. New York: Crossroad, 1989.

———. *Hearer of the Word*. Translated by Michael Richards. New York: Herder & Herder, 1969.

———. "History of the World and Salvation History." In *Theological Investigations*, Vol. 5, *Later Writings*. Translated by Karl-H. Kruger, 97–114. London: Darton, Longman & Todd; Baltimore: Helicon Press, 1966.

———. "Nature and Grace." In *Theological Investigations*, Vol. 4, *More Recent Writings*. Translated by Kevin Smyth, 165–88. London: Darton, Longman, & Todd; Baltimore: Helicon Press, 1966.

———. "The Order of Redemption within the Order of Creation." In *The Christian Commitment*. Translated by Cecily Hastings, 38–74. New York: Sheed & Ward, 1963.

———. *Spirit in the World*. Translated by William V. Dych. New York: Herder & Herder, 1968.

Ratzinger, Joseph. "Part I: The Church and Man's Calling, Introductory Article and Chapter I: The Dignity of the Human Person." In *Commentary on the Documents of Vatican II*, Vol. 5, *Pastoral Constitution on the Church in the Modern World*, ed. Herbert Vorgrimler, 115–63. Translated by W. J. O'Hara. New York: Herder & Herder, 1969.

Ray, James Lee. "The Abolition of Slavery and the End of International War." *International Organization* 43 (1989): 405–39.

Reus-Smit, Christian. "Beyond Foreign Policy: State Theory and the Changing Global Order." In *The State in Question: Transformations of the Australian State*, edited by Paul James, 161–95. St. Leonards, NSW: Allen and Unwin, 1996.

———. "Constructivism." In *Theories of International Relations*, 2nd ed., edited by Scott Burchill et al., 209–30. Houndmills, UK and New York: Palgrave, 2001.

———. *The Moral Purpose of the State: Culture, Social Identity, and Institutional Rationality in International Relations*. Princeton Studies in International History and Politics, edited by Jack L. Snyder and Richard H. Ullman. Princeton, NJ: Princeton University Press, 1999.

Rhodes, Anthony. *The Vatican in the Age of the Cold War, 1945–1980*. Norwich, UK: M. Russell, 1992.

Risse-Kappen, Thomas. "Collective Identity in a Democratic Community: The Case of NATO." In Katzenstein, *The Culture of National Security*, 357–99.

———. "Ideas Do Not Float Freely: Transnational Coalitions, Domestic Structures, and the End of the Cold War." In *International Relations and the End of the Cold War*, edited by Richard Ned Lebow and Thomas Risse-Kappen, 187–222. New York: Columbia University Press, 1995.

Rosecrance, Richard. *The Rise of the Trading State: Commerce and Conquest in the Modern World*. New York: Basic, 1986.

———. *The Rise of the Virtual State*. New York: Basic, 1999.

Rosenau, James N. "Citizenship in a Changing Global Order." In *Governance without Government: Order and Change in World Politics*, edited by James N. Rosenau and Ernst-Otto Czempiel, 272–94. Cambridge Studies in International Relations, edited by Steve Smith, 20. Cambridge: Cambridge University Press, 1992.

———. *The Study of Global Interdependence: Essays on the Transnationalization of World Politics*. New York: Nichols, 1980.

———. *Turbulence in World Politics: A Theory of Change and Continuity*. Princeton, NJ: Princeton University Press, 1990.

Rousselot, Pierre, SJ. *The Eyes of Faith*. Translated by Joseph Donceels. New York: Fordham University Press, 2006.

Ruggie, John Gerard. "Continuity and Transformation in the World Polity: Toward a Neorealist Synthesis." In Keohane, *Neorealism and Its Critics*, 131–57.

———. "Territoriality and Beyond: Problematizing Modernity in International Relations." *International Organization* 47 (1993): 139–74.

———. "What Makes the World Hang Together? Neo-Utilitarianism and the Social Constructive Challenge." In *Exploration and Contestation in the Study of World Politics*, edited by Peter J. Katzenstein, Robert O. Keohane, and Stephen D. Krasner, 215–46. Cambridge, MA: MIT Press, 1999.

Russett, Bruce. "The Democratic Peace: And Yet It Moves." In Brown, Lynn-Jones, and Miller, *Debating the Democratic Peace*, 337–50.

———. *Grasping the Democratic Peace: Principles for a Post–Cold War World*. Princeton, NJ: Princeton University Press, 1993.

Russett, Bruce, and John R. Oneal. *Triangulating Peace: Democracy, Interdependence, and International Organizations*. New York: W. W. Norton, 2001.

Ryan, Edward. "The Rejection of Military Service by the Early Christians." In *Christian Life: Ethics, Morality, and Discipline in the Early Church*, edited by Everett Ferguson, 217–48. Studies in Early Christianity: A Collection of Scholarly Essays, edited by Everett Ferguson, vol. 16. New York: Garland, 1993.

Sacco, Ugo Colombo. *John Paul II and World Politics: Twenty Years of a Search for a New Approach, 1978–1998*. Canon Law Monograph Series, edited by Rik Torfs, 2. Leuven, Belgium: Peeters, 1999.

Schindler, David L. "Christology and the Imago Dei: Interpreting *Gaudium et spes*." *Communio* 23 (1996): 156–84.

_____. "The Church's 'Worldly' Mission: Neoconservativism and American Culture." *Communio* 18 (1991): 365–97.

_____. *Heart of the World, Center of the Church: Communio Ecclesiology, Liberalism, and Liberation*. Grand Rapids, MI: W. B. Eerdmans, 1996.

_____. "Is America Bourgeois?" *Communio* 14 (1987): 262–90.

Schockenhoff, Eberhard. *Natural Law and Human Dignity: Universal Ethics in a Historical World*. Translated by Brian McNeil. Washington, DC: Catholic University of America Press, 2003.

Schreiter, Robert J. *Constructing Local Theologies*. Maryknoll, NY: Orbis Books, 1985.

_____. *The New Catholicity: Theology between the Global and the Local*. Faith and Culture Series. Maryknoll, NY: Orbis Books, 1997.

Sciolino, Elaine. "France to Veto Resolution on Iraq War, Chirac Says," *New York Times*, March 11, 2003. http://www.nytimes.com/2003/03/11/world/threats-and-responses-discord-france-to-veto-resolution-on-iraq-war-chirac-says.html (accessed May 24, 2010).

Second Vatican Council. Declaration on the Relation of the Church to Non-Christian Religions, *Nostra aetate*. 1965.

_____. Decree on Ecumenism, *Unitatis redintegratio*. 1964.

_____. Decree on the Apostolate of the Lay People, *Apostolicam actuositatem*. 1965.

_____. Dogmatic Constitution on the Church, *Lumen gentium*. 1964.

_____. Pastoral Constitution on the Church in the Modern World, *Gaudium et spes*. 1965.

Smith, Michael Joseph. *Realist Thought from Weber to Kissinger*. Political Traditions in Foreign Policy Series, edited by Kenneth W. Thompson. Baton Rouge, LA & London: Louisiana State University Press, 1986.

Suarez, Francisco, SJ. *A Treatise on Law and God the Lawgiver*. In *Selections from Three Works of Francisco Suarez, SJ: De Legibus, Ac Deo Legislatore, 1612; Defensio Fidei Catholicae, et Apostolicae Adversus Anglicanae Sectae Errores, 1613; De Triplici Virtute Theologica, Fide, Spe, et Charitate, 1621*, Vol. 2, *The Translation*. Classics of International Law, edited by James Brown Scott. Oxford: Clarendon Press, 1944.

_____. *A Work on the Three Theological Virtues: Faith, Hope and Charity*. In *Selections from Three Works of Francisco Suarez, SJ: De Legibus, Ac Deo Legislatore, 1612; Defensio Fidei Catholicae, et Apostolicae Adversus Anglicanae Sectae Errores, 1613; De Triplici Virtute Theologica, Fide, Spe, et Charitate, 1621*, Vol. 2, *The Translation*. Classics of International Law, edited by James Brown Scott. Oxford: Clarendon Press, 1944.

Swaim, J. Carter. *War, Peace, and the Bible*. Maryknoll, NY: Orbis Books, 1982.

Swartley, Willard M., ed. *The Love of Enemy and Nonretaliation in the New Testament.* Studies in Peace and Scripture. Louisville, KY: Westminster/John Knox Press, 1992.

Swift, Louis J. *The Early Fathers on War and Military Service.* Message of the Fathers of the Church, edited by Thomas Halton, vol. 19. Wilmington, DE: M. Glazier, 1983.

Tambasco, Anthony J., ed. *Blessed Are the Peacemakers: Biblical Perspectives on Peace and Its Social Foundations.* New York: Paulist Press, 1989.

Tambasco, Anthony J. "Principalities, Powers and Peace." In Tambasco, *Blessed Are the Peacemakers*, 116–33.

Tertullian. *Apology.* Translated by Sister Emily Joseph Daly, CSJ. Fathers of the Church: A New Translation, vol. 10, 7–126. New York: Fathers of the Church, 1950.

———. *To Scapula.* Translated by Rudolph Arbesmann, OSA. Fathers of the Church: A New Translation, vol. 10, 151–61. New York: Fathers of the Church, 1950.

Thompson, Kenneth W., and W. David Clinton. "Foreword." In Hans J. Morgenthau, *Politics among Nations: The Struggle for Power and Peace*, 7th ed., edited by Kenneth W. Thompson and W. David Clinton. Boston: McGraw-Hill Higher Education, 2005.

Thorn, William J., Phillip M. Runkel, and Susan Mountin, eds. *Dorothy Day and the Catholic Worker Movement: Centenary Essays.* Marquette Studies in Theology, 32, edited by Andrew Tallon. Milwaukee, WI: Marquette University Press, 2001.

Tierney, Brian. *The Idea of Natural Rights: Studies on Natural Rights, Natural Law, and Church Law, 1150–1625.* Emory University Studies in Law and Religion, 5. Atlanta, GA: Scholars Press, 1997.

Torre, Joseph M. de. "Maritain's 'Integral Humanism' and Catholic Social Teaching." In *Reassessing the Liberal State: Reading Maritain's* Man and the State, edited by Timothy Fuller and John Hittinger, 202–8. Washington, DC: American Maritain Association, 2001.

Tucci, Robert. "Part II, Chapter II: The Proper Development of Culture." In *Commentary on the Documents of Vatican II, Vol. 5, Pastoral Constitution on the Church in the Modern World*, edited by Herbert Vorgrimler, 246–87. Translated by W. J. O'Hara. New York: Herder & Herder, 1969.

Tuck, Richard. *Natural Rights Theories: Their Origin and Development.* Cambridge, UK: Cambridge University Press, 1979.

———. *The Rights of War and Peace: Political Thought and the International Order from Grotius to Kant.* Oxford & New York: Oxford University Press, 1999.

Vandervelde, George. "The Grammar of Grace: Karl Rahner as Watershed in Contemporary Theology." *Theological Studies* 49 (1988): 445–59.

Vattel, Emer de. *Le Droit de Gens, ou Principes de la Loi Naturelle, appliqués à la Conduite et aux Affaires des Nations et des Souverains*, Vol. 3, *Translation of the Edition of 1758.* Translated by Charles G. Fenwick. With an introduction by Albert de Lapradelle. Classics of International Law, edited by James Brown Scott, 4. Washington, DC: Carnegie Institution of Washington, 1916.

Vitoria, Francisco de. *On Civil Power.* In *Political Writings*, edited by Anthony Padgen and Jeremy Lawrance, 1–44. Cambridge Texts in the History of Political Thought, edited by Raymond Geuss and Quentin Skinner. Cambridge, UK & New York: Cambridge University Press, 1991.

———. *On the Law of War.* In *Political Writings*, edited by Anthony Padgen and Jeremy Lawrance, 293–327. Cambridge Texts in the History of Political Thought, edited by

Raymond Geuss and Quentin Skinner. Cambridge, UK & New York: Cambridge University Press, 1991.

Vives, Juan Luis. "Selections from the Commentaries of Joannes Lodovicus Vives on Saint Augustine's 'De Civitate Dei.'" In Augustine, *The City of God (De Civitate Dei)*, edited by R. V. G. Tasker, vol. 2, 409–44. Translated by W. Crashawe. Everyman's Library, 983. London: J. M. Dent & Sons, 1950.

——. *Introduction to Wisdom: A Renaissance Textbook*, edited by Marian Leona Torbinger, SNJM. Classics in Education, edited by Lawrence A. Cremin, 35. New York: Teachers College Press, 1968.

Von Balthasar, Hans Urs. *The Glory of the Lord*, Vol. 3, *Studies in Theological Styles: Lay Styles*. San Francisco: Ignatius Press, 1986.

——. *Theo-Drama: Theological Dramatic Theory*. 5 vols. San Francisco: Ignatius Press, 1988–98. First published 1973–83.

Von Rad, Gerhard. *Holy War in Ancient Israel*. Translated by Marva J. Dawn. Grand Rapids, MI: W. B. Eerdmans, 1991.

Wallerstein, Immanuel. *World-Systems Analysis: An Introduction*. Durham, NC & London: Duke University Press, 2004.

Waltz, Kenneth. *Man, the State, and War: A Theoretical Analysis*. New York & London: Columbia University Press, 1959.

——. "The Origins of War in Neorealist Theory." *Journal of Interdisciplinary History* 18 (1988): 615–28.

——. "Realist Thought and Neo-Realist Theory." In *Controversies in International Relations Theory: Realism and the Neoliberal Challenge*, edited by Charles W. Kegley Jr., 67–82. New York: St. Martin's Press, 1995.

——. "Reflections on *Theory of International Politics*: A Response to My Critics." In Keohane, *Neorealism and Its Critics*, 322–45.

——. *Theory of International Politics*. New York: McGraw-Hill, 1979.

Weigel, George. *American Interests, American Purpose: Moral Reasoning and U.S. Foreign Policy*. Washington Papers, edited by Walter Laqueur. New York: Praeger, 1989.

——. *Catholicism and the Renewal of American Democracy*. New York and Mahwah, NJ: Paulist Press, 1989.

——. "The Churches and the Gulf Crisis." In James Turner Johnson and George Weigel, *Just War and the Gulf War*, 45–90. Washington, DC: Ethics and Public Policy Center, 1991.

——. *The Cube and the Cathedral: Europe, America and Politics without God*. New York: Basic Books, 2005.

——. *Faith, Reason, and the War against Jihadism: A Call to Action*. New York & London: Doubleday, 2007.

——. *The Final Revolution: The Resistance Church and the Collapse of Communism*. Oxford & New York: Oxford University Press, 2003.

——. "The Free and Virtuous Society." In *Against the Grain: Christianity and Democracy, War and Peace*, 11–36. New York: Crossroad, 2008.

——. "From Last Resort to Endgame: Morality, the Gulf War, and the Peace Process." In *But Was It Just?: Reflections on the Morality of the Persian Gulf War*, edited by Jean Bethke Elshtain. New York: Doubleday, 1992.

——. "The Future of the John Courtney Murray Project." In *John Courtney Murray and the American Civil Conversation*, edited by Robert P. Hunt and Kenneth L. Grasso, 273–96. Grand Rapids, MI: W. B. Eerdmans, 1992.

_____. *Idealism without Illusions*. Washington, DC: Ethics and Public Policy Center, 1994.

_____. "Is America Bourgeois? A Response to David Schindler." *Communio* 15 (1988): 77–91.

_____. "Low-Intensity Conflict in the Post–Cold War World: The American Moral Cultural Environment." In *Legal and Moral Constraints on Low-Intensity Conflict*, edited by Alberto R. Coll, James S. Ord, and Stephen A. Rose, 251–64. International Law Studies, vol. 67. Newport, RI: Naval War College, 1995.

_____. "Moral Clarity in a Time of War." *First Things*, January 2003, 20–27.

_____. "The National Interest and the National Purpose: From Policy Debate to Moral Argument." In *The American Search for Peace: Moral Reasoning, Religious Hope, and National Security*, edited by George Weigel and John P. Langan, 1–25. Washington, DC: Georgetown University Press, 1991.

_____. "The Neoconservative Difference: A Proposal for the Renewal of Church and Society." In *Being Right: Conservative Catholics in America*, edited by Mary Jo Weaver and R. Scott Appleby, 138–62. Bloomington, IN: Indiana University Press, 1995.

_____. *Peace & Freedom: Christian Faith, Democracy, & the Problem of War*. 2nd ed. Washington, DC: The Institute on Religion and Democracy, 1987.

_____. "The Poverty of Conventional Realism." In *Might and Right after the Cold War: Can Foreign Policy Be Moral?*, edited by Michael Cromartie, 67–87. Washington, DC: Ethics and Public Policy Center, 1993.

_____. "Religion and Peace: An Argument Complexified." In *U.S. Security in an Uncertain Era*, edited by Brad Roberts, 241–55. Cambridge, MA: MIT Press, 1993.

_____. "Response to Mark Lowery." *Communio* 18 (1991): 439–49.

_____. *Soul of the World: Notes on the Future of Public Catholicism*. Washington, DC: Ethics and Public Policy Center; Grand Rapids, MI: W. B. Eerdmans; Leonminster, UK: Gracewing, 1996.

_____. "Talking the Talk: Christian Conviction and Democratic Etiquette." In *Disciples and Democracy: Religious Conservatives and the Future of American Democracy*, edited by Michael Cromartie. Washington, DC: Ethics and Public Policy Center; Grand Rapids, MI: Eerdmans, 1994.

_____. *Tranquillitas Ordinis: The Present Failure and Future Promise of American Catholic Thought on War and Peace*. Oxford and New York: Oxford University Press, 1987.

_____. *Witness to Hope: The Biography of Pope John Paul II*. New York: Cliff Street Books, 2001.

_____. "World Order: What Catholics Forgot." *First Things*, May 2004, 31–38.

Wendt, Alexander. "The Agent-Structure Problem in International Relations Theory." *International Organization* 41 (1987): 335–70.

_____. "Anarchy Is What States Make of It: The Social Construction of Power Politics." *International Organization* 46 (1992): 391–425.

_____. "Collective Identity Formation and the International State." *American Political Science Review* 88 (1994): 384–95.

_____. "Constructing International Politics." *International Security* 20 (1995): 71–81.

_____. *Social Theory of International Politics*. Cambridge Studies in International Relations, edited by Steve Smith, 67. Cambridge, UK & New York: Cambridge University Press, 1999.

Wendt, Alexander, and Raymond Duvall. "Institutions and International Order." In *Global Changes and Theoretical Challenges: Approaches to World Politics for the 1990s*, edited by Ernst-Otto Czempiel and James N. Rosenau, 51–74. Issues in

World Politics, edited by James N. Rosenau and William C. Potter. Lexington, MA: Lexington Books, 1989.

William of Ockham. *On the Power of Emperors and Popes*. Edited and translated by Annabel S. Brett. Durham, UK: University of Durham; Bristol, UK & Sterling, VA: Thoemmes Press, 1998.

_____. *A Short Discourse on the Tyrannical Government over Things Divine and Human, but Especially over the Empire and Those Subject to the Empire, Usurped by Some Who Are Called Highest Pontiffs*. Edited by Stephen McGrade. Translated by John Kilcullen. Cambridge Texts in the History of Political Thought, edited by Raymond Geuss and Quentin Skinner. Cambridge, UK & New York: Cambridge University Press, 1992.

Williams, Rowan, and George Weigel. "War & Statecraft: An Exchange." *First Things*, March 2004, 14–21.

Winiarski, Warren. "Niccolo Machiavelli." In *History of Political Philosophy*, edited by Leo Strauss and Joseph Cropsey, 247–76. Rand McNally Political Science Series, edited by Morton Grodzins. Chicago: Rand McNally, 1963.

Wink, Walter. "Neither Passivity nor Violence: Jesus' Third Way (Matt. 5:38-32 par.)." In Swartley, *Love of Enemy*, 102–25.

Winright, Tobias. "Gather Us In and Make Us Channels of Your Peace: Evaluating War with an Entirely New Attitude." In *Gathered for the Journey: Moral Theology in Catholic Perspective*, edited by David Matzko McCarthy and M. Therese Lysaught, 281–306. Grand Rapids, MI: Eerdmans, 2009.

Wolff, Christian, Freiherr von. *Jus gentium methodo scientifica pertractatum*, Vol. 2, *The Translation*. Translated by Joseph H. Drake. In Classics of International Law, edited by James Brown Scott, 13. Oxford: Clarendon Press, 1934. Reprint, New York: Oceana Publications; London: Wiley & Sons, 1964.

Wood, John A. *Perspectives on War in the Bible*. Macon, GA: Mercer University Press, 1998.

Woods, Kevin, James Lacey, and Williamson Murray. "Saddam's Delusions: The View from the Inside." *Foreign Affairs* 85 (May/June 2006): 2–26.

Yocum-Mize, Sandra. "'We Are Still Pacifists': Dorothy Day's Pacifism during World War II." In Thorn, Runkel, and Mountin, *Dorothy Day and the Catholic Worker Movement: Centenary Essays*, 465–73.

Zacher, M. W., and R. A. Matthew. "Liberal International Theory: Common Threads, Divergent Strands." In *Controversies in International Relations Theory: Realism and the Neoliberal Challenge*, edited by Charles W. Kegley Jr., 107–50. New York: St. Martin's Press, 1995.

Zartman, I. William. "Need, Creed, and Greed in Intrastate Conflict." In *Rethinking the Economics of War: The Intersection of Need, Creed, and Greed*, edited by Cynthia J. Arnson and I. William Zartman, 256–84. Washington, DC: Woodrow Wilson Center Press, 2005.

Zerbe, Gordon. "Paul's Ethic of Nonretaliation and Peace." In Swartley, *Love of Enemy*, 177–222.

Zwick, Mark, and Louise Zwick. *The Catholic Worker Movement: Intellectual and Spiritual Origins*. Mahwah, NJ: Paulist Press, 2005.

INDEX